For The
Library of
Ralph E.& Brenda M. Carrington
September 14, 1993

Presented by:

Pappys Jabba Seck
(WOLOFF)
Dakar senegal

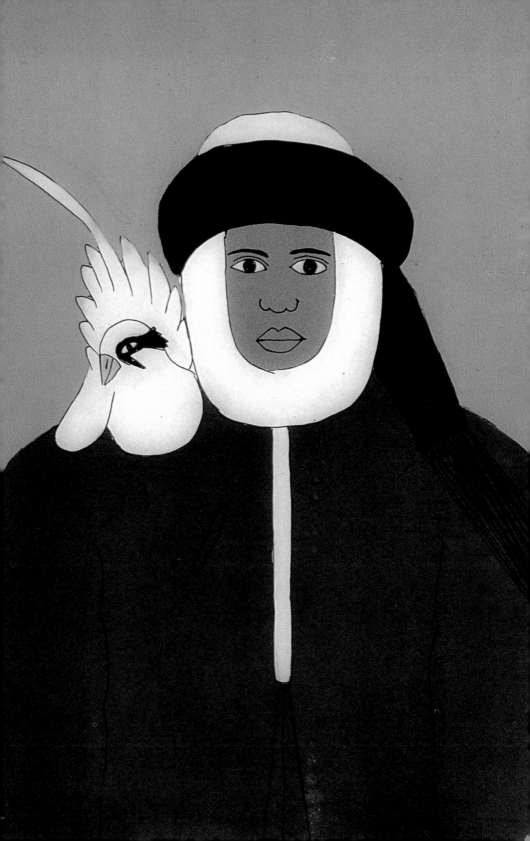

Created and Directed by Hans Höfer

INSIGHT GUIDES

The GAMBIA and SENEGAL

Edited by Philip Sweeney

Principal photography by Michel Renaudeau

Editorial Director: Brian Bell

HOUGHTON MIFFLIN COMPANY

APA PUBLICATIONS

NO part of this book may be reproduced, stored in or introduced into a retrieval system, or transmitted in any form or by any means (electronic, mechanical, photocopying, recording or otherwise), without the prior written permission of the copyright owner of this book, Apa Publications (H.K.) Ltd. Brief text quotations with use of photographs are exempted for book review purposes only.

As every effort is made to provide accurate information in this publication, we would appreciate it if readers would call our attention to any errors that may occur by communicating with Höfer Media (Pte) Ltd., Orchard Point Post Office Box 219, Singapore 9123. Information has been obtained from sources believed to be reliable, but its accuracy and completeness, and the opinions based thereon, are not guaranteed.

The Gambia & Senegal

First Edition (2nd Reprint)
© **1993 APA PUBLICATIONS (HK) LTD**
All Rights Reserved
Printed in Singapore by Höfer Press Pte. Ltd

Distributed in the United States by:	Distributed in Canada by:	Distributed in the UK & Ireland by:	Worldwide distribution enquiries:
Houghton Mifflin Company	**Thomas Allen & Son**	**GeoCenter International UK Ltd**	**Höfer Communications Pte Ltd**
2 Park Street	390 Steelcase Road East	The Viables Center, Harrow Way	38 Joo Koon Road
Boston, Massachusetts 02108	Markham, Ontario L3R 1G2	Basingstoke, Hampshire RG22 4BJ	Singapore 2262
ISBN: 0-395-66291-5	ISBN: 0-395-66291-5	ISBN: 9-62421-099-3	ISBN: 9-62421-099-3

ABOUT THIS BOOK

This new *Insight Guide* covers one of the world's less well-known destinations, but by no means one of its less interesting. The colours, sounds and, above all, the culture and philosophy of West Africa's closest neighbour to Europe offer fascinating possibilities for discovery. The region is a perfect subject for the award-winning Apa Publications formula of presenting the full picture of a country—the background to its life and traditions—rather than merely offering a tour guide's view of its territory.

The Right Staff

As with all titles in the series, a team of specialists was assembled to piece together the mosaic at its most vivid. When it came to recruiting the key member of this team, the project editor—whose job it is to find and coordinate the various talents—Apa's London-based editorial director **Brian Bell** thought immediately of **Philip Sweeney**.

The two had met through *The Observer*, one of Britain's top Sunday newspapers. Bell had been deputy editor of the paper's magazine section, for which Sweeney had been commissioned to visit Senegal and write a profile of the young singing star Youssou N'Dour, who was making news for his work with the rock singer Peter Gabriel. As a London-based writer and journalist—his work appeared regularly in several of Britain's national newspapers—Sweeney has visited West Africa frequently, partly to research a book on popular musics of the world.

The majority of the footwork—or, in this case, bush taxi work—was done by **Andy Gravette**, an experienced travel writer who first visited Senegal and the Gambia 20 years ago as a special correspondent for *The Sunday Times* of London. He has continued to return regularly to both countries, lured back by the charm of the Gambians and the stark contrasts to be found in Senegal. As a travel writer, Gravette contributes regularly to the Economist Intelligence Unit and produces articles, often supported by his own photography, to a variety of magazines and periodicals. He is the author of previous books on Cuba, the French and the Netherlands Antilles.

For an insider's view of Dakar, as well as for the most authoritative accounts of the religious and ethnic composition of the region and of its arts, Sweeney approached the Senegalese television journalist and producer **Amadou Moctar Gueye**. Gueye studied at the Universities of Dakar and Paris before taking a Masters in Mass Communication at the University of Leicester, England, during which period he polished his English to the level he later required as presenter of the nightly English language news on Senegalese television. In addition to his television work and his frequent visits on press delegations to Europe and the rest of Africa, Gueye finds time to write books (his latest on *Communications and Politics in Africa* is under preparation), participate in the running of Sud Communication, a Dakar press agency, and act as correspondent of the London specialist journal *West Africa*.

Few analysts are better qualified to describe the political structures and conditions of the region than *West Africa*'s editor-in-chief **Kaye Whiteman**. One of London's most experienced and respected commentators on African affairs, Whiteman broadcasts

Sweeney

Gravette

Gueye

Whiteman

regularly on the BBC and independent television channels as well as BBC World Service radio. A nine-year break from journalism as information officer for the Commission of European Communities in Brussels provided him with invaluable insight into the European perspective of interaction with Africa, not least during his work organising EEC delegations throughout the continent. His numerous publications include works on *Minority Rights in Chad*, the Lomé Convention and much more.

If Whiteman has few peers in London on Senegambian politics, **Nim Caswell** is equally pre-eminent as an analyst of the region's economics. Caswell has been working on Africa since 1980, when she abandoned a career as a high-flying civil servant in the British Ministry of Agriculture in favour of writing and research. This took her first to Dakar, where she investigated the downfall of the Senegalese groundnut marketing board, and thence to the BBC radio African Service. Four years as Africa Editor of the Economist Intelligence Unit followed, from where she moved to London's *Financial Times*. Caswell, who lives in north London, is also a director of a marketing and consultancy firm specialising in Francophone Africa.

Sweeney had met **Michael** and **Elizabeth Kelly** in Dakar where Michael Kelly was an English language teaching adviser attached to the Senegalese Ministry of Education. Having partaken of Kelly's hospitality in their flat overlooking the ocean, shared their Land-Rover on trips to St Louis and Banjul and benefited from their unerring taste and knowledge of the best places to sample Siné Saloum oysters or *thiof farci à la Saint Louisienne*, he knew they were natural choices to guide discerning visitors to the region.

Michael Kelly wrote the chapter on Banjul, where he moved from Dakar to advise the Gambian Ministry of Education. Apart from his career in education throughout West Africa, Kelly is a published poet and writer of short stories and a translator of African song lyrics from Wolof into English.

Elizabeth Kelly, a qualified teacher, has also held posts in schools throughout the region while simultaneously bringing up their large family. A keen cook currently preparing a book on African cuisine, she contributed the chapter on Senegambian gastronomy as well as painstakingly and meticulously assembling the Travel Tips section on the Gambia.

The Pictures

The majority of the photographs for the book were supplied by **Michael Renaudeau**, a Paris-based photographer who, either personally or via his agency and publishing company, has been responsible for more than 20 books on countries throughout Africa, the Caribbean and the Far East. Renaudeau's unrivalled archive of photographs from Senegambia was acquired over the 20 years he lived in Senegal, a country he first encountered during a spell as a technical adviser attached to the Senegalese Ministry of Tourism in the 1960s. Among the most attractive images he captured during his residence were his many photographs of the beautiful old colonial house he inhabited in the romantically faded island of Gorée.

Final thanks go to **Kaj Berndtson**, who drew the maps, to **Diane Fisher**, who proofread and indexed the book, and to **Jill Anderson**, who tamed the computer.

Caswell   *M. Kelly*   *E. Kelly*   *Renaudeau*

CONTENTS

TRAVEL TIPS

You can travel to the Senegambia region by car from Europe— across the Mediterranean, south over the great Sahara and into Black Africa. Budget for a month and a couple of good four-wheel-drive vehicles. Or you can fly the distance in six hours and be at a comfortable dining table overlooking a pool by suppertime on the day you leave.

The two methods illustrate the different extremes of the appeal of the region. It is exotic, redolent of the dark age of the slave trade and of the trans-Saharan camel caravans. At the same time, it is a thoroughly practical and convenient holiday destination, easily accessible to holidaymakers who want to see nothing more exciting than a hammock between two palm trees.

It is also relatively secure. Both Senegal and the Gambia are stable multi-party democracies with low crime rates and freedom of speech and information. Coupled with this, the cultural lives of both countries are rich, combining the best of Europe and of Africa, in a civilised intellectual climate which permeates the region's life.

Preceding pages: Sharing a joke on the bus home; washing sheep in St Louis; washing shoes in the River Senegal; pounding millet. **Left**: function follows form in the Sahel.

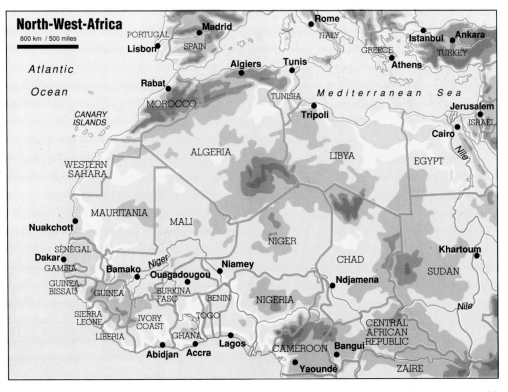

North-West-Africa

800 km / 500 miles

The Senegal Negro, male and female.

Engraved for the Encyclopædia Londinensis, 1818.

J. Chapman, Sc.

Before the Sahara Desert began to creep south and west, the great bulge of West Africa enjoyed a very different climate and landscape from today. Fossilised evidence shows the land between the Senegal and Casamance rivers to have been teeming with wildlife. Today descendants of those antelope and buffalo are conserved in a National Park near the source of the Gambia River.

Nomadic tribes, attracted by the profusion of game and lush vegetation of the river basins, began to establish permanent settlements by around 800 BC. A neolithic civilisation grew up in the area supported by a climate and environment conducive to a hunting and gathering lifestyle.

Left to their own devices, the Senegambian people developed their own kind of societies and religions. Sun worship and belief in natural gods evolved as the people settled into a more established way of life, combining hunting and fishing with the raising of crops. Almost lost are the beliefs and rituals of the ancient tribes that once lived in Senegambia. We know, however, that the supreme deity of West Africa was Wulbari, or Nyankopon. This god, who controlled the sun, moon, darkness and blindness, was also named Anansi.

Human sacrifice: In north Senegambia tribes worshipped Nyamia Ama, the god of rain, storms, lightning—and gold. In the south the people looked to the god Sene who was both kind and vicious. Also god of rain, thunderstorms and the rocks, Sene possessed the ability to make the sun bright and to dim the moon. Represented by a stool surmounted by an iron ball signifying a thunderbolt, the god Guruhi, in southern Senegambia, demanded human sacrifices and was said to torture his victims. His name derived from that of the god of war and of smiths, Gu in the south, Ogun in the north.

Other deities were Shango, the warrior/magician god, Sagbata the god of disease, Famien of fertility, Akovodun, god of the dead, and the panther god Agassu. Crocodile gods, tree fetishes, snake worship, river gods and social taboos distinguished a network of connected civilisations across Senegambia.

Mythology and magic mirrored everyday life and were well developed by around 500 BC when Hanno the Great, a Carthaginian navigator from near Tunis, visited the West African coast. In his *Periplus*, or Circumnavigating Voyage, he related encounters with elephants and hippopotami along the rivers he named "Chertes" (the Senegal) and "Bambotus" (the Gambia).

Less than 20 years after Hanno's visit, Euthymenes, a trader from Marseilles in France, voyaged around the "bulge" of West Africa, noting the mouths of the two rivers. By this time the Persian King Cambyses had occupied Egypt and, around 470 BC, the Persian Sataspes visited the Senegal River on a mapping expedition.

It was, however, Herodotus, the Ionic Greek historian, who gave the Senegambian region a name, "Garamandes". Tracing a short distance up the estuaries of both rivers, Herodotus noted that the natives practised "silent trade" with those tribes which were hostile. Goods were left in a certain place to be exchanged by passing traders from alien tribes. Herodotus also remarked that local people made a wine from the palm tree, a tradition maintained to this day—nearly 2,500 years later.

Following Herodotus' expedition to coastal Senegambia in 445 BC, little was written for 300 years about the region's exploration until another Greek, Polyibus, visited Senegal's coast in 146 BC. Further inland, civilised cultures had established large, prosperous settlements such as the one at Jenne-Jeno.

Even by Polyibus' time peoples from the interior of Africa were trading with the coastal Senegalese and Gambian iron workers. Slaves were taken from among the river folk to trade with merchants from the Sahara and further north. Gold, salt and iron became currency along with iron, Phoenician glass beads and copper ornaments. Several of the central West African kingdoms were destined to affect the development of Senegambia, particularly as the River Niger rose in the

Left, early English engraving—the European's idea of the African.

same Futa Djalon mountain range as the Senegal and Gambia Rivers.

Trade in the inhospitable countryside, still covered by dense forest, jungle and bush, demanded the use of river traffic as a means of communication and exchange. Townships like Jenne, recently excavated, show 16 centuries of occupation and trade with isolated settlements on the coastline of Senegal and the Gambia.

Contemporary clay utensils and weapons, burial urns and children's toys discovered in Mali are more advanced than the primitive implements, tumuli graves and lack of ornaments found in Senegambia. In the millennium before the birth of Christ there was

Sahara was then known only as Sudan, comprising one region which spread from Egypt to the Senegal River.

It was in the area just east of the arc of the Senegal that a powerful ethnic group evolved. Commanding a large territory of fertile land, the first major West African civilisation was the Empire of Ghana. Established around the end of the third century AD, it spread west from its capital of Kumbi Saleh in what is now Mali, embracing the country of the Zenega in the north and of the Wolof and Serer peoples in the south. Gold, slaves and ivory were bartered for salt from the Saharan mines.

Located at a vital cross-roads of African

little change for the tribes between the two rivers.

The people who moved into north Senegambia were known as the Zenega, a branch of the Berber tribes. The name Senegal may come from *Zenega*, although no conclusive explanation of the origin of the name is available—another common version is that the word comes from the Wolof *sunu gal*, meaning "our canoe".

Wicker shelters soon developed into more permanently established villages as primitive tribes were forging their identities and, further east, larger groups were founding empires. The strip of Africa south of the

trade, the Empire of Ghana flourished and Arab travellers described Ghana's king as "the richest man in the world". The Ghana Empire dominated part of Senegambia until the 10th century, during which time another kingdom was established by Soninke, or Tukulor, tribes. From around the 9th century, the Tukulors, who ocupied the Senegal River Valley, built up the powerful Tekrur Empire.

An important development of the time is closely associated with the Ghana Empire. Early in its evolution, the Empire was introduced to metal smelting. Iron, in large quantities, was found along the banks of the Gambia River. The discovery of mysterious circles of laterite megaliths associated with an iron smelting civilisation point to an advanced society based between the Gambia and Saloum Rivers.

Iron and Islam: Estimated to have been erected around AD 75, the Senegambian stone circles and the advent of West Africa's Iron Age preceded a cultural revolution which swept across the entire region. Islam reached Senegambia in the 11th century. Conflict between Muslim Arabs and the Ghana Empire accelerated the spread of the new religion when, in 1076, Abu Bakr, leader of the Almoravid religious order, defeated the Empire of Ghana and allied his

coast between the Gambia and Sine Rivers by the year 1235.

For almost 300 years the Mali Empire held sway over the leading tribes of Senegambia, initially under King Sundiata, then under his famous grandson, Mansa Musa. Mali was an Islamic empire and the Wolof, Serer and Tukolor tribes were quickly conquered and converted to the Muslim faith.

Between Cape Verde and the Senegal River, Fulani invaders established a new empire during the 13th century. On the coast another, smaller kingdom emerged at the beginning of the 15th century. Known as the Kingdom of Djolof, it was controlled by the dominant Wolof tribe. Later, this kingdom

forces with those of the newly-founded Islamic Empire of Tekrur.

The influence of Islam was not readily accepted by native Mandé tribes living in the southern part of Senegambia. For a short while, an Empire known as Songhai, founded by Mandingo and Sussu tribes, controlled the region from the Futa Djalon mountains in the south to the Gambia River. Filling the void between Abu Bakr's Kingdom, based east of Senegambia, its land extended from Niger to the West African

Left, European world map, circa 1500. **Above**, Tuareg slaves.

was divided into Djolof, Walo, Cayor and Baol states. Meanwhile, the Fulani and Tukolor tribes had created a Muslim imamate in the east called Futa Toro.

In the south, the Mande tribes were not so willing to adopt Islam. But, seeing the benefits of land and power bestowed on favoured tribes which turned to Islam, the people south of the Gambia River consolidated against the northern tribes under Sunni Ali from 1464, and under Mohammed Askia the Great from 1493. By this time, however, emissaries from Europe were beginning the exploration which was to have such a dramatic effect on the continent.

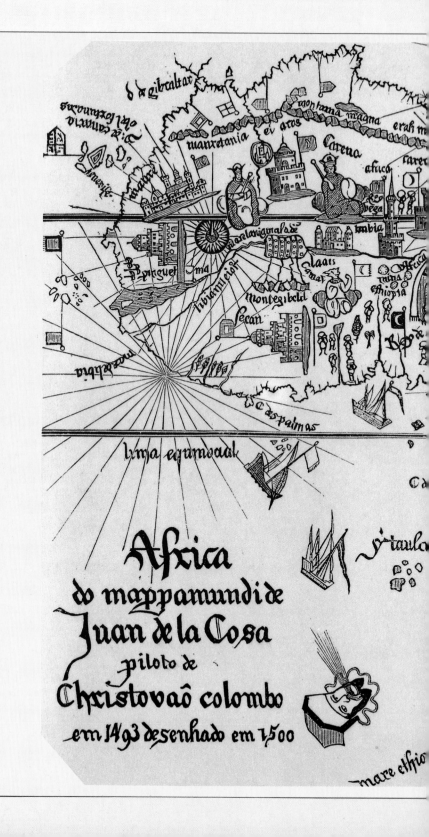

Africa
do mappamundi de
Juan de la Cosa
piloto de
Christovaõ colombo
em 1493 desenhado em 1500

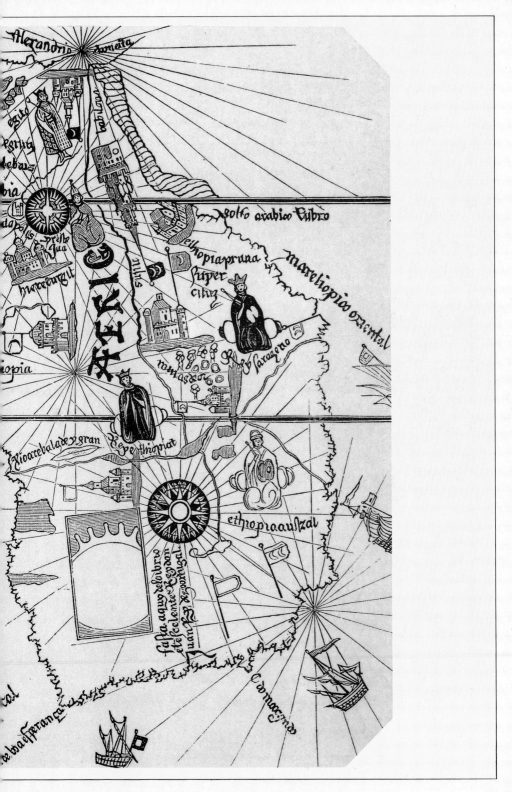

29

In the ceaseless search for trade and riches in the African continent, numerous early maps had been drawn up by the ancients. The first known chart of the Senegambian coast was drawn up in 141 A.D. The Romans, by this time, were establishing themselves in Africa north of the Sahara and had introduced the camel to travel to sub-Saharan regions, expanding their trading routes. In 150 A.D. Ptolemy mapped their known world showing quite accurately the courses of the Senegal and Gambia Rivers and locating a settlement he called Magiora, somewhere on the Senegal. This shows that even as the Romans were pushing Saharan tribes south, townships were growing up along the West African riverbanks.

Both the Phoenicians and the Vikings were thought to have drawn up sea charts of the West African coast in addition to the Romans' mapping of the settlements south of the Sahara. As the religion of Islam spread into Africa from 622 A.D. the world's most expert cartographers, the Arabs, documented each conquest and converted settlement.

By 1076 Islam had crept into the area south and west of the Senegal River. With the expansion of trade and education which followed in its wake, detailed Muslim charts defined new territories as the faith encroached into pagan Africa. Islamic missionaries, with Koran in one hand and scimitar in the other, were the first outsiders to explore Senegambia.

Imaginative charts: The first serious map of the region was produced in around 1300 by Abraham de Cresques. His cartographic efforts were based more on mariners' tales than on factual evidence and his map was soon superseded by a circular image of the globe made in 1307 and dubbed the Hereford map. Several of these early maps showing West Africa depicted kings seated on bejewelled thrones, rich palaces and camel trains of treasure, embellishments which owed as much to the over-excited imaginations of the cartographers as to any first-hand reportage.

Preceding pages: map of Africa by Columbus's pilot, circa 1500. Left, Prince Henry the Navigator.

These were the early maps which were studied by would-be explorers particularly by the Dieppois who are said to have reached Gorée Island in around 1364. Early voyagers were primarily inspired by the legends of immense riches in gold to be found in that part of the continent. Indeed, much of the known world's gold did come from West Africa at that time. As cartographers' imaginative illustrations actually materialised and gold began to filter back to Europe from the region south of the Sahara, explorers started to search for routes into the interior from the West African coast.

A leading light, master mariner and financier of ambitious expeditions was Prince Henry the Navigator of Portugal. One of the Portuguese king's champions, Nuno Tristão, reached the mouth of the Senegal River in 1443, and three years later, ventured another 200 miles (320 km) further south along the coast.

Another of Prince Henry's mariners, Dinaz Diaz, explored the Senegal River in 1444 and his contemporary Ca'da Mosto noted cotton, rice, exotic animals and the golden jewellery prevalent in the region.

On his 1465 journey up the Gambia River he received slaves and gold from a local chief. Ca'da Mosto opened up both major rivers of the Senegambia for exploration and trade—the word Gambia is itself thought to come from cambio, meaning exchange in Spanish. It was the practice of barter which brought tribal traders to the coast and to the rivers and attracted merchants from Europe to venture into the West African interior. French traders first sailed up the Gambia River in 1570 and, by 1588, Antonio, Prior of Crato, had won exclusive trading rights throughout Senegambia from Queen Elizabeth I of England.

Black ivory, bitter battles: The early Portuguese traders first developed the idea of sending labourers from Africa to the Americas. The cultivation of sugar cane which the Arabs had introduced to Southern Europe had become of such importance that new plantations were springing up as fast as fresh territory could be found. The slave trade from Africa to the West Indies was part of a triangle of trade, which involved trinkets shipped from Europe being exchanged for African slaves, who were sold to Caribbean plantation owners and replaced by the Antillean produce of sugar, rum and tobacco destined for the markets of Europe. The business depended on easy access to the sea from harbours and ports on the West African coast. Each settlement in the 1600s had its own "factory" or collecting station where slaves would be gathered to wait for the trading ships.

Each coast was named with reference to its produce—the Gold Coast, the Grain Coast, the Teeth Coast (Ivory), the Gum Coast (Gum Arabic) and the Slave Coast. `

Although the English were comparatively late in the succession of nations to exploit the riches of Senegambia—the first Portuguese slave ship to leave West Africa for the Americas sailed in 1510—Elizabethan mariners made up for lost time by organising trading expeditions backed by military force. By the time that the Portuguese had lost their interest in black slavery, preferring the trade in Far Eastern spices, both English and French had begun regular shipments of "black ivory" from the Senegalese and Gambian coasts. The famous English seadog Captain John Hawkins took the first British slave ship to the West Indies in 1562. From that time on, the competition for the

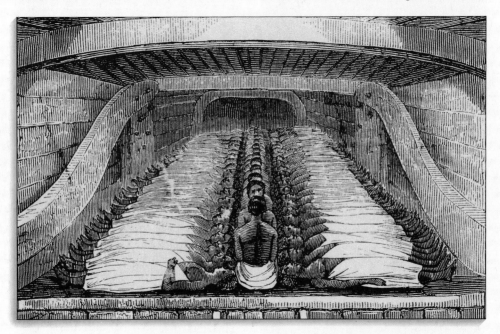

Even tribes were renamed according to their skills. The Kru, for example, were named for their rowing expertise. It is estimated that as many as 10 million slaves were shipped to the New World between 1526 and 1810. Brazil alone received more than three million as a result of Portuguese enterprise.

It was not only the Portuguese, Dutch, English and French who involved themselves in the lucrative business of trading in "black ivory". It had long been African custom to take and enslave workers from other tribes conquered in battle, and Arab and African marauders had captured and traded in slaves for centuries.

slave trade alternated between French, Dutch and English entrepreneurs.

In 1617 the first permanent European trading settlement was founded by the Dutch West Indies Company, securing a foothold at Gorée. By 1621 the French had dug in on the Senegalese coast at St. Louis, and built a fort there. France also built a slave factory on the island of Bocos off the Cape Verde peninsula. The demand for black African slaves to work the Caribbean sugar plantations was increasing and new slavery posts were set up at navigable points along the coast or on tidal waters of the major rivers.

French expansion was stimulated by the

1633 commissioning by Cardinal Richelieu of the Senegal Company. The Portuguese had built a trading post south of the River Gambia at Gereeja before the mid-17th century and this had been used by British traders. Once Portuguese traders had established half-way posts at Gereeja and Tankular on the river's south bank they were in a position, by around the mid-1600s, to trade with Sukutu. Situated 250 miles (400 km) up the Gambia River, this Djolof city numbered 4,000 inhabitants in 1507. Gold from the interior, iron from the Gambia, slaves and gum Arabic were bartered by British, French and Portugese traders.

Florence had been producing gold coinage explored the Gambian coast in 1652, attacking British Commonwealth shipping until the newly-founded "Royal Adventurers Trading in Africa" Company was established in 1661.

Island Forts: The Portuguese first named a tiny island in the Gambia River estuary after a sailor who was buried there. Ilha de San André became one of the most strategic bastions in the battles of the slave trade. The first fort on the island was built by the Duke of Courland, Germany, in 1651. For nine years the Duke traded from his island for slaves which he shipped to Tobago in the Caribbean. French privateers seized the island in 1659 but Courland recaptured it in the

since 1252, and the Almoravid dinar was the basis of both Spanish and Portugese gold coins. Several Portuguese trading locations had been established in the region of the Senegal River and the English planned similar posts in the Gambia. At this time more gold from West Africa was being used by Europe than from any other source.

Charles II of England had heard the legends of "El Dorado", the fabled gold lands of West Africa and his supporter Prince Rupert following year. In 1661 the English named the island after the heir to their throne— James Island.

The English were ousted by the Dutch the following year, having hardly had time to build the little fort. But, they had made a deal that same year over Gorée Island with the Dutch. And the English kept a contingent at the island fort until the French conquered it in 1695. Again the English replaced the French usurpers in 1713 and held the position until 1719 when the privateer Hywel Davis ransacked the fort.

Six years after the pirate attack, a powder magazine blew Fort James into the river,

Left, an Atlantic slave transport, 1844. Above, exercising slaves to keep them healthy.

ALEX HALEY AND "ROOTS"

It was the height of the wet season on the north bank of the River Gambia in 1681 and, through lashing October rains, one could make out the hump of the fort on James Island out in the wide, muddy waters. British men of war stood out in the roads, facing the spit of land near the large building at Juffure. On the point the tricolour of the French flew over a hurriedly built drywall fortress and two French frigates stood off the shore. This spot, Albreda, was almost a double of Juffure and its neighbouring plot, Sanchaba, the last two in English territory.

All three were built as slavery "factories". The high walls of the compounds contained cells, a courtyard and a slave master's quarters. In the centre of the compound stood a row of iron-ringed posts to which captives and prospective merchandise would be shackled for inspection by the slave ships' buyers.

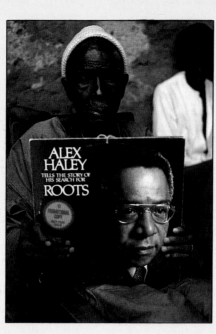

In the centre of the large quadrangle stood a mast from which the British Union flag flew. In later days, any slave who risked his chances against the soldiers' muskets and reached the flagpole would be granted instant freedom. Around the Battlement walls cannon bristled, powder and ramrod at the ready. This was Juffure, only one year after it was constructed.

Many thousands of bewildered tribesmen, women and children were to pass through the iron-studded doors in the baked mud walls to certain death in the billows of the Atlantic Ocean or the burning cane fields of West Indian plantations over the next 126 years. Manacled in the scant shade of the dusty factory square the families, often from different tribes, beliefs and tongues, had been marched to the station from many miles up country, often in pairs, with double-forked sticks tied to their necks. Their captors may have been Arab merchants, European privateers or soldiers, or other West African tribes.

From the 500 or more factories similar to Juffure up and down the West African coast, millions of slaves were shipped by Portuguese, French, British, Spanish, Dutch and German slave boats to toil in the fields of the Americas—Brazil, the Caribbean, Central America or the southern states of the USA.

One such slave, brought from Juffure to a cotton plantation in the deep south was named Kunta Kinte. Captured from his forest village as a small boy, the Mandinka youth could remember the circumstances of his kidnapping quite vividly. He remembered being brought to Juffure by the river, his last walk on African soil, from the slave compound to the longboat, being hauled on board the great sailing ship and the last glimpse of light and breath of fresh river air as he was thrust into the gaping hold, and finally interminable weeks below decks in stifling conditions with little or no food and water.

Separated from family, tribe and homeland, Kunta Kinte was sold onto a Southern plantation and put to work on the fields. The boy never forgot his heritage back in Africa. Every detail he put to memory and, in his mind, retained the thoughts, sounds, smells, rituals and traditions of family life back in the Gambia. More importantly, he passed on every detail to his sons, their sons and their sons in turn, until in the 1960s, a writer called Alex Haley found that he was able to trace his ancestry back to Kunta Kinte himself.

In a moving book, Haley painted a vivid picture of the saga of his ancestors from their village in the Gambia to the present day in the USA. *Roots*, both a literary success and a block-busting film series, was one of the 1970s' best-selling books, making Haley's ancestral home of Juffure a Gambian national monument and place of homage for both fans of the book and those who identified with the story of Kunta Kinte.

Today, on the teetering jetty at Juffure, a chattering group of little children gathers as each *pirogue* or ferry unloads visitors at the doors to the old slave station. To the right of the village the crumbling remains of the "holding station" can be seen. Directly ahead, as the path forks off by an ancient cannon, the compound of Kunta Kinte is a low huddle of corrugated iron-roofed huts. Visitors make their way up to the central hut followed by eager villagers. An elder relates the saga—and gifts, souvenirs and money change hands.

requiring another remodelling exercise. Soon it became redundant as a fort and was abandoned about 50 years later. In the 300 years of European occupation, James Island had changed hands at least 10 times.

Similarly, a tiny, baboon-infested island near to James Island, also in a commanding position in the River Gambia, was fortified in order to protect slave shipping lanes. Dog Island, named after the barking of the baboons, was occupied by the English in 1666 and Fort Charles was established. Although impressive remains of the fortifications exist on James Island, nothing of Fort Charles is now visible on Dog Island.

Across a narrow stretch of the Gambia

Further north, in Senegal, the Swedes had taken the island of Gorée in 1655, the Dutch having retired to Rufisque a few miles away. The Dutch had also constructed a "factory" at Arguin Island north of the Senegal River and the French had, by 1659, fortified their base at St Louis in the far north of Senegal. Skirmishes over trade and territory occurred almost monthly during these times until, in 1677, the French Admiral, d'Estrées, drove the Dutch from Senegambia by capturing the Isle of Gorée (or Cape Coast Castle as the English called it).

The British Royal African Company was chartered in 1684 and the Royal Senegal Company was founded by 1696. By this time

Camp de Podor. 1853

River from James Island there was another strategic outpost called Albreda by the French. Here they built a little slave trading station on the northern shores of the Gambia River in 1670. By 1681 France's soldiers had fortified the post and it was held for almost 175 years, until 1857. Just behind this French enclave in English territory, an English trading post was built at Juffure in 1680. Twice the English forces overran Albreda, but they were only able to defend it against the French for a few months.

Left, village chief at Juffure. **Above**, traders camp at Podor, Senegal.

there were more then 10 main slave trading posts and forts in the Senegambian territory, including St Louis, Gorée, Rufisque, Portudal, Jaol, Albreda, James Island, Juffure and, on the Senegal River, Podor, Matam and Bakel.

By the late 1600s, the Portuguese had either been ousted from West Africa or moved on to better trading grounds. Ancient Portuguese factories were being rebuilt and fortified by the English and several remain as ruins, signifying the extent of river trade in the early 1700s. Gereeja and Tankular are particularly of note on the south bank of the Gambia River. Another fortification is at

THE WRECK OF THE MEDUSA

A tragic shipwreck off the coast of modern-day Mauritania, not far north of Senegal inspired one of the world's most celebrated works of art. Horrific details filtered through to 19th-century France of the loss of the brigantine "Medusa" on its way to Gorée, which had been restored by the Treaty of Paris to the French the previous year. In shark-infested waters many French families were drowned by the raging Atlantic waves. The ship had left the mother country in the summer of 1816 with 400 crew and soldiers on board as well as the new Governor of Senegal, going out to take up his post. Its life-boats were scandalously inadequate:

to build a replica of the raft using details described by the few souls who survived the wreck. Géricault even invited individuals to pose for his sketches on the makeshift platform.

The painting, now in the Louvre, portrays a classical pyramid formation of the living and dead desperately clinging to the disintegrating raft. Because of the graphic depiction of the survivors, the public of France were affronted. The storm of criticism paralleled the storm illustrated on the canvas when it was first shown in the "Salon of 1819", in Paris.

A famous artist of the day, Michelet, dubbed

they could cope with barely half the numbers actually travelling.

Some survivors clung to wreckage in the vain hope of rescue away from regular shipping lanes, while 150 people took refuge on a large improvised raft. Only 15 were left alive when a passing ship picked them up weeks later. It was this desperate scene which caught the imagination of an eminent French painter.

Aided by numerous sketches, a few of which are in the Louvre Museum, Paris, and studies of corpses and human limbs made in the Hôpital Beaujon, Théodore Jean-Louis André Géricault created what has become one of France's most treasured exhibits. Between 1818 and 1819, the artist worked on his huge canvas, going so far as

Géricault the "Corregio of suffering". Delacroix enthused over the painting as one of the first French Romantic period masterpieces to be exhibited. The giant canvas accompanied a travelling exhibition to England, where it received high acclaim.

Equal in technique, but simpler in subject matter, is Géricault's *Portrait of a Negro*, a vivid and moving portrayal of a young Senegalese. This noted classical study is now on show in the Denon Museum, Chalon-sur-Saône, France. Remaining, however, his most celebrated historical work, *The Raft of the Medusa*, initially named simply *Shipwreck Scene*, gives an insight into the reportage style introduced into French art by the master Géricault.

Tendaba, 62 miles (100 km) upstream and there is another at Berfet.

Slavery's lengthy demise: By 1758 the British had almost ousted the French but, by 1763, the French were back in Gorée. All this time, the English had been keeping up a regular trade in slaves to the West Indies and exploring more of the interior. Asserting their power on the coast, the English eventually controlled Senegal in 1765. The Crown Colony of Senegambia, the first British colony in Africa, was created by 1768.

St Louis was given over to the French in 1776 and an attack on James Island from Gorée destroyed the entire fort, driving the British to concentrate on the south banks of the Gambia in 1783. At the subsequent Treaty of Paris, France relinquished its hold on all but the slave factory of Albreda, and French troops were re-stationed north of the Gambia River.

The advent of the 19th century should have been a relief for the indigenous inhabitants of West Africa. Instead, the 1800s saw increasing racial and religious strife overshadowing the fact that Britain had imposed a ban on slavery throughout its territories in 1807. The French continued to trade in slaves for another 41 years and, as the British Navy was entrusted with the task of cleaning up the "black ivory" business, they had ample excuse to harass the French along the West African coastline.

Without immense numbers of men, however, it was impossible to prevent the Arabs and tribal chiefs from persisting in the lucrative trade. Although the French had temporarily introduced emancipation before the English, slavery had returned with a vengeance on the orders of Napoleon in 1802. During the first few years of Britain's anti-slavery policy, more than 100 slave vessels were captured off the Gambian coast, bound either for Cuba or Brazil.

Resettlement townships were set up in the Gambia for slaves captured from the traders. It was discovered, through this scheme, that some powerful tribes in the hinterland were selling off entire weaker tribes to traders from the French coast. The trade in slaves appeared to be increasing until the British founded an encampment at Banjul (Bathurst) from which to rid the coast of slavers. In 1816 Captain Alexander Grant entered into a treaty with Kobo's chief for the island of Banjul, renamed St Mary's Island, which was eventually to become the Gambian capital.

From 1821 until 1843 the British territory on the Gambia River was ruled from Sierra Leone. In 1826 the strategic Point of Barra, opposite Bathurst was strengthened by the construction of Fort Bullen. In 1828 Grant negotiated for MacCarthy Island, which was later renamed Georgetown. Plots of land on the north shore were procured from local chiefs and peanuts were introduced in 1829.

Both sailing and steamships had plied the

waters of the four great rivers of Senegal and the Gambia shipping goods far into the hinterland. Navigable for about 200 miles (320 km), the River Gambia narrowed after MacCarthy Island but still proved to be one of the most important waterways in West Africa. Trading with the far interior was facilitated through this point at the settlement of Georgetown and, in Senegal, similar success had been achieved on the Casamance and Senegal Rivers which were also navigable for some miles upstream. However, real exploration, not just for the opening up of trade routes, did not begin in the Senegambia region until well into the 19th century.

Left, Géricault's *Radeau de la Méduse*. **Right**, shackles in the slave-house on Gorée.

EXPLORERS OF THE INTERIOR

"...So geographers, in Afric-maps,
With savage-pictures fill their gaps;
And o'er unhabitable downs
Place elephants for want of towns."
— Jonathan Swift 1667-1745

Long before Swift the satirist penned these words, European sorties into West Africa had opened up lands which lay adjacent to the larger rivers. Portuguese, Italian, French and Dutch expeditions had charted the Senegambia coastline and traced the courses of several major rivers. From the Hereford Map of 1307, the Lennox Globe of 1510 and European traders' charts of the early 17th century, the pattern of waterways, deserts, tribal villages and colonisers' settlements evolved slowly over the centuries.

Few adventurers trekked far into the interior, however—unless, like George Thompson in 1619, it was to chart river banks. Thompson explored as far up the River Gambia as Tenda (Tendaba), around 60 miles (100 km). Just a year after Thompson's trip, Richard Jackson followed the English explorer's maps and succeeded in penetrating deep into the Gambia between 1620 and 1624. In search of legendary riches said to be located near the source of the river, Jackson wrote of his expeditions in his book *The Discovery of the Land of King Solomon*—the first detailed account of life in the Senegambian hinterland.

In Senegal, the French made few efforts to venture into the country's interior, even though the Senegal, Siné and Saloum Rivers were all comfortably navigable. Arab warriors from the Mauritanian wastes to the north and Moorish aggressors in the east deterred serious exploration. The region also harboured a daunting selection of diseases which decimated early settlers attempting to establish bases from which expeditions into the continent could be launched. For a century, from Jackson's heroic voyage up the Gambia River, only a few Europeans ventured further inland than the slave trading

stations located conveniently near the estuaries of both the Senegal and Gambia Rivers.

In the late 17th century, territorial squabbles had deterred any serious explorers from venturing into lands which were constantly changing hands. Exploration began in earnest as soon as the tension between France and England was thought to have died down and, in 1723, the adventurer Captain Bartholomew Stibbs was attracted to sail further up the Gambia in search of the legendary gold mines near its headwaters.

Twelve years later another intrepid explorer, Francis Moore, the travel writer, wrote of his escapades in the Gambia in *Travels in the Inland Part of Africa, 1735*. Then in 1745 a British military expedition constructed one of the earliest up-country fortresses at Podor, Senegal. The British explorer Daniel Houghton made an epic journey up the Gambia River in 1790, crossing the Senegal and reaching the settlement of Simbing before being left to die in the desert by marauding Arabs. The place were he died was visited by the famous West African explorer, Mungo Park, six years later.

Park in the wilderness: The story of Mungo Park in West Africa is among the best tales of exploration. It typifies all that came to be thought of as stout and British, even though his adventures precede those of the Victorian era. With little or no knowledge of the area and with archaic maps, the Scottish doctor took on the daunting task of searching for the secret of the vast Niger River. Daniel Houghton had already sacrificed his life to the quest and it was this fatality which induced the African Association to support Park in his ambitious undertaking.

Park was no novice to the tropics, having been assigned at 21 years of age as medical officer on board the *Worcester* bound for Sumatra on the East Indies trade route from 1792-93. The young surgeon studied Javan wildlife and its botanical curiosities. On 22 May 1795, having convinced the Association that he was the man for the job, Park boarded a vessel to Bathurst and from there proceeded up the Gambia River to Pisania (Karantaba). Here, 200 miles (320 km) inland Park, who was still in his early twenties,

Preceding pages: men of war off the West African Coast. Left, Mungo Park loses another jacket.

spent five months learning the Mandingo language. On horseback, with two helpers, he headed upstream. An obelisk marks the spot where Park left the village in early December.

The story of the "Mambo Jambo" talisman has long been associated with Park's journey through eastern Senegal. Thought to be an idol in the shape of a grotesque snake—similar to the "Rainbow Snake" worshipped by tribes further down the West African coast— the talisman was used by the Woolli River people to regulate all their village disputes by making sacrifices to the image. Park said that he found a mask of the Mambo Jambo spirit somewhere near Tamba-

almost died of a tropical fever. But seven months later he was helped back to Pisania by friendly tribespeople.

In Pisania Park sheltered in a "slave factory" and wrote an account of his first expedition. The book was published in 1799 under the title *Travels in the Interior Districts of Africa* and attracted considerable attention. The same year, Park married and the British Government invited him to lead a party of 45 explorers along the route he had taken from Pisania. Seven of the party backed out before leaving the Gambian outpost, but Park and the 38 remaining struggled into the interior. From Bamako, on the Niger River in Mali, Park sent his last

counda, towards the confluence of the Rivers Gambia and Kouloufou. His story of the rituals associated with the fetish so confused his listeners back in Britain that the phrase *mumbo jumbo* meaning hocus pocus or superstitious rigmarole was born.

Park pressed on eastwards. The following year, 1796, Moorish Arabs imprisoned his company in Upper Senegal. Escaping his captors on 20 July he reached Ségou in Mali on the Niger River. Eventually he ran out of supplies in a place called Silla. From here he travelled alone, reaching Kamalia (Kourémalé), south of Bamako in the Kingdom of Malinke, where he was taken ill and

missive to the outside world in November 1805. The package contained letters and his journal giving accounts of native domestic life, botanical and natural history notes.

Pressing ever further up the Niger, Park and his nine surviving companions were set upon by natives and killed. One slave oarsman of the canoe in which the expedition travelled made the journey back to Pisania, relating the story of the disaster to those at the Gambian trading station in 1812.

An account of Mungo Park's second journey to the Niger River was published in London in 1815 and several years later Park's son died in an attempt to discover the whereabouts of his father's remains. Mungo Park was significant for the great persistence of his exploration, the clarity and abundance of his observations of native life and customs and, above all, for his discovery that, unlike any other West African river, the Niger, which rises in mountains adjacent to the sources of the Gambia and Senegal, does, in fact, flow east.

An unsuccessful attempt to reach the important Saharan trading town of Timbuktu was made by the French explorer René Caillé in around 1816, the same year in which an English expedition managed to reach the town of Bakel. A few years later, between 1819 and 1822, J. Ritchie and G.F.

Lyon made an expedition through Gambia and Senegal in search of the Niger source. Following them, a succession of Victorian explorers ventured inland—Dixon Denham, Hugh Clapperton, Walter Oudney and, in 1825, Major Alexander Gordon Laing, whose company reached Timbuktu.

Meanwhile Caillé twice returned to the seaport of St. Louis in Senegal to replenish expedition funds from the coffers of the Governor, Baron Roger. It was not until 1827 that Caillé, disguised as an Arab trader,

Left, **Mungo Park crosses the Niger. Above**, **René Caillé en route to Timbuktu.**

eventually reached Timbuktu. By this time naturalists were increasingly visiting West Africa in order to obtain specimens of plants and wildlife. Hardly plentiful in Senegambia, but certainly more widespread during the early 19th century, Africa's greatest beast, the elephant, roamed forest and river areas causing fear among early explorers and excitement among wildlife experts.

A hunter named Schmidt, with the support of the French authorities, managed to capture a live elephant. Triumphantly the animal was shipped to Paris and exhibited in the Zoological Park. In 1865 the elephant, which was named "Jumbo", was presented to the London Zoological Gardens—the first African elephant to reach the United Kingdom and the longest-lived elephant ever kept in captivity.

A number of ambitious adventurers were still searching for either the source of the Niger, elusive gold mines, or purely the fame of new discoveries right through the 19th century. The German Heinrich Barth made excursions in the area between 1849 and 1855; French explorer Henri Duveyrier travelled inland during the 1850s, followed by another German, Gustav Nachtigal from 1869 to 1874. Gerhard Rohlfs pursued a number of ancient trade routes from 1862 to 1878 and Oskar Lenz entered the headwaters of the Senegal River in 1879-80, tracing it down its estuary.

The great adventurer Sir Richard Burton, who visited the Gambia in 1863, gave a lengthy account of his travels in *Wanderings in West Africa from Liverpool to Fernando Po*. He wrote the book under the pseudonym F. R. G. S. (Fellow of the Royal Geographical Society). In his account he referred to the region as "the white Man's grave" and an "anti-paradise". Thirty-five years later, Mary Kingsley, in *Travels in West Africa* commented: "When you have made up your mind to go to West Africa the very best thing you can do is to get it unmade again and go to Scotland instead!"

Whatever the impressions those early explorers had of this part of the African continent, it was their persistence which highlighted Senegambia. The arrival of river steamers and the construction of railways— the first of which was the Dakar to St Louis line in 1886—brought an end to the real period of pioneering and discovery.

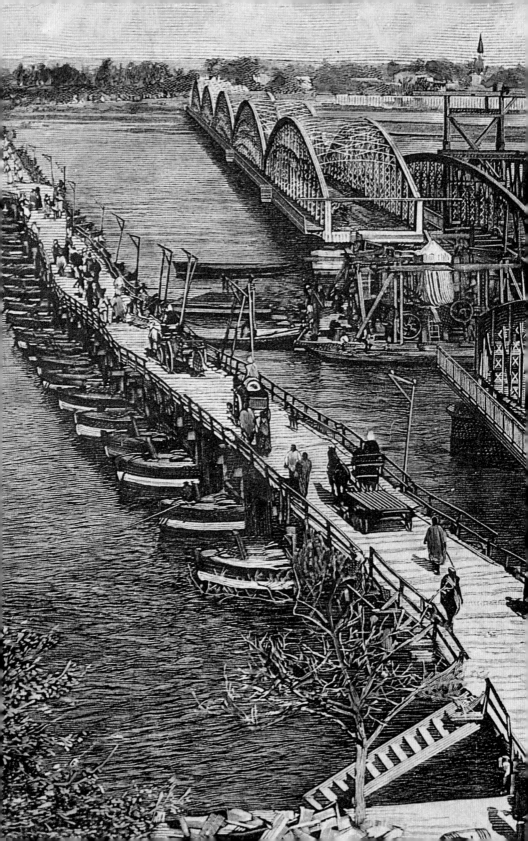

"Ex Africa semper diquid novi" wrote Pliny. ("There is always something new coming from Africa.") Colonialism proved the Roman philosopher right. Ancient Rome first colonised northern Africa but it was French and English colonialism in Senegal and the Gambia which underlined Pliny's comment 2,000 years on.

Both countries experienced similar problems in the years of colonialism; either opposition from the original inhabitants or the difficulty of administrative development. In Senegal, Louis Faidherbe's story illustrates the problems and successes of colonialism in West Africa.

Born in Lille, France, in 1818, Louis-Léon-César Faidherbe found himself in 1852 in a country where his exploits would bring him fame. After two years in Senegal the Deputy Director of Engineers was promoted to Major and appointed Governor of the colony. Flouting orders from Paris, Faidherbe took the initiative against opposition from Tukulor chiefs like El Hadj Omar.

Across Senegal, Islamic African leaders such as Samori and Lat Dyor were conducting a jihad, or holy war, against the largest colonial presence in Africa. With a strong base in Dakar and a system of forts and trading posts across the colony, Faidherbe set about negotiating terms with the tribes.

Marabouts versus the military: Since the advent of Islam the *marabouts*, or religious leaders, had exercised enormous power. Throughout Senegal these leaders stirred up an animosity against the French which had endured since 1798, when the Tidjaniya sect had appeared on the scene from North Africa. Other sects, such as the Mourides and the Khadriya, participated in what were known as the Marabout Wars against the foreign colonialists. The running battles between the *marabouts* and the military spread into the Gambia between 1850 and 1887, although fighting there amounted to little more than a series of skirmishes.

The Marabout Wars delayed and hindered

Preceding pages: building the Faidherbe Bridge, St. Louis. **Right**, Faidherbe's statue in St Louis. **Right**, a *signare* and her servants.

exploration of both Senegal and the Gambia after slavery had been abolished in Senegal in 1848. Governor Faidherbe instigated many exploratory ventures into the interior provoking numerous battles with warring tribes and necessitating the construction of a series of forts in strategic locations throughout the region.

In 1857 Faidherbe founded Dakar and the same year the French relinquished Albreda to the British. From this time both the French and the English pushed deeper into their re-

spective, barely explored, territories.

Faidherbe had likened the Senegambia region to that of Canada or India and planned his strategies with this in mind. Saving Napoleon III the expense of another Mexican or Indo-Chinese campaign, the young Governor set his enemies against each other, even getting his arch-rival, Lat Dyor, to fight for the French in 1870.

Over a period of 37 years from 1850, a Pan-Islamic surge encroaching from the north set local tribes and even families against each other. Faidherbe quelled numerous uprisings incited by the *marabouts* by systematically establishing forts along

MERMOZ AND THE AVIATORS

The world began to open up to Europeans with the advent of commercial air travel in the 1930s. Imperial Airways flew south and east—to Egypt, East Africa and India. Regular flights to New York from Europe made the continent of North America more accessible and, in the late 1920s, airlines even considered flights to South America. But a direct, non-stop flight from Europe to Brazil was impossible as early aircraft had a limited range. Senegal and the Gambia, however lie almost exactly half-way between London, or Paris, and Recife, or Rio de Janeiro. Ideal locations for crew and refuelling stop-overs,

and Dornier flying boat across the Atlantic from Germany to the United States, but the demand for a fast route to South America prompted the construction of an airfield on the site at Jeshwang.

Jeshwang airfield was Lufthansa's West African base for four years, until the outbreak of World War II. The first Zeppelin stopped over here in 1934 on its inaugural flight from Frankfurt to Brazil. Both airships and Dornier aircraft were employed by the German airline on this route until 1938.

British South American Airways' flying boats established a link to Brazil in the latter part of the

both St. Louis—Senegal's capital in the 1930s—and Bathurst (now Banjul) in the Gambia, the furthest points west on the African continent, became important air staging posts.

A French aviator, Jean Mermoz, was the first to open air routes from Paris to Senegal, and from there to South America. Aeropostale's depot was established on the narrow spit of land between St Louis and the Atlantic Ocean. Mail was delivered from Guet N'dar's point—now known as the Hydrobase—to within two miles (three km) of the mailing station.

Lufthansa, the German airline, purchased a piece of land in the Gambia, just outside the capital of Bathurst (Banjul), in 1932. Already the company was operating regular flights by airship

1930s and their aircraft also used the Jeshwang airfield. In 1939, a crash killed 23 people and brought services to a halt. During World War II the British Royal Air Force needed an effective base in West Africa and the Gambia was strategically very suitable. Twenty Sunderland flying boats operated a shipping protection service from Banjul itself throughout the war and the RAF constructed two landing strips at Yundum, 17 miles (27 km) from the capital.

Five years later, the new replacement airport at Yundum, today the Gambia's only airport, was visited by President Franklin D. Roosevelt on his way to Brazil. Senegal, today, has eight airports.

Above, 1930s airline poster.

the Senegal River. The Governor's theories of "assimilation" were adopted by his successor, Admiral Jauréguibéry, who pushed French boundaries as far as Niger by the year 1880. Faidherbe had ensured his name a place in the history books of African colonialism. Almost as prominent is the place of his fiercest adversary, El Hadj Omar Tall, who returned from a youthful pilgrimage to Mecca fired with zeal to convert his pagan home region to Islam. During his brilliant but brutal forty-year warrior career, he succeeded in forcibly converting a vast tract of Senegal and Mali before Faidherbe finally crushed him with a coalition of French and African forces.

the British negotiated control of the River Gambia. In the same year, the Casamance area south of the Gambia River belonging to Portugal was separated, coming under Senegalese jurisdiction and surrounding British Gambia with French territory.

By 1900 France had extended its colonial power as far east as Niger, into Dahomey, Chad, the Ivory Coast, Guinea, Upper Volta and north into parts of Mauritania, Algeria and Tunisia—a total land area of 3.29 million sq. miles (8.52 million sq. km), the largest foreign colonial region on the African continent.

Africa's largest colonisation: From the mid-19th century France had granted privileges

Louis Faidherbe went on to higher roles in French politics and was instrumental in raising funds for the first railroad in Senegal—from Dakar, the city he founded, to St Louis. Dedicated to the emancipation champion, Victor Schoelcher, Faidherbe's best known book, *Le Senegal, la France dans l'Afrique occidentale* (1889), describes his objective of creating a truly Francophone African state and his work as Governor of Senegal.

Faidherbe would have been disappointed to learn that, in the year of his death, 1889,

to its favourite protectorate in Africa. Law decreed that any Senegalese born in the townships of St Louis, Gorée, Rufisque and Dakar automatically became full French citizens—a policy unheard of in other colonial empires. Each region was entitled to locally elected representation in the French parliament.

As part of the "assimilation" process of adopting its Senegalese subjects into French society and politics, the country's first deputy was elected to the French parliament in 1848, serving until 1852. The post became permanent in 1871 but it was not until 1914 that the first African was elected to deputise.

Above, St Louis quay in its heyday.

His name was Blaise Diagne. Born in 1872, he held the post for 20 years, until 1934.

The sliver of land on both shores of the Gambia River followed suit. The Gambia had been plagued by civil disturbances and *marabout* uprisings prior to the British and French destruction of the *marabout* fort at Sukuta (Sabiji) near present-day Banjul. At times the country was placed under the jurisdiction of Freetown in the British colony of Sierra Leone. In 1852, the embryo of the current House of Representatives, the Gambian parliament, was established with both Gambian and white members and Sierra Leone ceased to administer the colony. The British in Gambia had not had the continuing

problem of slavery since its abolition there in 1807, but it was as late as 1895 that the last local leaders and Chiefs agreed, with some reluctance, to desist from the practice of keeping slaves.

By the turn of the century, both Britain and France had quelled the native populaces sufficiently to establish viable colonies. The French in Senegal had smoothed out most local and racial boundaries, maintaining a strict control through networks of forts and trading stations.

Preoccupation with colonial issues blinded both sides to economic development. It was not until the construction of the first railway, instigated by Faidherbe, Governor of Senegal, that real commerce came to the region. Trains swiftly covered distances which took road or river traffic much longer. With the completion of the Dakar—St. Louis line in 1886 a network of rail routes began to take shape with major townships linked to the coastal ports.

Although during the latter half of the 19th century great strides were made in opening up the interior, it was not without the tenacity of successive intrepid explorers backed by military might. Faidherbe had also been responsible for an upturn in the region's economy by promoting the groundnut—introduced in the 16th century by the Portuguese, with manioc and maize from Brazil—into a cash crop.

Towards independence: The entire territories of French West Africa were governed from St Louis on the Senegal River until, in 1902, Dakar became the administrative capital because of its central and coastal location. By 1920 the communes of Dakar, Gorée, St Louis and Rufisque boasted a "colonial council" which consisted not just of local dignitaries and representatives but also tribal chiefs from the interior.

During World War II many Gambians were enlisted to fight for the British, mostly in Burma, while companies of Senegalese infantry swelled the ranks of the French. Just after the war, in 1946, France extended the offer of French citizenship to the colonies, making all French West African states full overseas territories. The same year Léopold Senghor, aged 40, became the first African to sit in the French National Assembly as representative of Senegal. In 1947, and again in 1954, the constitution of the Gambia underwent changes.

Two years later, in 1956, universal suffrage was established in Senegal under the *loi-cadre* reforms aiming at the eventual formation of an independent government. Between General Faidherbe's vision of a wholly French enclave slotted into the map of West Africa and Captain Alexander Grant's earlier attempts to form a liberated coastline, the mould was being created in which two fully independent countries would be formed.

Above, colonial architecture in Thiès. **Left**, Lat Dyor in full cry.

VIVE LE PRESIDENT SENGHOR

Senegal never expected to enter independence as one country. Because Dakar had been the capital of France's West African Federation (*Afrique Occidentale Française*, the AOF), nearly all Senegal's political leaders had favoured maintaining the federation in some form.

On the one hand, Senegal had infant industries that needed the wider hinterland the federation offered; on the other, Dakar itself was a big city designed as the capital of a much wider unit than simply Senegal, and has always seemed top-heavy in relation to the rest of the country. It also housed a large bureaucracy designed for a federation, and, although most of the other nationals returned to their territories on the break-up of the federation, Senegal's main problem in the years of independence has been adjusting downwards.

It actually became independent on 4 April 1960 as part of the Mali Federation. This federated the territories of Soudan and Senegal, and was all that was left of the eight-territory AOF after its collapse following the events of 1956-58. At that time autonomy was largely devolved to the territorial capitals, and Guinea dealt Charles de Gaulle's proposed Franco-African community a body-blow by taking full independence. It was at this time that the nationalist leader (and later despot) of Guinea, Sekou Touré, made his famous speech in front of the visiting de Gaulle.

Touré opted on behalf of his country for independence and poverty over what he considered to be demeaning reliance on France. The subsequent French withdrawal from Guinea was notable for its completeness involving the virtual dismantling of the country's infrastructure (the fact—true or not—that certain officials even took the light bulbs with them was quoted at the time as an example of alleged French pique).

Power struggle: The Mali Federation, named after the ancient African empire, lasted four and a half months before internal stresses forced a power struggle. This caused

the Senegalese to secede from the federation on 29 August, creating two separate republics, Senegal and Mali.

The first President of the Republic, Léopold Senghor, thus came to power in a political crisis. He experienced several more over the first decade of independence, although in the end his position was consolidated.

In December 1962 he faced a major challenge to his authority from his Prime Minister, Mamadou Dia, in a power struggle in which Senghor dismissed Dia (who claimed the party had sovereignty over the state), and then tried and jailed him for treason. An even greater challenge came in May 1968 when a combination of student-worker demonstrations (echoing those in Paris of the same month) paralysed the government and gave Senghor a crisis of nerve, in which he depended on the armed forces to stay in power.

On both occasions he relied on two of Senegal's key levers of power. Firstly there was the endorsement given to the regime by the Islamic brotherhoods, especially the Khalif-General of the Mourides. In 1968 they mobilised their supporters from the countryside to demonstrate for Senghor

Preceding pages: flag-portrait of Senghor. **Left,** patriotic majorette, Dakar. **Above,** the Senegalese national flag.

THE POET WHO REWROTE POLITICS

Among all the African leaders of the independence generation, Léopold Sédar Senghor has a very special position. Others may have equalled and even surpassed his international prestige, or have been more loved by their peoples, but Senghor's place in history comes from the way he managed to combine the role of writer and poet with that of practical politician and statesman.

He is also that rare phenomenon, a successful intellectual in politics. This gave him that sense of historical perspective which enabled him to see the need to withdraw from political power in good order and prepare his succession. He has always taken delight in his mixed ancestry (part Serer, part Mandinka, part Peul) with a name from the Portuguese Creole culture of Casamance. It illustrates the notion of cultural *métissage* (crossbreeding) which has been a recurrent idea in his writing and thinking.

His education, initially with the Holy Fathers in Senegal and, after 1928, in France, profoundly marked him with French culture. Critics who have singled him out as a black Frenchman have failed to appreciate his basic duality. Hence the idea of *négritude* he helped to launch in Paris was a kind of reaction to the weight of the French culture that he had experienced. And, although an uncompromising theory of the assertion of black African values, *négritude* still bore the mark of a Parisian literary movement. Much of Senghor's intellectual, literary and even political career revolved around both promoting and redefining *négritude*—an expression which, though he did not invent it, will always be linked to him.

After studying, he stayed in France teaching and, a supporter of General de Gaulle (in part as reaction to the racism of Hitler and of the Vichy regime), he was taken prisoner of war in 1940. With the Liberation he entered politics, building on the prestige of his reputation as the first African to achieve the academic qualification of *agrégation*, qualifying him to teach in a *lycée*.

In 1945 he was elected one of the two deputies of Senegal in the French National Assembly, and it was a short step from there to achieving ascendancy in Senegal's complex web of party politics. He was also leader of one of two groups of Africans in the assembly in Paris, and was a minister in the 1955 government of Edgar Faure.

With independence, he became President of Senegal, and experienced the drama of life at the top of the greasy political pole, going through a series of crises before establishing confident supremacy over the Senegalese political scene. The high level of political consciousness among Senegal's diverse and numerous educated élite makes it a particularly difficult country to run, with a volatility that changes from week to week.

Senghor used his own intellectual reputation, and his undoubted access to French political circles, for all they were worth, but he also became a master of Machiavellian manoeuvre, that *politique politicienne* he affected to despise.

While the support of the French was important at key moments, he knew he needed to retain the allegiance of the *marabouts*, the leaders of the Islamic brotherhoods dominant in the rural areas. Although for a time these were alienated through difficulties over groundnut production, he was able to use his being a Catholic to present himself as a neutral force between the different powerful brotherhoods.

He has always stressed the importance of culture as the basic politics, and sometimes seemed to be dwelling on culture at the expense of economics. The present vibrancy of Senegal's culture certainly owes much to his patronage—seen, for example in the first world festival of Black Arts held in Dakar in 1966, arguably the most successful large-scale arts festival ever held in Africa.

Sometimes his intoxication with ideas made him seem remote, especially when he took up with the "universal civilisation" idea of Father Teilhard de Chardin. His advocacy of *la francophonie* (a colonial language, after all) also seemed to some Africans to be questionable.

His rationale was, in part, that it was a way of tying Europe to Africa, fitting in with another concept he had consistently advocated—Eur-Africa, two continents tied together in symbolic relationship, a nexus he has well represented in his own personality.

against what was primarily an urban disaffection. Secondly, the armed forces stayed more or less solidly behind Senghor as a result of a defence agreement with France and the presence (psychologically important) of a French base in Dakar.

After the turbulences of the 1960s, the 1970s were a period of consolidation. But the education system—the teachers' union, the University of Dakar and even the schools—was a continuing focus of discontent.

Having beaten back organised political opposition either by assimilating or banning other parties, Senghor was strong enough by 1974 to permit one legal opposition party,

retirement created a more favourable climate for his chosen successor. This was Abdou Diouf, a technocrat who had served a long apprenticeship of 10 years as Prime Minister.

A new president: In his first two years in power, Diouf enjoyed a real honeymoon. He was helped by Senghor's refusal to continue to dabble in politics, and by the presence at his side of Jean Collin, a French-born Senegalese with vast experience of both administration and politics, who has held the key position of Secretary-General to the government for all the Diouf years.

The favourable start of Diouf's rule also came from his lifting of Senghor's restric-

then two, and finally three while trying to dominate the centre-left by changing the name of the ruling party to Parti Socialiste (PS). The President's advancing years also helped consolidate his supremacy, because of the respect Africans accord to age.

When, in 1980, he decided to announce his retirement, what had at times appeared to be a highly volatile political situation had become relatively stable. Predictions of a violent demise of the regime proved unfounded, and the mere fact of Senghor's voluntary

<u>Left</u>, Léopold Sédar Senghor. <u>Above</u>, Gambia's Sir Dawda Jawara.

tion on the number of political parties. This permitted Senegal to describe itself as a multi-party democracy.

This image became tarnished after the 1983 elections, when there were widespread allegations of rigging. In the view of most observers Diouf would have won the election anyway, but he was handicapped by the activities of his own party.

Much of the history of the Diouf years has been of the President's struggles with the barons within his own party. If he has been able to dominate the party old guard, he still has difficulty adapting himself to the special skills needed to survive in politics.

This was seen again in the elections of 1988, which, although his victory was probably more honestly won than that of 1983, led to an outburst of violence by disappointed youthful opposition supporters. The frustrations of a worsening economic situation seemed to produce a higher risk of social conflict. Again, the educational system was the most sensitive sector.

The troubles in the schools and university during the months leading up to the 1988 election are worth summarising, as they give an excellent insight into the political and social feel of the country. In few other African nations does one see such a degree of student politicization, leading to a confron-

on what President Diouf with some justification described as an economic rather than a political problem. The decline of the economy had increased pressure on the education system in two ways. Dwindling government income meant that equipment and books were more and more inadequate or non-existent, while fewer teachers were available for the large classes. At the same time decreasing job prospects were undermining the sense of purpose of the whole system.

The student strikes became more and more bound up in a general movement of opposition to the government. The opposition leader Abdoulaye Wade was arrested for incitement. It was only after his trial, when

tation of the scope of the one which took place. This is partly because many governments elsewhere on the continent deal more harshly with their would-be opponents.

In Dakar University, although a number of heavy-handed police raids on the campus took place, students had both sufficient liberty and sufficient motive to organise their lengthy protest movement. The strikes of '88 began over a relatively trivial matter—a disciplinary measure against a student in Thiès—but rapidly escalated to become an expression of dissatisfaction with a whole range of issues.

Perhaps the most basic complaint centred

he was released with a suspended sentence in May 1988, that tension relaxed. Although subsequent attempts at a reconciliation through a "political round-table" seemed to founder, the government had recaptured the initiative.

The Gambia: In the Gambia, independence came five years later than in Senegal. It was also the last British colony in West Africa to attain independence—mainly because, as it was the smallest and poorest of those colonies, the British had doubts about its economic viability.

However, the wave of independence that came in 1960 (including especially Senegal) and the independence the following year of Sierra Leone made the question of breaking links with Britain more significant. The possibility of closer ties with Senegal—even leading to a merger—came on to the agenda, but contacts (discreetly encouraged by both British and French) foundered on the difficulty of working out power-sharing arrangements. Thus the Gambia became an independent sovereign state on 18 February 1965, with Dawda Jawara as Prime Minister. As *Sir* Dawda (he was knighted in 1966), he became President when a Republic was proclaimed in 1970. He had been Chief Minister since the success of his ruling PPP (People's Progressive Party) in the first uni-

ways depended on government resources and patronage to help keep its ascendancy.

The only major crisis President Jawara and his party have faced has been the putsch of 29 July, staged by elements in the Field Force (the paramilitary arm of the police— the Gambia until 1981 had no army). This unambiguously exposed the dangers of one party and its ruler staying too long in power.

The coup attempt was quelled with the assistance of Senegalese troops, invited in under a defence and cooperation treaty. But the violence of the event produced a reaction in favour of established authority, and dented Jawara's image.

Although the PPP was able to resume its

versal franchise elections in 1961 and the party has stayed in power ever since.

This was based on the support that the PPP has always had in the rural areas, although the capital Bathurst (which changed its name to Banjul in 1973) and surrounding areas, have tended to be more diverse politically.

The PPP has always worked through traditional means, especially among the Mandinka people (the majority group in the Gambia) and since attaining power has al-

dominance and continued to win elections, the shadow of 1981 still lingers. In its wake came the formation of the confederation of Senegambia in 1982. But 500 Senegalese troops remained unobtrusively in the Gambia, a guarantee of the continuity of the present regime.

The Confederation of Senegambia, limited though it was in scope, made sense in many ways, not least of them economic. It was totally unexpected, therefore, when the short-lived union was summarily abandoned as "a waste of time and money" by President Diouf in 1989 in response to a critical speech by Sir Dawda Jawara.

Above, President Abdou Diouf inspects the Guards in London.

The first constitution of Senegal was technically that of January 1959, when the Mali Federation, autonomous within the then Franco-African community, was set up. This was adapted for the independence of the Federation in April 1960, but the first proper constitution of the independent Republic of Senegal was that voted by the Senegalese National Assembly on 25 August 1960. Modelled on General de Gaulle's 1958 Constitution of the Fifth Republic in France, it provided for a president, prime minister and a national assembly elected by universal suffrage.

Following the crisis between President Senghor and Prime Minister Dia in December 1962, the constitution was changed in a referendum in March 1963. The prime ministership was abolished, and the president became chief executive with undivided powers.

This was changed again in 1970, with the post of prime minister once more created, so as to permit President Senghor to delegate the day-to-day running of the country to the new premier Abdou Diouf, and to concentrate more on affairs of state, especially foreign policy. In 1976 the constitution was changed to make the Prime Minister the successor, instead of the National Assembly President.

The situation remained stable for the next 10 years. Then, in December 1980, Senghor resigned as President. Under the constitution, it was provided that the prime minister should carry out the remainder of a presidential term in the event of the president resigning, so Diouf stepped into Senghor's shoes on 1 January 1981. A new prime minister was appointed, Habib Thiam.

He remained until after the elections of 1983, when the post of prime minister was again suppressed. This was partly because it had proved to be a bone of contention in the party. It had only been re-established in 1970 to take care of the question of the Senghor succession, and Diouf estimated that at this

period in his rule it was again unnecessary. It was also a signal that he intended to be in full control of his government.

New parties: The only other major constitutional changes over the years of independence have related to political parties. Initially these were freely permitted, even if by 1966 Senegal was *de facto* a one-party state.

In 1974 a second political party was given recognition—the Parti Democratique Senegalaise (PDS), led by Maitre Abdoulaye

Wade. In 1976, Senghor, still in pursuit of what he called a "normal" opposition, amended the constitution to limit the number of political parties to three, with the ruling Parti Socialiste (PS) representing a "socialist democratic" tendency, the PDS a "liberal democratic" and the leftist PAI (Parti Africain de l'Independance), which had been banned in 1960, a "Marxist-Leninist" tendency.

Mahjemout Diop, the PAI leader, returned from exile in Mali to lead the party, but the majority of his followers preferred to remain in "clandestinity", so the party fragmented. Later a fourth party ("conservative" ten-

Preceding pages: Senegalese Republican Guards. **Left**, ambassadors of the holy city of Touba. **Above**, soldiers entering a mosque.

dency), the Mouvement Republicain Senegalais (MRS), was recognised.

This period of limited multi-partism came to an end in 1981 when the new President, Abdou Diouf, pushed through a constitutional amendment lifting the limit on the number of parties, as well as removing the need for any ideological pigeon-holes. By the time of the 1983 elections, 15 parties were manoeuvering for position. By 1988, there were 17.

Various attempts have subsequently been made to bring the opposition parties together, notably from 1986 onwards. But they have been inhibited by an electoral law forbidding alliances and coalitions, and by the

personal rivalries among opposition leaders.

The French legacy: The constitution affirms the rights of man, the liberty of the person, and religious freedom. French is the official language. The President and the 120-seat National Assembly are both elected by universal suffrage every five years, in elections that take place simultaneously.

There is an Economic and Social Council, after the French pattern, and a Supreme Court, which also acts as Appeal Court and government audit office. From 1988 the Supreme Court took over from the Interior Ministry the function of administering elections, partly because the judiciary had a

reputation for being a more impartial body.

The country is divided into eight regions (Cap-Vert, Thiès, Djourbel, Siné-Saloum, Louga, Fleuve, Casamance and Senegal Orientale), each run by a governor. Each region is divided into *départements* run by prefects, and each of these is divided into *arondissements* and *communes*.

Regional and departmental councils are elected, although they include nominated members of "socio-economic" groupings. The structures have been decentralised and democratised since the days of the French colonial administration.

Press problems: Although it isn't specified in the constitution, Senegal enjoys a considerable press freedom. This is an historic tradition, but it has been encouraged by both Senghor and Diouf regimes, by means of liberal legislation that makes it relatively easy to start a publication. The main obstacles are economic rather than political: most publications have too small a circulation to be viable.

There is still only one daily, the government-owned *Le Soleil*, but there is a host of opposition weeklies and monthlies, as well as a satirical press (*Le Politicien* was the pioneer, and more recently there has been *Le Cafard Libéré*).

There are also Islamic publications, representing different tendencies, and a younger generation of professional journalists have formed a cooperative to put out the independent *Sud* magazine (quarterly) and *Sud-Hebdo* (weekly).

Senegal maintains embassies in nearly 30 countries and is a member of the United Nations and its specialised agencies, as well as the International Monetary Fund, the World Bank and a variety of other international organisations. It has also contributed troops to the UN Peace-keeping forces in the Congo and the Middle East, most recently in Lebanon.

It is a member of the Non-Aligned Movement, and is associated with the European Community through the EEC-ACP Lomé Convention. In Africa, it belongs to the Organisation of African Unity, and a number of regional groupings and bodies, such as the 16-nation Economic Community of West African States (ECOWAS), the seven-nation West African Economic Community (essentially the countries of the former Federation of French West Africa), the West African Monetary Union, and the Development Organisations of the Senegal and Gambia Rivers.

The Gambia's constitution: Worked out at a conference in London in 1964, the Gambia's independence constitution provided initially for a "Westminster model" type of constitution. This retained the link with the British crown, with Queen Elizabeth II as nominal head of state.

A Governor-General was to be on the spot holding sovereignty. For a year after independence, this post was held by the last British Governor Sir John Paul; then a Gambian, Falilu Singhateh, was appointed.

Thus, on 24 April 1970, Sir Dawda Jawara became the first—and so far the only—President of the Republic of the Gambia. The new republican constitution broke the connection with the British crown, although the Gambia, as other countries had before, remained a member of the Commonwealth.

The constitution provided initially for the President to be elected by the new House of Representatives. In 1982 this was changed so that, as in Senegal, the election of the President is by universal suffrage at the same time as the elections for the House of Representatives, every five years. The House now has 49 members, 35 elected by universal suffrage, as well as five traditional chiefs,

The head of government was a Prime Minister, the head of the majority party in the House of Representatives.

This arrangement did not prove workable for very long, partly because other African countries doubted the real independence of a country that retained the British monarch as head of state. A referendum to change to a republic soon after independence in 1965 failed by only 700 votes.

When re-submitted in April 1970, the project was approved overwhelmingly.

Left, a much decorated veteran. **Above**, Dakar's Assemblée Nationale.

eight non-voting nominated members and an Attorney-General. The President appoints a Vice-President, who is head of government business as well as formal successor.

Parties and institutions: The formation of an unlimited number of political parties has always been allowed in the Gambia. Apart from the ruling People's Progressive Party, there is now the National Convention Party (NCP) started by former Vice-President Sheriff Dibba in 1975, and the Gambia Peoples Party (GPP) formed in 1986 by a number of former ministers.

Another party of young radicals, the PDOIS (Peoples' Democratic Organisation for Independence and Socialism) was formed in July 1986. It was said to have close links with the MOJA-G (The Movement for Justice in Africa—The Gambia) one of the groups banned after the 1981 coup attempt. In the 1987 elections the opposition still failed to make an impact, as it had failed in 1977 and 1982.

The Gambia has a free press, although resources are painfully few and even the *Gambia News Bulletin* published by the Government comes out only once a week. Most independent publications are cyclostyled broadsheets—though they can be lively, or even scurrilous. An attempt in 1985 to produce an English version of *Le Soleil*

called the *Senegambia Sun* failed financially after a year.

The Gambia belongs to the UN and its specialised agencies, as well as the OAU, ECOWAS and regional African organisations. Its only overseas missions are in London, Brussels, Washington (covering New York) Dakar, Jeddah and Lagos.

Senegal-Gambian relations: Following the failure of pre-independence merger attempts, a Treaty of Association was signed between Senegal and the Gambia in 1967, which established a Senegalo-Gambian Secretariat in Banjul. Tensions emerged in the early 1970, especially over smuggling between the two countries (sometimes referred to euphemistically as "traditional trade"), and any attempts to bring the two countries closer together seemed doomed to frustration.

Although an organisation for the Development of the Gambia River was established in 1978, this was partly because of the continued refusal of the Gambians to accept Senegalese pressure for a bridge over the Gambia linking Dakar to the separatist-minded southern province of Casamance, unless it was combined with a dam. This became a symbol of continuing Senegambian misunderstanding, and some Senegalese openly vented their frustration with talk of forcible annexation.

The 1981 coup in Banjul changed the situation dramatically. From the point of view of both Dakar and Banjul, the threat to stability reinforced the arguments for a much closer relationship.

The forming of a Confederation of Senegambia established a constitution which provided for consultation and cooperation on foreign defence and economic policy. It also established the theoretical framework for a future single government, even while stressing that each of the states maintains "independence and sovereignty".

The President of Senegal was the President of the Confederation and the President of the Gambia was the Vice-President. A joint confederal legislature, with members drawn from the national parliaments, was established, and between 1982 and 1985 protocols were agreed on common policies in the field of defence and security, external relations, communications and information. Once the institutions were fully functional, it was decided to close down the Senegalo-Gambian secretariat, regarded as redundant.

The protocol of defence was particularly important. It provided for a new Gambian Armed Forces, with a small gendarmerie equipped by France and trained by the Senegalese to replace the Field Force (dissolved after the 1981 coup). The cooperation in external relations provided for coordination of policies and some joint representation, but little sovereignty was ever surrendered.

Above, the world press in Dakar. **Right**, an elegant Socialist Party worker. **Following pages**: street prayers.

Of the major religions of Senegal and the Gambia, animism is the oldest and Christianity the newest, but much the most important is Islam, which claims over 90 percent of the population.

Animism is the ancient belief system which considers that all earthly things possess spirits or souls. A tree, an animal, even an inanimate object such as a stone—each contains its own spiritual force. Certain creatures may have particular significance. In the Kaolak region, for example, the wild lizard is particularly revered and people of the region never harm one of these reptiles.

Strictly speaking, animism as a formal and principal belief has died out except in parts of Casamance, Eastern Senegal and the Gambia. However, a residual attachment often lives on even among Muslims or Christians, underpinning the newer religions. When modern medicine, prayer and the semi-magical, semi-religious remedies of *marabouts* fail to cure an illness, people may turn to the old ways as a last resort.

Among the Lébou of the Cap Vert peninsula, for example, the ritual/ceremony known as *Ndeup* is still held from time to time, though not on set dates. The *Ndeup* is a mystical therapy aiming to extract the evil spirit from a patient. It is held in public in the open, often conducted by women, and involves dancing and drumming. In fact, it has always been the case that older, so-called pagan belief systems mesh surprisingly well with the newer religions. Christian or Muslim saints may become identified with older deities, allowing the two to be worshipped simultaneously.

Christianity comes: Arriving with the first Europeans, the Christian religions were for a long time confined to exclusively European trading and military settlements. Only relatively late did Christianity begin to spread to the indigenous population. In the early 19th century a small French Catholic mission was established on Cap Vert, where the Lébou had declared an independent republic.

Elsewhere, missionaries were fiercely resisted, as Christianity was seen as an attribute of the invading Europeans, while Islam became strongly identified with the resisting kingdoms and their leaders. It was not until Lat Dyor Ngoné Latyr Diop was defeated by the French in 1886 that the Catholic church established itself on Gorée, the Little Coast, in St Louis, and in the Gambian townships of Banjul, Georgetown and Basse Santa Su.

Today, Christianity is well established but

very much a minority religion, its adherents numbering around five percent of the population. In Senegal, Catholicism is predominant, with the large congregation of Dakar Cathedral lead by Cardinal Hyacinthe Thiandoum. In the Gambia, with its English influence, the Anglican church is more important. Banjul's little Anglican Cathedral, more like an English village church in size, in no way compares with Dakar's grandiose structure.

In a number of churches throughout Senegal and the Gambia, it is possible to attend services adapted linguistically and musically to African practice. The best

Left, a provincial church. **Right**, Muslim prayer beads.

known is the Catholic church at Keur Moussa, near Dakar, where a mass accompanied by traditional instruments such as the kora and balafon takes place. So popular has this amalgam become that the Keur Moussa services often attract a substantial tourist congregation armed with cassette recorders.

Islam: It is more than a millennium since the conquering Almoravids swept down into Senegal from Morocco and Mauritania, bringing their new religion. Islam, with its simple rules and method of worship, took root quickly. By the 19th century it was thoroughly identified with the political and social structure of the region and the great

are considered by certain theorists to have been inherited from Pharaonic Egypt.)

With the advent of Islam, elders began to acquire knowledge of the written word, as embodied in the Koran. In a totally oral society, the knowledge of reading and writing had a power verging on the magical, and the priest-leaders became the marabouts, of whom the most famous are held in great awe and consulted by the highest in the land. It is not surprising that, of all the forces in the region, it is the marabouts who are most respected and courted by the government.

The second distinctive feature of Senegambian Islam is the existence of

anti-colonial leaders such as El Hadj Omar Tall and Lat Dyor Ngoné Latyr Diop were also religious leaders.

Although the basic teachings and practices are universal, West African Islam has developed certain attributes not found elsewhere. One of these is the existence of *marabouts*, often charismatic figures who are a combination of priest, sage, prophet and mystic. The marabouts—the word comes from the Arabic *marabutin*, meaning Almoravids—arose out of the ancient Senegambian practice of regulating society by means of councils of elders. (These councils, similar to those in Ancient Greece,

brotherhoods of disciples known as *talibé* who follow individual leaders known as *khalifé*. Entry to a brotherhood may be a hereditary matter (for example, members of the M'Backé families are traditionally Mourides, the Sy are Tidjianes, and so on) or one may join voluntarily. Although there is sometimes a regional aspect to brotherhoods (for instance, the Layènes belong very much to the Cap Vert area), the Senegambian brotherhoods are multiracial, and anyone may join. Lately a small number of Europeans have joined the Mourides and the Layènes.

There is no formal entry or standard

membership fee to a brotherhood. Followers pay whatever tribute, in money or goods, lands and services, to their leadership they can afford. This may involve working unpaid on a marabout's land for a certain time. In addition, talibé attend the pilgrimages and other ceremonies of their order and observe its specific rites and customs. The brotherhoods work together temporally as well as spiritually and members help each other to get on in the world.

The largest and earliest of the brotherhoods, the Mourides, was founded in the 19th century by Cheikh Amadou Bamba, who, in addition to being a great religious unto themselves, but compensate for their unconventional appearance and behaviour with their extreme piety and capacity for very hard work in the service of the order, either in the fields or begging alms in the streets.

Mouridism is noted for its insistence on the importance of work, which is rather similar to the Protestant work ethic. Mourides have always been heavily involved in agriculture and the care of their land. They were largely responsible for the development of the peanut industry and many of the workers and landowners of the great Senegalese peanut areas are Mourides. The French encouraged this activity, giving

leader, was implacably opposed to French colonial rule. This led to his being deported and exiled on several occasions by the French. The descendants of Bamba, the M'Backé family, have continued to provide the leadership of the brotherhood. There are factions and disagreements over specific items of dogma within the M'Backé family, but the Grand Khalif, Abdou Khadr M'Backé, is accepted ultimately as spiritual guide and source of authority. The sub-group, the Baye Fall, are something of a law

landowners free rein to cultivate large tracts of land in exchange for the trade of exporting the resulting peanut oil. Many poorer Mourides work for minimal recompense on the land of their marabouts as part of their religious devotion.

The decline of peanut production and the deterioration of the land meant that large numbers of Mourides were obliged to join the drift to the towns. But they perpetuate their strong social structures and commitment to helping each other wherever they are.

In the streets of Dakar, the great majority of small traders are Mourides, and they are

Left, a Baye Fall steward at Touba. **Above**, Magal pilgrims arriving, Touba.

often sponsored and protected by the bigger retailers and wholesalers who also belong to the fraternity. Three times a year (at the end of the Ramadan fast, at *Tabaski*, the "feast of the sheep", and at *Magal*) commercial activity in the Senegalese capital is at a standstill as the Mouride shopkeepers attend to their religious duties.

The great annual pilgrimage of the Mouride Brotherhood, and the greatest pilgrimage in the country, is Magal (meaning "return voyage"). It celebrates the symbolic return of the order's founder, Cheikh Amadou Bamba, to the holy city of Touba, which he founded in the 1880s. Bamba was exiled by the French colonial

administration to the Gabonese island of Mayombé in 1895 and spent his last years also exiled from Touba, in Djourbel.

Magal, like other Islamic feasts, is moveable, falling between the 10th and 11th days of the 11th month of the Muslim calendar. The core of the feast is a night of prayer either in the great mosque with its tall minaret or among the followings of individual marabouts.

Hundreds of thousands of pilgrims descend on Touba, travelling by car and bus, on foot or swarming over the special trains. Non-Muslim visitors are permitted to attend, but as there is no accommodation in the town (the nearest hotel is in Djourbel) and as the roads and railways are jammed with traffic, it is not an easy excursion.

All visitors should naturally expect to observe the ban on smoking and drinking in Touba. If they don't, they may well attract the attention of the imposing Mouride stewards, the Baye Fall, with their dreadlocks, colourful patched tunics, clubs and calabashes (used for drinking and collecting coins). The Baye Fall were originally the followers of Cheikh Ibra Fall, one of Amadou Bamba's most dedicated disciples.

Legend has it that Ibra Fall and his followers were excused observance of the traditional Islamic obligation to pray, etc., because of their extraordinary zeal. Recently the movement has regained impetus, attracting numbers of young men, who combine a rather wild appearance with a position of some distance from conventional society. Apart from policing the pilgrims at Magal, groups of Baye Fall work in the fields or walk the streets of towns chanting and begging.

The second largest brotherhood, the Tidjianes, was founded by the Algerian Cheikh Ahmed Al Tidjiani in the early 19th century, and brought to prominence by the Senegalese leader El Hadj Malick Sy. Its spiritual headquarters is the town of Tivaouane. Another Northern brotherhood, the Khadriya, founded by the Mauritanian Cheikh Saad Bou, is headquartered in Nimzatt, Mauritania.

The Layènes are a small but very active brotherhood localised in Cap Vert, near Dakar. Their centre is the fishing village of Yoff, near Dakar's international airport. Virtually all of the inhabitants of Yoff adopt the name Laye in addition to their original family name, the word being synonymous with the name of God. Around the Cap Vert peninsula are a number of sites venerated by the Layènes, including a cave in Yoff which is said to be the site of a miracle and a number of stones held to bear the miraculous image of the sect's leader, Seydina Limamou Laye. Distinctive features of the Layènes are their all-white attire and their custom of holding mass marriage ceremonies.

Above, women healers in N'Deup ceremony.
Right, the Mouride leader Cheikh M'Backé.

According to the late Cheikh Anta Diop, the great Senegalese historian and anthropologist, the main groups of human inhabitants of Senegambia have their origins in Ancient Egypt. To support his theory, Diop draws on a number of disciplines from archaeology to linguistics, and a variety of sources, from African oral traditions to the writings of the Greeks and Arabs.

The half dozen major tribes of Senegambia are subdivided into some 20 distinct ethnic groups. Much intermarriage has taken place, so that it is often difficult for an outsider to discern any difference between, say, a Serer and a Tukulor. For Senegambians, the matter is easier.

Although proud of their common national identity and conscious of the links between the groupings—the tradition of *gamou*, meaning roughly cousinship, stresses the connections between peoples—Senegambians are always aware of each others' backgrounds. A complex set of social and linguistic details, gestures and manners makes it easy for people to recognise each others' ethnic groups and to communicate across the divisions.

Humour is, as always, a great intermediary. A Serer might remind a Tukulor that he used to be his slave in days gone by. Family names and histories are also subjects for fun. When a Seck meets a Gueye, it won't be long before one of them refers to the other's excessive appetite for rice. This is taken in good part—it's better to be greeted warmly with a joke, even at your own expense, than coldly or distantly. The ethnic groups found in Senegal are mostly to be found also in the Gambia, although certain tribes are especially concentrated in particular regions. The exception to this is the Aku, who live solely in the Gambia.

The Wolof: This large grouping, numbering about two million, is found throughout Senegambia. The Wolof language has come to be Senegal's main indigenous tongue, spoken by 80 percent of the population. The Wolof are believed to have spread into the central regions of the country between the 12th and 15th centuries, establishing the Djolof Empire. Along with the Mandinka, they were among the earliest and most devout converts to Islam. Virtually all the Wolof are still Muslims.

The Wolof had a clearly defined hierarchical caste system, which still persists, though obviously in diluted form. At the top were the *geer* (nobles) and *badolo* (something between free peasants and gentry). Lower down the social scale were

the artisans, whose crafts were hereditary; this group included blacksmiths, tailors and *griots*, or minstrel-historians. At the bottom came the *jaam*, or slaves.

Theoretically, marriage is forbidden between castes. It is even banned between certain categories of artisans. Although the modern era has seen this prohibition largely relax, one still finds even in the cities family arguments about a proposed marriage with a member of a family of different hereditary position.

In their recent history, the Wolof have excelled at farming and agriculture, having been instrumental in the development of

Preceding pages: a tribal kaleidoscope. **Left,** Tukulor man. **Right,** Serer youth.

groundnut cultivation (even to the exclusion of other, equally necessary, crops). Unlike other groupings, it is the men who work the fields, while the women take care of the home, the kitchen and the children.

The Lébou: Sometimes described as a subgroup of the Wolof, the Lébou are concentrated in the Cap Vert region, where they are believed to have arrived from the north around four centuries ago. They are farmers and expert fishermen, though in earlier times they had a strong sideline as ship-wreckers and looters. As mentioned in the Dakar chapter of this book, the Lébou are unique in operating their own mini-government, which is recognised by the Senegalese

Upper River district. Their origin is unknown, but one hypothesis traces them back East, to Nubia and Ethiopia and perhaps even further.

The Peuls are typically nomadic cattle herders and their large herds of hump-necked zebu are of immense importance to their culture. Although the cattle are never killed for food, the size of a family's herd marks its social prestige. Great efforts are made to build up and conserve herds, therefore, and marriages between rich families involve the exchange of large numbers of animals in dowry.

The Tukulor: These people, the second wing of the Alpularen, are also major cattle-

government, in the Cap Vert region. This represents the continuation of a tradition founded in the early 19th century, when the French colonial government recognised the legitimacy of a fledging Lébou "republic" before the existence of the city of Dakar.

The Alpularen: This large grouping of light reddish-skinned people is subdivided into two tribes, each between 600,000 and 700,000 strong.

The Peuls are found particularly in the River Senegal region but are spread throughout West Africa, where they are also referred to as Fula, Fulani, Foulbé, or Poulo. In the Gambia, they are most numerous in the

breeders, but increasing numbers of them are having to abandon their inhospitable Sahelian homelands for the cities. They were among the earliest converts to Islam, and still remain almost wholly Muslim.

The Sarakholé: These pale-skinned people are the descendants of the 14th-century Ghana Empire, which stretched from present-day Ghana to Senegal and Mali in the east. Their hereditary qualities are military skill, independence and a readiness to travel. Nowadays many Sarakholé have been obliged to emigrate as far as Europe where they constitute one of the main groups of Senegalese residents in France. They have a reputation for resourcefulness and solidarity, sticking together in their European communities and helping out new arrivals. They are profoundly Muslim.

The Serer: The second largest ethnic grouping in Senegambia, the dark-skinned Serer are mainly to be found in the Thiès and Siné-Saloum regions, where they inhabit forested areas and till the land. They and the Diola are the major adherents to Christianity, though the traditional animist beliefs still retain a strong hold. Their ceremony of *pangal*, which venerates the souls of ancestors, is one of the most distinctive of animist rituals still practised. Léopold Sédar Senghor, the founding father

murmurings of anti-Government nationalism in southern Senegal have come chiefly from the Diola.

The Bassari: The third grouping still deeply attached to animism is the small Bassari tribe who live in the region of the Niokolo Koba National Park. Their traditional thatched hut dwellings and colourful ceremonial attire have made their image a familiar one on postcards and in guidebooks.

The Mandinka: This minor but substantial grouping (around 300,000 members) comprises the descendents of the Muslim warriors who swept into the Gambia and Casamance regions after the break-up of the Mali Empire. They are still found through-

of modern Senegal, came from this tribe.

The Diola: Also great animists, the Diola comprise a number of subgroups, all of whom inhabit the region of Casamance. Small and dark-skinned, they grow rice and live in forested areas. Despite threats from other tribes, especially the Mandinka and from Portuguese and French colonisers, they have survived partly by withdrawing to the forests, to develop a fierce independence. It is not surprising, therefore, that the recent

Opposite page: left, Malinké woman; **right**, Diola man. **Above: left**, Mauritanian man; **right**, Peul woman.

out Guinea, Mali and the Gambia. Members of the Mandinka griot musician caste play the unique harp-lute known as the kora which has, in the hands of popular musicians such as Mory Kante, made increasingly common appearances in the concert halls and even the record charts of Europe.

The Aku: The descendants of former slaves from Sierra Leone, the Aku are found exclusively in the Gambia. They are an English-speaking tribe.

The Mauritanians: Also known as Moors, these pale-skinned men of Berber stock are distinctive in their voluminous pale blue robes. Some cross the border from their homelands in Senegal's northern neighbour herding cattle, sheep and goats. Many others are craftsmen, particularly silversmiths, and traders. Their dominance of the small shop commerce of Dakar led to riots in 1989.

Other peoples: As in most of West Africa, Senegal and the Gambia both have significant, although small, populations of Lebanese, who are invariably involved in commerce large (banking, vehicle distribution) or small (running the ubiquitous *shawarma* restaurants). And, there is a relatively small number of French, although most Europeans tend to be on limited duration contracts.

Ethnic cohesion and strife: Centuries back,

the tribal pattern of the territory of Senegambia was one of wars in which one grouping conquered another, ruled, interbred and established complex new social structures before being in turn conquered, driven away or overlapped by a newly dominant tribe. With the advent of Islam, consolidation of peoples and territories into Muslim and non-Muslim blocs occurred. The arrival of European colonisers further brought together peoples formerly divided into many small groupings.

By the late 20th century, the mix had developed to such an extent that great cohesion and mutual tolerance between the

different ethnic groups was the norm. But this order broke down in 1989, resulting in hundreds of deaths, great destruction of property, and serious damage to the goodwill between two communities.

At the beginning of 1989, Nouakchott, the capital of Senegal's northern neighbour Mauritania, contained many hundreds of Senegalese, mostly working as labourers. There already existed considerable resentment among the black population at what was seen as discrimination against their Mauritanian brothers. At the same time, Senegal's capital contained several thousand Mauritanians, who mostly worked as silversmiths but, more significantly, controlled almost all the little corner shops and stalls selling groceries.

The hard-working Mauritanians, known to the Senegalese as *Naar*, sold small quantities of goods — a single cigarette or a spoon of coffee — and, more significantly, also acted as money-lenders. In this way, they had come to dominate commerce at a street level and to be familar figures to the Senegalese population at large. Their prosperity in a worsening economic situation had already attracted resentment from the populace when a series of events sparked off full-scale rioting. An argument over land rights on the border between Mauritanian cattle herders and Senegalese farmers resulted in skirmishing which spread to Nouakchott, where Senegalese were attacked by local people. Rumours reaching Dakar of Government-approved attacks on their countrymen provoked young men to take to the streets and attack anything resembling a Mauritanian shop.

Within days, large-scale rioting had torn through Dakar and Nouakchott. At one point, Dakar's main mosque was pressed into service to shelter thousands of Mauritanians seeking refuge from the mobs and awaiting repatriation to the north.

By the time troops restored order in both capitals, hundreds of lives had been lost. In the aftermath, during which Mauritania and Senegal nearly came to war, almost the entire population of Senegalese and Mauritanians were evacuated from each other's countries, while the border remained closed seemingly indefinitely.

Left, Wolof girl. Right, Bassari youth.

THE ECONOMICS OF ANGUISH

Jimmy Carter, the former US President, may have got rich on peanuts, but the peasants of Senegambia, for whom the crop has been almost the sole source of revenue since Britain and France started showing an interest last century, have very little to show for their labours. For the first thing to know about the economies of Senegal and the Gambia is that they are among the poorest in the world.

The statistics mean less in a country where only a minority can read and write and where very little is counted than they do in the developed West. They can nevertheless give an order of magnitude. Gross national product—the economists' measure of total national wealth—was estimated at just $230 per head in the Gambia in 1985 and $370 in Senegal, against $17,600 in the US.

Stark contrast: To put it crudely, the average US citizen was nearly 80 times better off than his or her Gambian counterpart—in terms not only of food, housing and clothes, but also of health care, education and all the other necessities of life. The tourist, pursued by ragged little boys asking for coins, might well wonder how families get by at all.

It is less easy to comprehend this from the bustling Senegalese capital, with its modern high-rise blocks and traffic jams. "Were it not for the black faces, the vendors with their cola nuts, sweets and tiny twists of peanuts on every corner, the deformed beggars on their wooden trolleys," said one recent visitor to Dakar, "were it not for a certain untidiness, the boulevards could almost be in any French provincial town." Less easy, too, when a minister's wife goes by in her chauffeur-driven Mercedes, richly dressed in embroidered cloth and adorned with gold.

Don't be taken in by such appearances, for this is very emphatically Africa. The ragged urchin may well have a distant cousin who lives in one of the elegant villas surrounding the capital, with all the trimmings of Western affluence. His father or elder brother may well be in Europe, working as a road sweeper

or on a ship, earning a little something to send home.

But, even if he was born in the city, the lad may be called home to a village during the rainy season, to live in a hut made of dried mud and thatch, without water or electricity, to tend cattle or crops. Diversification is the key to survival where there is no social security system, no national health service or Medicare; each influential or wealthy relative, however distant, is another brick in the wall of insurance against unemployment or

death from a simple, curable disease.

Senegambia's natural resources are limited, to say the least: an Atlantic coastline, a climate prone to drought, phosphates and thus-far unexploited iron ore deposits in Senegal, and the possibility—also as yet unexploited—of oil and gas. Senegal, as the former centre of colonial French West Africa and the larger of the two states, has a more developed industry and infrastructure. Both countries remain, however, overwhelmingly dependent on agriculture, and both suffered acute economic troubles during the 1980s.

Atlantic coastline: Senegambia's long At-

Preceding pages: groundnut conveyor on River Gambia. **Left**, cement works, Senegal. **Right**, groundnut sorting, Senegal.

lantic coastline is the one thing distinguishing it from even poorer states such as Mali and Burkina Faso to the east. Something like 100,000 fishermen make a living from the waters, mainly using motorised dugouts (the northern fishing communities are a world apart and do not like strangers—beware of venturing onto their picturesque fishing beaches without advice).

Soumbedioune beach in Dakar is the place to see the fruit of their labours—hammerhead sharks, in season; tunny and seabream; giant prawns, lobsters and hideous spider crabs. With the small industrial fleet, these provide a growing proportion of exports. There are agreements too with the European

bill represents goods destined for Senegal and beyond.

Some of the trade is official—carried in railway goods wagons, taxed and documented. A vast network of clandestine trade also, however, remains. The Dakar-Bamako "express", that tortuously slow train inland to the Malian capital, resembles nothing so much as a modern-day camel caravan, as fish, fruit, soap and stock cubes are traded in and out of its windows the length of the track.

Tourism's growth: Winter sun, a hospitable people and beaches so long and empty you could spend all day deciding which patch to sit on are the makings of a natural tourist paradise. Tourism is now one of Gambia's

Community, providing tax revenues in return for the right of European boats to fish Senegambian waters. But factory ships still sometimes plunder the oceans, dodging the few patrols and landing their catches clandestinely, far away.

The coast also means trade; it was indeed the arrival of the Europeans and the subsequent establishment of trading posts such as St James' Island, Gorée and St Louis that marked the beginning of modern Senegambia. The ships that unload at Dakar port will as likely as not be carrying cargoes for the landlocked neighbouring states such as Mali, and much of Gambia's massive import

main sources of revenue, although development of the industry has not always been smooth. Government loans for hotel construction were not always fully accounted for or repaid, and tour operators creamed off almost the whole of the price paid for holidays in Europe.

The sudden influx of foreigners in the 1970s also gave rise to social problems—prostitution and petty crime—while all too often, the hotels imported food and other goods for their guests even when they could be locally produced. In a way, therefore, the sharp drop in the number of visitors that followed the 1981 coup attempt, though painful, offered a pause for thought about the way tourism should develop in future. That, and a World Bank-backed recovery programme has brought about a reorganisation of the industry and increased efforts to ensure that it brings greater benefits locally.

The colonial legacy is, naturally, alive and well in tourism as elsewhere, and the predominantly British package tourists basting themselves on Gambia's beaches have their French counterparts across the border in Senegal. There the industry is less important to the overall economy, accounting for only 2 percent or so of total activity, but more widely diversified, ranging from Dakar's luxury, business-oriented hotels to the mass

the precarious way of life. A few large and sophisticated farms exist—a vast new irrigation scheme is under way in the Senegal river valley, potentially bringing true agro-industry to the region for the first time.

For the most part, however, production is by peasant producers, using animal-drawn equipment or even digging the ground by hand with *dabas* or hoes. (Hoes, in the hands of the muscular Mandinka women farmers of the south, can be formidable tools.)

Crops vary with the rainfall, but most farmers grow grain for their own consumption—predominantly millet in the north and rice or maize in the south—and a surplus for sale. In most of Senegambia the main cash

tourism of the Petite Côte.

Senegal also boasts a highly successful experiment with village *campements* for the more adventurous traveller interested in learning how ordinary Senegalese live (most *campements* are in the southern Casamance region—go to the tourism compound in Ziguinchor for details).

Rural hinterland: In the vast hinterland stretching away from the coast, where despite rapid urbanisation some three-quarters of Senegambia's population live, farming is

<u>**Left**</u>, mending the nets. <u>**Above**</u>, tourism, the big earner.

crop is the humble peanut, or groundnut to give it its proper name, so called because it grows underground like a potato. This is not, however, the peanut for nibbling along with a cold beer—not usually, at any rate, though there are far worse ways of spending a Senegambian evening—but for pressing into high-quality cooking oil much favoured by French housewives and British fish-and-chip fryers.

Between the harvest in October-November and the onset of the rains in June, huge piles of groundnuts can be seen along the main roads and rivers, awaiting transport by lurching lorries and barges to the crushing mills and export. Elsewhere, cotton is making inroads, and local projects have encouraged production of other crops such as cashew nuts, fruit and vegetables.

Economic difficulties: Dependence on farming and unreliable prices for a few export crops provide the clue to many of the economic difficulties that both Senegal and Gambia have suffered. In essence, they stem from the fact that both governments were spending more than they earned in taxes, and importing more than they were exporting, through most of the 1970s.

The reasons why will be a matter of argument for a long time to come. Sharp fluctuations in world prices for oil and groundnuts

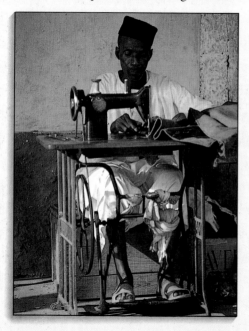

undoubtedly had a part to play, and even more so a series of severe droughts. Beyond that, some point to bad management and corruption in government; others to the inherent imbalance in relations between the rich "north" and the underdeveloped nations of the "south".

Whatever the truth, there came a point where the banks would no longer lend to either country to tide over what was obviously no longer a temporary problem.

With literally no money in the kitty—Banjul was almost without petrol for months on end because oil companies could not be paid—both governments eventually applied to the World Bank and IMF for loans to support economic restructuring programmes. The details differed in each case—the Gambian dalasi was, for instance, devalued sharply while Senegal's CFA franc, part of a much larger monetary system, retained its 50-to-1 parity with the French franc. But in both countries there has been a sharp cutback in public spending and collapse of uneconomic industries, bringing rising urban unemployment.

Increased resources for rural development and good rainfall for four successive years (1985-88) meanwhile laid the basis for what both the governments and their backers hope will prove a sustained recovery.

Economics of confederation: The long queues that existed until recently of lorries waiting to cross the river on the way from northern Senegal into Casamance, and the hours wasted in customs checks at the Senegal-Gambia border, are ample testimony to the logic of an economic union between the two states. Yet it is no coincidence that this lagged behind political aspects of the short-lived confederation.

However illogical the border, it expresses two very different colonial legacies that survive to this day. At its simplest, these are reflected in the fact that France remains by far Senegal's most important trading partner and the UK is Gambia's.

Senegal's traditionally protected economic environment, in juxtaposition with Gambia's low-tariff regime and a long, porous border, means that smuggling has always been rife. Confederation did nothing to end this, despite talk of customs union, and the rows of traders at the ferry landing in Banjul cater not for the Gambians, but for the Senegalese shopper, stocking up on basics such as rice, cooking oil and tomato paste that can cost up to twice as much at home.

There are strong vested interests on both sides of the border in maintaining the situation as it is. Yet if Senegambia has a more prosperous future ahead, there are few who would argue that closer cooperation is probably inevitable in the long run. In the meantime, the average Senegambian knows that only God can decide whether the rain falls and things get a little bit better.

<u>Left</u>, a tailor hard at work. <u>Right</u>, work and family mixed in Senegal.

It may be difficult to believe when you're being mobbed by the persistent young touts of Dakar's open markets, but the peoples of Senegambia are extremely hospitable and lay great store by public and private manners. These are very different from those of the developed West, making contacts in some ways a minefield for the visitor; but don't forget also that your hosts know a great deal more about Western manners and morals than you probably do about theirs.

If you show goodwill but put your foot in it by mistake, any unintended slight will immediately be forgotten. Keep your eyes and ears open, and you will be received with extraordinary generosity. Act arrogantly and the human landscape will freeze over. And never, ever lose your sense of humour—it can get you out of any number of scrapes.

Take a break during your probably exhausting wanders around Dakar or Banjul to watch two—preferably oldish—men greeting each other in the street. They will first shake hands. Then, hands still loosely clasped (emphatically *not* a signal that the pair are homosexual), the formal litany of greeting will begin.

First, a repetition of names, thus:
"Smith."
"Jones."
"Smith."
"Jones."

Then, gazing sightlessly at the horizon, somewhere over each other's shoulders, an interrogation which might be translated very loosely as follows:
"How are you?"
"Fine."
"The family?"
"Fine."
"Everything all right?"
"Thank God."
"How's the wife?"
"Fine."
"Kids?"
"Fine."
"Job going okay?"

Preceding pages: Glass painting of rich couple with their family *griot*. **Left, passing the time of day, St Louis.**

"No problems."
"How's your mother?"
… and so on.

Then the roles may switch over, with the answerer posing the same series of questions. With Senegambia's northern ethnic groups, the process may go on for several minutes, and be restarted half-way through the subsequent "proper" conversation. It is a way of reaffirming a relationship, conceived at least partly as one between two family or clan groupings rather than between two isolated individuals. Sociology apart, it has made Senegal's Wolofs, scattered throughout French-speaking Africa, the butt of jokes featuring imaginary inquiries as to the state of health of the family goat or chicken.

The detail of the greetings, which are numerous and complicated, need not concern the casual visitor. What is worth retaining is first, that human—and particularly family—relationships are accorded much more weight in the region than they are in Western Europe or North America. Introduce your elderly parents, for instance, to a Sengambian family and it will be regarded as a great honour.

The drumming and dancing you may see in the streets is probably a baptism to which the whole extended family and neighbourhood is invited. Do not be shy to go and say hello; the odds are that you will be pushed into the circle, amid much laughter and clapping, to execute some few halting steps of Senegambian dance.

Second, drum it into yourself that any contact, however casual, will expect to be greeted before you launch into the matter of conversations. Friends and business acquaintances will expect to be shaken by the hand, and even the most mis-pronounced *"Nanga' def"* or *"Kassoumaye"* that you can retain from the glossary will give great pleasure—even if it is in the wrong language for the listener.

A woman's place: Senegambian societies present to the European or North American traveller an unexpected mix of strength and oppression among women. Much of the legal framework is heavily weighted against them; yet one look at the confident, laughing girls of the region's towns and villages, or the fierce *madames* of the market place tells another story.

It is not at all uncommon for a man to have more than one wife, a source of constant fascination for outsiders and fertile potential ground for an African soap opera. This can be a legally enforced marriage, or a looser arrangement without guarantees for the woman concerned. In the towns, it all too often poses problems: of jealously among women increasingly brought up on Western-ised notions of romantic love, and among men who create financial problems for them-selves by taking on the social kudos of a second or third wife. Some of the best Sene-

galese literature, such as Mariama Ba's *Une Si Longue Lettre* or Ousmane Sembene's *Xala* (both available in English), deal with such difficulties.

In the countryside, however, sharing a husband may be the only way to cope with almost constant pregnancy and childbirth, the demands of farming and family. Remem-ber, too, in looking at the crowds of children, that labour is often a family's only asset and that death all too often carries off the young.

Women remain very much members of their own families, even after marriage. Often they retain what Westerners would regard as their maiden name, or use both interchangeably: Gambia's Mary Joof and her Senegalese sister Marie Diouf (the two names are, of course, the same but spelled differently in English and French) will probably not change their names on mar-riage, but will sometimes be introduced as Mrs Jallow or Madame Diallo.

In a traditional milieu, and sometimes also in sophisticated society, the wife's family will normally be paid a bride price (a sort of reverse dowry) to compensate for her depar-ture. Marriages are organised by the two families, although only rarely against the wishes of the couple. A woman has little status until married.

The vast majority of Senegambians may be Muslims, but almost no women cover their faces and only Beydane women from across the border in Mauritania are kept indoors. Practices vary between country and town, and from north to south, but across the area the women have a good deal of eco-nomic independence from their husbands: they farm, travel and trade on their own, and carry considerable weight in the household. A Senegambian man will think more than once before crossing his mother, and even the most cosmopolitan Wolof male will profess himself helpless before his wife's or lover's sexual wiles.

All this makes travelling in Senegambia a real pleasure for a single woman and far less hassle than, say, in the Mediterranean coun-tries. As far as clothing is concerned, there are no taboos about arms or shoulders, and bare breasts are considered far less indecent than in the West—though no Senegambian could begin to understand why anyone should wish to lie out half-naked in the sun. Almost all local women wear headscarves, though this is not expected of the visitor. It is, however, frowned on for women to expose their legs above the knee—mini-skirts are out—and only young boys would normally wear shorts in public. Otherwise, more or less anything goes.

Most Senegambian men, at least in the towns, enjoy a pretty active sex life and a woman moving around on her own can expect to be propositioned every now and then. This is almost never meant aggres-sively, and is best brushed off as a joke; invent a husband along the lines of boxer Mike Tyson, if you haven't got one already, or suggest some other time when the sun is not quite so hot. Either way, expect some very direct questioning, even from total strangers, about your family status: "Are you married?" or "where is your husband?"

Rude encounters: Finally, remember that, however charming most people will be, the occasional Senegambian can be rude. Southern ethnic groups—and particularly the Diola of parts of Gambia and Senegal's Casamance region—are exceptionally easy-going and have manners that resonate well with those of Europe. The Wolof, the dominant group in northern Senegal, have more aggressive manners and a more raucous sense of humour. They also tolerate a certain amount of institutionalised bad behaviour—

of your wristwatch or to the housewife offering you yet more of her best cooking.

There are many beggars on the streets, often damaged by tuberculosis, polio or leprosy. These have their place in Muslim society, which places great store on alms-giving (Aminata Sow Fall's delightful novel *La Grève des Battus* suggests devastating results if the beggars went on strike). Give them your small change if you feel like it.

But be wary of the over-persistent stranger. Dakar also has its share of more or less sophisticated con-men, who will spin you a yarn about having had their wallets picked on the way from the airport. It has street vendors who will pester you merci-

for instance, from members of the *griot* musicians' and praise-singers' caste.

Perhaps because of the long economic crisis, a sort of half-institutionalised begging has become common in Dakar, and is much decried by older Senegalese. It is possible that people may come up to you asking for money or to take your possessions, to which the response is a laughing "It's not mine" ("*C'est pas pour moi*") or "Next time" ("*La prochaine fois*"). A direct "No" would be rude, whether to an overenthusiastic admirer

Left, short back, sides and top. **Above**, plaiting big sister's hair.

lessly to purchase tacky or overpriced wares. And it has pickpockets and thieves—though stealing is very heavily censured and a thief caught in a market may even be beaten to death by the crowd if he is caught.

Outside Dakar's tourist haunts and highways, the odds are that any contacts will be made from genuine friendship and hospitality. The young boy who offers to show you around Banjul's market may be hoping for a present, but he is also out for a more interesting afternoon than he would have otherwise; and he will know of others who have even been invited to Europe by tourists they have befriended on the way.

By comparison with some African countries, Senegal and the Gambia are a little short of natural wonders to attract tourists, so culture plays an important part. One example is the village campments experiment in Casamance, in the south of Senegal, where tourists are invited to experience the economic and cultural realities of their hosts. Away from the luxury ghetto of hotels, the tourists learn to live the villagers' daily routine, thus achieving direct contact with the cultural aspects of the life of their hosts. This, the Senegalese authorities believe, avoids presenting cultural details as reflections of the tourists' own preconceptions and fantasies about Africa.

Spoken traditions: A great African philosopher once said that, in Africa, "when an elder dies, it is as if a whole library has burned down." African history and culture have been kept alive mainly by word of mouth passed from generation to generation. In the Sahel region to which Senegambia belongs, the *griots* or story tellers are the ones entrusted with the task of preserving the memory of the family, the clan or the village.

In Senegambia, all "noble" families (*geer* in Wolof) had one or more *griots* (*gewel*) attached to them. The griot is an historian, a musician, a specialist in genealogy, and the role is passed from father to son within a restricted class of families. Thus the spoken word is an important element in social relationships and interaction. Because the words have been kept alive, the group can recall its history, philosophy of life and mode of survival. The spoken word keeps tight the social bonds and aids society's equilibrium.

Senegambian peoples' perception of their history cannot be understood without the contribution of oral tradition, which is used to explain and interpret natural phenomena such as the two hills named Les Mamelles at Almadies Point on the Atlantic coast just outside Dakar.

This is how the writer, the late Birago Diop, explains their origin as presented by

oral tradition: "There once was a peasant named Momar who had two hunchbacked wives. Khary, his first wife, had a very tiny hunchback, which made her envious of all normal women. Koumba, his second wife, was badly deformed, but her heart was warm and open to everyone. Unfortunately, Khary was not touched by Koumba's pleasant nature and never forgave her for being reconciled to her deformity.

"One day, Momar and Koumba were sleeping under a tamarind tree which was

frequented by genies. An old woman appeared to Koumba and showed her a trick that would unburden her of her great hunchback on to a genie. As soon as Khary saw what had happened to her rival, she pestered Koumba to learn the secret, which she at once set to use. Alas, the genie was delighted to find someone on whom to unload the heavy burden she had acquired and she placed on Khary's back Koumba's hump. Khary, in desperation, threw herself into the sea. But the sea could not completely cover her and poor Khary's two humps surfaced alongside Cap-Vert. These humps are what we call the Mamelles."

Preceding pages: Senegalese artist Souley Keita. Left, painting on glass by Gora M'Bengue. Right, actress Younoussé Seye.

Music and Dance: As early as 1960, the Senegalese government gave priority to the development of the cultural activities of the different ethnic groups. The same policy was adopted to a lesser extent in the Gambia.

A national theatre, the Théâtre National Daniel Sorano, was created in Senegal with the primary purpose of conducting research into traditional music and dance forms in order to recreate them for a modern audience. It took the lead in Africa for a number of years with its dynamic *Linguere* and *Sira Badral* ballets which travelled the world. The national drama company takes part in every major international competition and has performed succesfully plays such as *Le*

situations are used to perpetuate the musical traditions of the country. Modern forms of communication such as radio and television are used to carry the city culture with its many Western influences. Television drama has grown increasingly important. Popular music, much influenced by American, French and Cuban musics, moved in a more authentically African direction in the 1970s.

While the *griots* continue to be important—influential men are still praised by their families' *griots* on ceremonial occasions—a new class of professional, non-hereditary popular musicians has appeared. The traditional instruments, the kora, a 21-string harp-lute, the balafon, a wooden

Roi Christophe by the French West Indian Aimé Cesaire, *L' Os De Mor Lam* by the late Birago Diop and *L' Exil D' Alboury* by Cheik Ndao, also of Senegal.

The music and dance performances which are staged in the tourist hotels are often far from being authentic. The so called "traditional" groups recreate for the mainly Western tourists the manifestations of a mythical single culture: the music is no longer Diola, Serer or Wolof but simply Senegalese. This is, of course, an illusion.

Popular music and dance depict daily activities. Women working in the fields, men building a house, children playing—all these

gourd—resonated xylophone and the xalam, a sort of basic banjo/guitar, are sometimes used in modern groups as well as in traditional music. A number of groups and singers such as Youssou N'Dour and the Super Etoile de Dakar, Super Diamono, Xalam, Baba Maal and Ismael Lo are becoming known outside Africa.

Modern writing: Dakar as former colonial capital of French West Africa has long been in the region's intellectual vanguard. Head of State, Léopold Sédar Senghor, was a fine poet and a staunch defender of African cultural values. He spread the idea of *négritude* or blackness, which he had developed in

Paris in the 1940s with West Indian activitists and writers Aimé Cesaire and Léon Damas. At the same time, Cheikh Anta Diop was creating his theory of the anteriority of African civilisation in world history, which is still provoking highly emotive debates in intellectual circles.

In 1966, the World Black Arts Festival in Dakar placed Senegal at the centre of Africa's cultural map. The Senegalese government gave strong support to the publishing industry and indigenous publishing houses were flourishing. Wolof, the principal language in Senegal, was being written in Arabic letters, a testimony to the influence of Islam in the country.

literature, but the oral traditions are just as strong and vital.

Painting traditions: Before Independence, Senegalese painting was carried abroad by representatives such as Papa Ibra Tall, who later became National Director of Tapestry and Decorative Arts. Senegalese painting is very rich indeed with extremely diversified sensibilities, as demonstrated by an annual National Exhibition of Fine Arts in Dakar.

At the beginning, the country's art borrowed a great deal from the West. But from 1962, the centre for research into black fine arts of the former Art College encouraged a modern African style called the *Ecole de Dakar*. Its best-known representatives are

But most important is the literature written in French which includes poetry, novels and history, both colonial and post-colonial. The new generation of writers, typified by Boubacar Boris Diop, is however more critical of its own times. If the literature scene has been monopolised by male writers, this is not to say that there are no women in the field. Mariama Bâ and Aminata Sow Fall are among the leading feminist writers.

The Gambia, as a much smaller country, has less activity and influence in the field of

Dioutta Seck, Maodo Niang and Amadou Ba. The pictorial conception of the *Ecole de Dakar* is deeply rooted in the concept of *négritude* and "back-to-roots" philosophy which swept Africa and the black diaspora in the late 1960s. Pape Ibra Tall and Pierre Lods represented this trend.

Nowadays, the younger generation of Senegalese painters is departing from that form in favour of letting the mind travel more freely in an imaginary world, abstract and free of any rigid definition. Here, the colours have more say than the shapes. Souley Keita, El Hadji Sy, Zulu Mbaye embody the new current.

Left, star Dakar singer Youssou N'Dour. **Above**, griot playing a "talking drum".

Beside the formal fine art, there exists a "naive" art which explodes in every corner of the city. Barbers' shops, the bodies of buses and all manner of other spaces are adorned by simple vivid paintings depicting religious or domestic themes.

These traditional drawings are famous, especially in St Louis and Rufisque where the longest French colonial presence is recorded. Notice, for example, the recurrent theme that makes fun of the ridiculous husband, or the one where the hunter is being pursued by the lion, his gun flying high in the air. These themes are mostly developed by self-taught painters who use transparent glass on which to draw and paint. This technique, known as "sower", a deformation of the French *sous verre* (under glass), however, it is not as widely known as it should be. Its best-known practitioners are Babacar Lô and Gora Mbengue.

Film-making: Film production in Senegal is something of a miracle as there is neither a film studio nor post production facilities. Yet Senegalese film makers rank among the best in Africa, partly because the government has provided loans, a cinema office, film library and distribution company to encourage local film making. Senegalese film makers have also received substantial help from the French Ministry of Cooperation for post-production in French studios. But, first and foremost, the development of this art is the result of the singlemindedness of the early film makers.

One of these is the writer and director Ousmane Sembene, who has spent over a quarter of a century developing his techniques. He above all others put African cinema on the world map, and with other producers such as Paulin Vieryra, Ababacar Samb and Majamat Johnson Traoré, formed the first group of ambassadors of African cinema abroad.

In view of the scant state budget, the Société Nouvelle de Production Cinématographique (SNPC) was created in 1984 to look for outside sponsors. A highly successful co-production exercise with Algeria and Tunisia was the making of *Camp de Thiaroye* by Ousmane Sembene and Thierno Faty Sow, which won the 1988 Jury prize of the Venice Mostra festival.

<u>Right</u>, on stage at the Sorano theatre, Dakar.

Food and its preparation are an essential part of a country's culture. Conditioned by its geography, shaped by its history and traditions, cooking reflects a country's social organisation of the moment.

This is particularly true of Senegalese cuisine, which stands out on its own. While not restricting themselves to aboriginal ingredients nor repudiating their culinary heritage, the Senegalese have used great imagination and style to create an eclectic cuisine, drawing on the Arabic, French, Portuguese, Antillean and, more recently, Vietnamese influences on their country's history.

Similarly, as a result of the intermingling of races, easier means of transport and job mobility, dishes from other African countries, once limited to a particular ethnic group, can be sampled, with indigenous variations, all over Senegal. Couscous, for example, originally from North Africa and made with wheat, is made with millet in Senegal and, with local additions such as baobab leaf (*lalo*) in the stew, has become a standard Senegalese dish.

Being in the arid Sahelian zone, Senegal cultivates as its staples grains such as millet and sorghum which can survive the dry climate. Rice is grown in the wetter regions and is rapidly supplanting millet to become the major staple food crop. It is much easier to cook than millet, which first needs long hours of pounding.

The staple Wolof dish in Senegal is *cheb-ou-jen* (*thie-bou-dienne* in the French transliteration) — rice with fish — and is a must for the midday meal, particularly in the St Louis region. However, millet is essential for certain dishes such as *ngalakh* (millet, groundnut paste and baobab fruit, sweetened and liquefied with orange flower water), *chakri* (steamed millet balls consumed with sweetened yoghurt) or *lakh* (millet porridge). The array of bowls you see in the market each contains a different type of millet—half-steamed millet, millet meal, millet flour, unpounded millet, de-husked millet — for the connoisseur housewife.

The base of this gustatory alchemy is fish, of which there is an abundance in Senegal and the Gambia and which, together with the large variety of vegetables available, gives people a regular balanced diet. Barracuda, tuna, groupers (sea bass, the Senegalese *thiof*), mullet (*dem*), Nile perch (*capitaine*), swordfish (*espadon*), devilfish (*lotte*) and sole are the most common.

In addition, the local shellfish is excellent. There are enormous prawns, crabs, lobsters,

crayfish, sea urchins and oysters (grown on mangrove roots in the creeks but taken to oyster beds off the Pointe des Almadies to be washed clean by the Atlantic tides and thus made safe for eating). They should be tried by the discerning visitor, whether freshly grilled over an open fire, deep-fried, sautéed, boiled in stews, baked in foil with herbs, stuffed *à la St Louisienne* or, in the case of oysters, uncooked.

Dried in the sun (a smelly process) or smoked, fish can be kept without refrigeration. A speciality in St Louis *cheb-ou-jen* is dried mollusc, *yète*, whose strong flavour is not to everyone's taste.

Left, the tea ceremony. **Right**, Dakar bistro, interior.

Lamb is the most common meat used, together with beef. Only Christians and animists, an estimated 10 percent of the population, eat pork. Small bars called *dibiteries* serve grilled lamb, beef or liver kebabs (*brochettes*) with bread and perhaps a pepper sauce. Choose your own piece of meat when you go in, watch it being cut, seasoned and grilled for you.

Along the coast of Senegal, between the sand dunes, in little allotments called *niayes*, irrigated by subterranean fresh water, a profusion of vegetables is cultivated—cabbage, carrots, spring onions, leeks, turnips, pumpkin, aubergine, spinach, garlic, parsley, mint and fresh coriander as

Delicious local drinks, as an alternative to the alcohol forbidden to Muslims, are *bissap*, made from red sorrel flowers, *ginger* drink (from pounded fresh root ginger), *ditakh* (a green fruit infused in water—full of Vitamin C), *citronnelle* (lemon grass tea) and *kinkeliba* (drunk at breakfast and medicinally good for one).

Senegalese tea (derived from China via Mauritania) is drunk after a meal. A young man of the family heats gunpowder green tea, fresh mint and water in a metal teapot over charcoal. Skilled pouring from a great height from teapot to glass and back dissolves the sugar and forms a white froth on the surface through which the tea is drunk.

well as the usual onions and tomatoes. Other popular vegetables in Senegalese cooking are green leaves such as sorrel (*bissap*), dried baobab leaf (*lalo*) and okra (*gombo*) which is used in *soupikandia*.

Celebrations and thirst quenchers: Festive dishes include *ngalakh* (see above), to be eaten on Korité (end of Ramadan) before Mosque prayers (Christians make and eat this on Good Friday) and *lakh* with *sow* (sweetened soured milk), served as the first dish at baptisms. At *Tabaski*, the Muslim Feast of the Lamb (remembering Abraham's sacrifice), a whole sheep is slaughtered and grilled for family and friends.

There are three brewings and if you accept the invitation to tea, you must stay for all three. The first is strong and bitter, the second sweeter and the third even sweeter, milder and more minty.

In Casamance, the traditional drink is palm wine, tapped from the oil palm. Drunk fresh or fermented, it can be both refreshing and potent. Distilled, it becomes *cana*. Lethal, unless modified by syrup, in which case it becomes "punch".

Gambian specialities: Gambian cooking has been less influenced by Western or Arabic ideas but the presence of Yoruba and Sierra Leonean immigrants stretching back several generations has helped create a syncretic but distinct Gambian cuisine. The overlap of ethnic groups in both Senegal and the Gambia means that many of the dishes and drinks mentioned above are enjoyed in Gambia as well as Senegal but with a Gambian name.

Benachin, a Wolof dish (bena = one, chin or kin = pot, i.e. a one-pot meal—Gambians say the Senegalese serve their rice and sauce separately!) resembles *cheb-ou-jen* but is often made with meat instead of fish (Senegalese *cheb-ou-yap*). *Domoda*, made best by the Mandinkas who grow most of the groundnuts, may remind one of the widespread West African dish *mafé*. *Sisay*

A feature of both Senegal and the Gambia is the *nyama-nyama* or *"amuse-gueules"* (finger food, sometimes known as "small chop"), sold and eaten at all times of the day. Examples to be tried are *akara balls* (*accra* in Senegal) and *oleleh* (Gambia only), both made from black-eyed beans (*nyébé*), *pastels* (small hot pastry fritters stuffed with spiced fish) and fish balls (*boulettes*), both from Senegal, fish cakes from the Gambia (a larger version of pastels), *fataya* (meat-filled pasties of Lebanese origin) and, of course, roasted groundnuts, prepared daily and which should be bought hot and loose, not languishing in a plastic bag left over from the day before.

yassa is the same as *chicken yassa* (chicken marinaded in lemon juice and onions and then grilled). Yet all three are completely Gambian dishes.

Red palm oil goes into *plasas* (a corruption of Sierra Leonean "palaver sauce", itself coming from the Portuguese "*palavra*"), a stew made with smoked fish and greens and eaten by the Akus. Fish is fresh and plentiful and should be enjoyed but beware the oysters which have not had the advantage of sea-washing.

Left, Dakar bistro, exterior. **Above**, fish, the national dish.

Traditionally, neither Gambians nor Senegalese eat prepared desserts. The meal is rounded off with a piece of pineapple or pawpaw (*papaye*), a fresh orange cut into quarters or one of the many delicious fruits found locally: mangoes, watermelons, melons, guavas, passion fruit, grapefruit, limes, bananas or soursop (*corrosol* in French—a large green-skinned fruit with black "prickles" but with a delicious scented white flesh).

Cooking and eating in both Senegal and the Gambia are based on the tradition of hospitality. Meals are copious, geared to feeding a large family and always having enough for the unexpected guest. Food is served on a large flat tray, rice underneath and vegetables arranged over the top, with careful attention to final presentation. (It must appeal to the senses of sight and smell as well as to taste.) This is placed on a mat on the floor and the family sits grouped round.

Traditionally, eating is done with the right hand, so a bowl of water is provided before and after the meal for handwashing. A little rice is rolled up in the fingers, squeezed into a ball and popped into the mouth. If you feel you cannot manage this, a spoon will be provided. Succulent pieces of fish, meat or vegetables are broken off by the hostess and tossed in front of the visitor because

jen, *domoda* and *mafé*, chicken *yassa*, groundnut soup and stuffed mullet (in Senegal only) are sometimes offered. But even then, a certain freshness can be lacking, which may be due to overcooking and keeping warm or perhaps to the fact that it is men who cook in hotels rather than the housewives who are experienced in cooking on a large scale at ceremonial family gatherings. The gourmet visitor will have to seek out the smaller bars and restaurants or be lucky enough to be invited to a Gambian or Senegalese home for lunch.

A few recipes: The following two recipes are in African-style quantities, suitable for a large family:

stretching is not good manners.

French influence in Senegal, though relatively unobtrusive in the cooking, has left the Senegalese with a predilection for fresh French bread, dressed salads and *hors-d'oeuvres*. British culinary practices have fortunately not affected Gambian cuisine but have regrettably left their mark on some modern hotel kitchens. These have a tendency to serve unimaginative meat dishes in bland sauces, chips with everything and fiddly unseasoned garnishes.

Regrettably also, not enough traditional Gambian or Senegalese dishes find their way on to hotel menus. *Benachin* and *cheb-ou-*

Chicken Yassa
2 chickens
6 limes
6 large onions
ground red pepper
salt/ground black pepper
bayleaf
oil for frying
Cut chickens into eight large pieces. Squeeze juice from the limes, and mix with salt, peppers and bayleaf. Pour over the chicken pieces. Slice onions finely, spread over chickens and mix in well together with two spoons of oil. Leave for minimum two hours (or overnight) to marinade.

Later: drain chicken pieces and grill lightly, preferably over charcoal or wood. Heat the oil in a frying pan. Drain onions and sauté gently in the oil till soft. Add the marinade and cook for five minutes. Then add chicken pieces and one glass water. Check seasoning. Cover and simmer for 45 minutes. Serve with rice.

Benachin/Cheb-ou-jen (thie-bou-dienne)

3.5 lbs (1.5 kgs) thiof or other white fish cut in steaks
    4 oz (125g) tomato puree
    12 oz (400g) cooking oil
    2 hot red peppers
    4 oz (125g) dried fish (if possible)

3 large onions
2 cloves garlic
parsley, salt, black pepper, bayleaf
1 small piece yète (optional)
3.5 lbs (1.5 kgs) rice (pref. small grain)

Chop half a red pepper, spring onions, garlic and parsley and pound together (or blend) with a pinch of salt to make a paste. Stuff a small amount into a slit made in each fish steak. Slice onions and fry gently in oil, add dried fish, then the stuffed fish slices and fry until golden. Remove fish, add tomato puree diluted in three litres water and bring to the boil. Add prepared vegetables and the fish pieces. Season to taste, float the remaining pepper on top, bring back to the

8 oz (250g) carrots
1 small cabbage, cut in quarters
10 oz (300g) cassava root, peeled and cut in pieces
10 oz (300g) sweet potatoes, peeled and cut in half
6 oz (200g) pumpkin, peeled and cut in chunks
10 oz (300g) aubergines, unpeeled, cut in halves
6 oz (200g) turnips, peeled and cut in chunks

Left, buffet by the pool. **Above**, beach restaurant in St Louis.

boil and simmer, covered, for 20 minutes. Remove the fish pieces, then the vegetables as they become cooked. The cassava will take the longest. Place in a dish, pour some of the sauce over them and keep warm until all have been cooked. When everything has been removed from the sauce, put aside a little of the sauce, then pour the rice into the remaining liquid (there should be approximately twice the amount of liquid to rice) and cook until absorbed. No liquid should remain. Turn rice on to a large platter with the fish and vegetables attractively arranged on top. Serve with lemon quarters and extra juice in a jug.

As fast as the popularity of soccer spread in Europe, so it did in its former colonies and, today, both Senegalese and Gambians are enthusiastic players, often competing internationally. Youngsters can be seen on any open patch of ground or on the beaches playing barefoot. Regular inter-West African matches are held at the Parc des Sports in Dakar, and the Box Bar Stadium or the new Friendship Stadium, built by the Chinese, in Banjul. Football attracts great crowds wherever it is played and the spectator charges are not expensive.

Although football appears to be the most popular sport throughout Senegambia, the traditional national sport of both countries is wrestling. Dating back to the days of the Mali Kingdom in the 11th century, the sport was once reserved for those of royal lineage. Now most villages have a cleared area of ground where this "no holds barred" sport is practised—usually on Saturday or Sunday afternoons. While opponents kick, bite and punch each other until one lies in the sand, spectators, including many women, shout, cheer, sing, whistle, and hurl abuse. Most hotels and tour companies offer a visit to a wrestling bout as a half-day excursion.

Teeing off: Of the most popular Western participant sports, most are represented in the two countries, but often only as a service to visitors. On the outskirts of Dakar, on the Route de Camberène there is a nine-hole golf course and Club Mediterranée at Cap Skirring has its own mini-golf course. In the Gambia, golf is played on the 18-hole course of the Banjul Golf Club in Fajara.

Tennis players are much better catered for, although most courts are attached to hotels or resort complexes. There are two tennis clubs in Dakar; the Tennis Club Dakarois at Les Marinas, Hotel de N'Gor and the Union Tennis Club; the University along West Corniche Road also has tennis facilities. Almost every beach hotel of more than 20 rooms in Senegal and the Gambia provides tennis courts for residents or guests. In the

Gambia there is a tennis club at The Cedars, Serekunda, and the Reform Club in Banjul has tennis courts.

A wide variety of sports are available at the hotels, from Hobie-Cat sailing, windsurfing, surfing, water polo, water-skiing, skin diving and surfboarding, to tennis, volley ball, squash, golf, horse trekking, walking, cricket, football, fishing, hunting, pirogue trips and safaris. Whatever your choice, remember that physical exertion in the climate of West Africa takes more toll on

the stamina than similar activity in temperate zones. Salt, lost through excessive perspiration, must be replaced and salt pills are a suggested supplement. Headgear of some sort is recommended, as is sun protection.

Watersports: It is in watersports that West Africans excel. Both Gambians and Senegalese are born swimmers. Just watch the local children diving off rocks, jetties or boats and playing in the Atlantic surf. Most swimming pools are reserved for residents but, since both countries have miles of attractive coasts, Senegalese and Gambian families make long treks to spend the day on the beach. Apart from some specifically des-

Preceding pages: wrestling bout in progress. Left, wrestler taking "magic potion". Right, calisthenics on a Senegalese beach.

THE DAKAR RALLY

Each Christmas Day, competitors converge on Paris from more than a dozen countries to participate in a motorsport event which has become notorious for its danger and excitement. The "Dakar", as the rally is known, tests the stamina and endurance of man and machine in a 21-day trek through eight countries and over 6,370 miles (10,200 km) of daunting terrain.

Since a small group of adventurous Frenchmen started it in 1978 as a means of escaping from the northern European winter, the Dakar has gone on to attract the biggest names in rally driving and sponsors from every walk of life. Cigarette and

Thierry Sabine, died when the helicopter in which he was travelling crashed in the desert. In 1988, the number of accidents on the rally, including six fatalities, caused the Pope to criticize the safety standards of the event.

The route of the Rally snakes via Barcelona to Tunis, down into the Fezzan region of Libya, where Colonel Gadhaffi offers free fuel for the vehicles and permits the (generally banned) consumption of alcohol by participants in the race. From Ghadames on the Libyan-Tunisian border, the track winds across Libya to Sebha and down to Termit. From the oasis town of Agadez

clothing companies' decals, along with those of hi-fi and watch manufacturers, adorn the 250 cars, 170 motorcycles and 70 support trucks which nowadays make up the field. For manufacturers such as Peugeot, which has a major export market in Africa, the publicity generated by success in the rally is immensely important. Their vehicles' frequent high placings have contributed greatly to Peugeot's reputation for toughness and reliability.

Among the numerous controversial mishaps which have dogged the rally's short history have been the temporary loss and expensive rescue of Mark Thatcher, the accident-prone son of Britain's prime minister, while he was participating. In 1986, the originator of the event,

in the Aïr mountains of Niger, a now straggling line of battered machines makes it way to Niamey, the capital of Niger, and thence to Gao and Timbuktu in Mali.

From Timbuktu the race hots up—as if temperatures are not hot enough. The route is downhill, south, through the Sahel to Bamako, capital of Mali. The race has now only three days to get to its final destination, Dakar. By this time the field has usually narrowed to around half the original number of vehicles.

Champagne, the victor's trophy and a laurel wreath await the winners. Prizes go to both motorcyclists and cars, and all who compete the course get the accolade of "Dakeurs", survivors of the world's most harrowing rally.

ignated "safe" beaches, strong currents and undertows can be a hazard.

Pointe Bernard, in Dakar, has a famous swimming pool overlooking the beach. The Lido on Route de la Corniche, L'Ocean, Domaine de Ouarer and Sub-nu-Gab are other popular pools. In the Gambia, Cape St Mary and Barra Point are both good, safe beaches and the Atlantic Hotel in Banjul has a fine pool, as do all of the major tourist hotels on the coast.

Sporting activities at most resort hotels are well organised and often centre around the pool or the beach. A favourite in Senegal but unknown in the Gambia is the traditional French game of *boules*, almost obligatory

hiring is available at the Atlantic Hotel and most of the main hotels along the Gambian coast. St Louis and Dakar are fast becoming popular with yacht sailors and more yachts are visiting the Gambia in recent years, the favourite moorings being at Denton Bridge.

Rod and line: The waters off the Senegambian coast are some of the richest and most varied in the world when it comes to fishing. Sports fishing in both countries is a favourite pastime and boats can be hired or trips arranged to follow the great game fish like marlin, barracuda, sailfish, bonito, swordfish and capitaine. See the Angling Centre in Dakar, or the Sports Fishing Centre on Gorée Island for rentals in Senegal.

for holidaymakers at any of Senegal's beachside hotels. Popular in both countries are beach games such as volleyball and table tennis. Some hotels even have squash courts.

In resort areas and on hotel beaches one can hire a variety of watersports equipment for skin diving, water skiing, sailing, boardsailing and para-sailing. In Dakar watersports equipment can be rented at L'Océan, Le Lagon, Les Marinas, Cercle de la Voile and at the Plage de Hann. In Banjul

Left, Jacky Ickx negotiates a splash, Dakar Rally. <u>Above</u>, Dakar stadium with wrestling match under way.

In the Gambia, Sportsfishing Ltd operates both from the shore and in the river. Based at Denton Bridge, the company runs barracuda trawling half-day excursions and a full-day "All Species" trip.

In Senegal, similar facilities are offered through a number of tour operators. Around Dakar Les Almadies (Club Mediterranée), offers deep sea fishing facilities daily. Club Mediterranée at Cap Skirring and the Hotel de Paris in Kaolack arrange regular trips, as does the Domaine de Nianing and the nearby Centre Touristique de la Petite Côte. In Casamance, at the Hotel-village de la Pointe St George, special river and sea angling excursions can be organised. Most fishing trips depend on enough people—generally four or five—being present in order to make the excursion viable.

Horse riding is unusual in the Gambia, where there are few horses. In Senegal, however, this sport is followed avidly. At L'Hacienda near Dakar there is a riding school; other stables are at Palm Beach, Hotel Saly and at Club Adiana. In Mbour, the Domaine de Nianing has horse riding facilities, as does the Ranch de Doli hunting lodge out in the Djourbel Region. At Camp Retba, near the lake of the same name, a riding school offers long treks along the dunes.

Hunting: This is a popular sport in Senegal but few hunting trips are organised in the Gambia where there are limited opportunities. Some hotels in Senegal specifically provide for hunting expeditions; Les Paletuviers has established a hunting camp in the Siné-Saloum region. Nearby is another hunting centre, known as Medine Djicoye, and the Gîte d'Etape at Richard Toll provides for hunting enthusiasts.

There is a camp at the reserve of Maka Diama for hunters and, in the Casamance region, the camping centre of Khobe, near Kolda, offers hunting facilities. At the Hotel de la Poste in St Louis, at Le Relais Fleuri hotel in Badioure, and at L'Hacienda just outside Dakar hunting parties can be arranged. On the steamship cruises of the *Bou el Mogdad,* which plies the Senegal River, hunting excursions are part of the cruising activities. Firearm permits, mandatory for those not hunting with a licensed guide, are best applied for in advance.

The Water and Forests Bureau in Dakar issues hunting permits to those with insurance, firearm certificate, regulation permit papers and dues. Permits come in three categories. The Small Game Permit is issued for one day's shoot taking not more than 15 stone partridges, guinea-fowl, bustards, francolins or hare. The Medium Game Permit includes the small game but also the shooting of one of each of the following: gazelle, oribi, waterbuck, cob, warthog or two great bustards. A Big Game licence is issued only through authorised hunting guides. The hunting season runs from mid-December until the end of April.

Right, canoe race, St Louis.

119

Visitors should not be discouraged by reports that West African wildlife is less extensive than East or Southern African. There are more than 20 national parks, game reserves, forest preserves and nature conservation areas throughout Senegambia. Senegal claims one of Africa's most important game reserves, the famed Parc National du Niokolo Koba.

More than 450 different species of wildlife live in these and other regions of natural beauty. Nearly all the great animals typical of the African bush, forest and veldt are to be found in some of West Africa's most interesting reserves.

The fringes of the Sahara desert which cut across the north and east of the region are known as the Sahel and the expansion of this barren region has affected the wildlife of Senegal and the Gambia. Many thousands of years ago the topography was quite different from that of today. The Sahara and its adjacent lands once supported a rich collection of fauna and flora.

Much of West Africa resembled the teeming plains and forest regions now more usually associated with East Africa. Elephant, buffalo, giraffe, lion and herds of wildebeest roamed the area. Evidence of the variety of wildlife remains in prehistoric cave paintings in the desert. Hunting all manner of forest creatures and savannah herds, neolithic man wandered among a tropical assortment of trees and plants, beasts and birds. A millennium of drought caused vegetation to die out and in a great migration animals left Senegambia.

Gradually the Sahel took hold. Great tracts of land, which were once rich in vegetation, succumbed to the seas of sand which moved south from the Sahara. River banks and isolated outcrops of more fertile land remained to support the dwindling wildlife population. Coastal and estuarine areas still encourage the complex variety of plant and animal life associated with mangrove swamps, and oases in the north provide succour to palm groves and camel herds.

Africa suggests images of great herds of wildebeest thundering across plains dotted with giraffe, elephant and zebra. This was once the scene across most of West Africa, but the tsetse fly drastically reduced the numbers of the larger mammals.

Further depleted by indiscriminate hunting and climatic and topographical changes, herds of antelope dwindled and, except in some isolated regions, the classic African wildlife disappeared. Action by conservat-

ionists and the establishment of a network of national parks and reserves has saved Senegambia's animal life from extinction.

Creatures of the sands: It's not easy to define accurately the territorial limits of the region's wildlife. The territories of the desert-dwelling animals and birds have, in some areas, overtaken the habitats of riverside creatures. But the traveller hardly ever sees desert wildlife, apart from vultures wheeling in the distance and huge flocks of migratory birds.

Doom palm and date groves dot the territory of small gazelle, roan antelope, striped and spotted hyena, desert wolf, civet

Preceding pages: Gazelle demonstrating its camouflage. **Left**, hunting is much reduced but not eliminated. **Right**, the king of Niokolo Koba.

cat and rare golden cat. Lappet-faced vultures and kites soar overhead. And the shifting dunes provide a home for a number of venomous creatures such as the Gabon viper, the puff adder and also several varieties of scorpion.

On the edges of the sandy wastes and in small oases, domesticated animals such as the goat and one-humped dromedary are herded under the shade of tall palmetto palms, cropping the sparse grass. In rocky outcrops the nocturnal crested porcupine shares its lair with the curious rock hydrax— a relative of the elephant, although hardly longer than 18 inches (45 cm). Other scavengers of the desert are the fennec, or

desert fox, jackals and lizards.

Less common, in this inhospitable environment, is the hartebeest, the smaller, chestnut-coloured Sassaby—usually off the plains—and the rarer addax, a beautiful white antelope with great twisted horns and a preference for wild, rocky terrain. Also a dweller of the open wastes is the aardvark which feeds off termites, ant-sized creatures responsible for the spire-like earth mounds dotted across the countryside. Termite mounds can often reach twice the height of a man and house many millions of industrious insects. Care should be taken when inspecting them as often discarded mounds

are adopted by snakes such as the mamba or python. Termites are also a favourite of the armour-plated giant pangolin.

Visitors journeying through the Sahel should be careful when camping out and take the usual precautions of knocking out clothes and shoes before dressing, checking for scorpions, spiders and other insects. Where there is water, butterflies and dragonflies are usually prolific; so are mosquitoes. Creams and sprays can deter most insects but the desert dust is a haven for midges and ants.

The Grasslands: The savannah, consisting mostly of brown elephant grass, is the habitat of a more varied selection of wildlife. Ghekkoes and multi-coloured lizards bask on exposed rocks, watched keenly by the unblinking stare of black-and-white palm nut vultures.

Where there is any source of water, the hardy Senegal date palm grows, harbouring numbers of exotic birds; fire finch, red-cheeked cordon bleu, red-headed grossbeak and red bishop weaver birds whose nests dangle like silk stockings from the trees' lower branches. Another favourite of the weavers, particularly the buffalo weaver, is the thorn tree, which is abundant throughout the savannah. Standing out like giants among the sea of scrub are gaunt baobabs and immense kapok trees. Here the hornbill, widow bird, swift and African emerald cuckoo take shelter.

Strutting by the roadside, the Senegalese snake bird or the larger secretary bird hunts for ground squirrels, gerbils and reptiles, while any areas of grassland sport flocks of cattle egrets picking off grasshoppers and insects disturbed by the hooves of grazing zebu. Lifeless stumps of palms make ideal perches for shrikes and rare golden-tailed woodpeckers. Bulbuls, flycatchers, pipits and wagtails share the savannah with Egyptian plovers, larks, guinea-fowl and flocks of black piapiacs.

Standing, sentry-like, in bush or short grass, the weird marabou stork waits patiently, poised to strike at passing frogs and small reptiles with its huge spear-shaped bill. Flashes of colour in the treetops indicate the presence of peach-faced lovebirds or African grey parrots.

The river environment: Around the mouths of Senegambia's four major rivers mangrove, swamp and marshland provide ideal cover for a great variety of animals and birdlife. Some of the animals are difficult to see because of the dense undergrowth in these regions but, where the bush meets the river, wildlife spotters can sometimes catch a glimpse of the wild forest boar. Around five ft (1.5 metres) in length, this is a particularly mean animal and it can do severe damage with its curved tusks.

In the hinterland small deer and the occasional waterbuck can be seen at the water's edge, the best place for wildlife watching. The African finfoot, like a large darter, takes its Latin name, *Podica Senegalensis*, from its native country.

bolongs or built-up river banks, meanding streams have created islands. Most are completely overgrown with dense vegetation and tall trees. Usually the islands are ringed by mangrove and almost inaccessible, but breaks in the foliage created by mudflats can be used as a landing for canoes. Skirting the islands by boat one can see a great deal of wildlife including olive baboon colonies, families of green-coated vervet monkeys with their white "bibs", red-jacketed Patas monkeys, and the rarer red colobus monkeys.

Wildfowl in great flocks rise from their perches in the upper branches of the mangroves as one approaches the islands.

A curious crested bird, often found near water, is the hoopoe, or its less common cousin, the green wood hoopoe. Glossy ibis nest in the gnarled branches of mangrove and one might catch a glimpse of the rabbit-sized water chevrotan, a little deer even smaller than the tiny duiker which also come to the riverbanks for fresh water. Here, francolins sun themselves, waders tiptoe across mud banks and one might see a rail stalking between reed beds.

Inland, where the rivers snake through

Often seen slumbering on a mudbank, the crocodile is becoming less common in the lower reaches of the rivers. There are three species of crocodile in this part of West Africa. The most common is the Nile crocodile which can reach 15-16 ft (five metres) in length. The West African Dwarf and the Bottlenose crocodiles are rarely seen, or more correctly, rarely identifed.

Few hippopotamus inhabit the region, although some have been seen far up the Gambia River and in parts of the Parc National du Niokola Koba. Most river banks have their snake population and numbers of monitor lizards. Both the lizards, which can

Left, pelicans in Djoudj, Senegal. **Above**, a crocodile in the Gambia River.

grow to four ft (1.2 metres) long, and pythons, are good swimmers and can often be seen crossing from bank to bank.

Inland from the river banks, where the jungle is thick, small deer may be seen. The Duiker and Oribi are typical forest mammals. Another inhabitant of the dense undergrowth is the warthog, which is now becoming rare because of the relentless hunting. This is also baboon territory and troops of them can sometimes be observed as they cross roads between one forest shelter and the next.

The variety of birdlife in high forest includes hawks and eagles. Diligent ornithologists may spot the harrier, kite,

lizard buzzard, harrier eagle or goshawk. In between forest and river the West African river eagle might be seen, or the osprey.

Parks and reserves: Situated within a day's flight from Europe, Parc National du Niokolo Koba in southeast Senegal is the nearest location in Africa where one can view the continent's larger animals in their natural habitat. This extensive reserve is not only the major game park of Senegambia, but also the only one in the region to rival the great reserves of East Africa.

The park's lions are among the largest known and the magnificent Derby Eland is the world's largest antelope. Both are easily

seen on guided safaris in the park, as are buffalo, gazelle and black antelope. Leopards are rare in Niokolo Koba but their traditional food, bushbuck, roan antelope, waterbuck, cob and the little duiker are plentiful. A variety of apes can be spotted, and also hippopotamus, crocodile and warthog. More than 300 species of bird have been logged, 70 species of animal and at least 60 of fish.

Senegal contains six more national parks, if one includes the Lac de Guiers, famed for its waders, Scoter duck, rail and teal. Djoudj is famous for its pelicans, flamingo, crowned cranes, wagtails and storks. The Parc de la Langue de Barbarie is noted for two things: the thousands of birds which migrate from Europe during the winter, and its turtle breeding grounds. The Parc du Delta du Saloum is known for the abundance of migratory birds and the seabirds that use the wide estuary waters.

The Parc de la Basse-Casamance attracts visitors for a wide variety of wildlife, including the stately Derby eland, the Buffon Cob and numerous monkeys; there are about a dozen wildlife-watching lodges in the Casamance region. The national park of the Ile de la Madeleine was established to protect its vast colony of seabirds from disturbance by amateur archaeologists visiting the site.

In the Gambia there is only one nature reserve open to visitors at Abuko, but many regions of forest and river have been designated protected areas. These include Bijilo Forest on the coast and five other fenced-off areas up-country: Salaji, Nyambai, Kabafita, Furuya and Gambia's largest reserve, the Kiang West.

Park areas in the Gambia are warden-protected and closed to visitors. UNESCO's World Heritage scheme has listed both the Djoudj National Park and the Niokolo Koba Parks as areas of world importance. Senegal became party to the World Heritage Convention in 1976 and the Gambia joined in 1987. The "Banjul Declaration", issued by the President of Gambia, Sir D.K. Jawara, in 1977 for the protection of the country's flora and fauna has become a guideline for both Gambians and visitors to the country.

Above, rehabilitated chimpanzees, Gambia.
Right, a mighty baobab.

THE BAOBAB TREE

The most prominent feature of the West African landscape, the baobab tree, dominates the savannah of Senegambia. Not a giant compared to the kapok, which can grow to over 160 ft (50 metres) in height, the baobab rarely exceeds 70 ft (21 metres). Its barrel-like, grotesque trunk, however, often acquires a girth of more than 30 ft (nine metres). The angular branches of the baobab look more like roots—giving rise to the Senegalese tale that the devil must have uprooted the baobab and plunged it back into the earth upside-down.

This is not the only myth to be associated with

traditionally used for curing rheumatic ailments and inflammations. The acidic fruit can be made into a sherbet-like, refreshing drink; the pulp has long been known as a remedy for various ailments, particularly circulatory, and the gourd-like shell is used as a container.

Musical instruments are fashioned from the bark, which can also serve as packing paper and be woven into rope or even cloth. In this region, were malaria is rife, the bark is also believed to have quinine-like properties and the seeds, which are rich in phosphates, are used in the manufacture of fertiliser and soap.

the baobab. Because of its ability to store water in an immense trunk, it has magical properties in the eyes of desert dwellers. Because of the pulpy nature of the baobab's large yellow fruit Africans call it the "monkey bread tree". Few villages in Senegambia are without an aged baobab and some are estimated to be more than 1,000 years old. Superstition surrounds the tree because, like humans, the baobab, in ageing, does not increase its stature; in fact it decreases in size—unlike any other tree.

The baobab has no shortage of practical uses. The sweet-smelling, white flowers provide decoration in times of festival. The leaves are eaten either fresh or dried. When powdered they are known as *alo*, a preparation which is

Wandering nomads have found a temporary home in the hollow trunks of venerable baobabs. When dead, the tree is a source of precious firewood or materials with which to construct canoes or fishing floats because of its light, spongy consistency. In places it is therefore known as the "cork tree".

The baobab features in countless folk tales and myths. It has also given its name to numerous hotels and restaurants, and to one of Senegal's most early "roots" music groups. The strongest use of all for the baobab has been as a burial place. In certain communities, members of the griot minstrel class could not be interred beside other castes and the massive hollow trunks came to be their traditional mausolea.

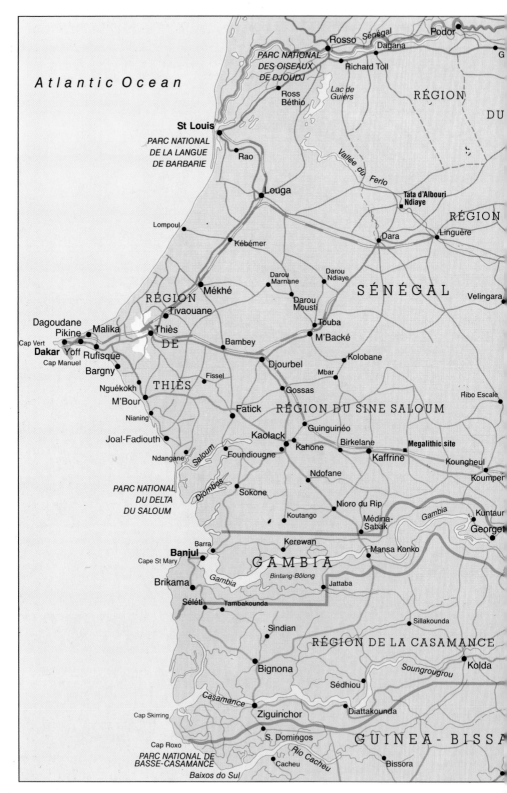

Atlantic Ocean

Rosso   Sénégal   Podor
PARC NATIONAL   Dagana
DES OISEAUX   G
DE DJOUDJ   Richard Toll
Ross   Lac de   RÉGION
Béthio   Guiers   DU

St Louis
PARC NATIONAL
DE LA LANGUE   Rao
DE BARBARIE

Louga   Tata d'Albouri
Ndiaye

Vallée du Ferlo   RÉGION

Lompoul   Dara   Linguère
Kébémer

Darou   Darou   SÉNÉGAL   Velingara
Marnane   Ndiaye
Mékhé   Darou
RÉGION   Mousti
Tivaouane   Touba
Dagoudane   DE   Thiès   Bambey   M'Backé
Pikine   Malika
Cap Vert   Kolobane
Dakar   Yoff   Rufisque   Djourbel
Cap Manuel   Mbar
Bargny   Gossas   Ribo Escale
Nguékokh   Fissel
M'Bour   THIÈS   Fatick   RÉGION DU SINE SALOUM
Nianing   Guinguinéo
Joal-Fadiouth   Kaolack   Birkelane   Megalithic site
Kahone   Koungheul
Ndangane   Saloum   Foundiougne   Kaffrine   Koumper
Ndofane
PARC NATIONAL   Diombos   Sokone   Nioro du Rip   Kuntaur
DU DELTA   Koutango   Médina-   Gambia   George
DU SALOUM   Sabak
Kerewan   Mansa Konko
Barra
Banjul   GAMBIA
Cape St Mary   Bintang-Bôlong   Jattaba
Brikama   Gambia
Séléti   Tambakounda
Sindian   Sillakounda
RÉGION DE LA CASAMANCE
Bignona   Kolda
Soungrougrou
Sédhiou
Cap Skirring   Casamance   Diattakounda
Ziguinchor
Cap Roxo   S. Domingos   GUINEA - BISSA
PARC NATIONAL DE   Rio Cacheu
BASSE-CASAMANCE   Cacheu   Bissora
Baixos do Sul

134

The Gambia/Sénégal

80 km/ 50 miles

Bogué

Sénégal

Ngoni

Kaédi

Mbout

EUVE

MAURITANIA

Guirvas

Matam

Maghama

UGA FERLO

Sénégal

Fourdou

Ranérou

Sélibabi

Mboune

Bakel

Loumbi

Sénégal

Nayé

Kayes

Goudiri

Kolomba

RÉGION

MALI

DU

Koussanar

Tambacounda

SÉNÉGAL

ORIENTAL

Gouloumbou

Missira

Gambia

Dialakoto

SÉNÉGAL

Basse
Santa Su

Médina
Gounas

Vélingara

PARC NATIONAL
DU NIOKOLO KOBA

Kounkané

311
▲
Assirik

414
▲
Goléakouto

Saraya

Koulontou

Salémata

Youkounkoun

Kédougou

Gabú

Kandika

Koundara

Fongolembi

Koliba (Tominé)

GUINEA

One of the first impressions you get of the Gambia is its quaintness. Whether you arrive by air at the little Yundum Airport with its open-air concrete tables for baggage collection, or by ferry over the river from Senegal, everything seems small, homely and rather jolly. There is little sign of extreme poverty—though virtually none of wealth either. The people are for the most part friendly and relaxed, certainly by comparison with the citizens of Dakar, who have all the stresses and strains of an overcrowded city life.

Particularly if you have come from Senegal, you will notice the British colonial legacy everywhere. The navy-blue police uniforms, the Silk Cut cigarette logos and the street vendors' tattered sunshades, the Express Fish and Chips shop in Banjul with its bougainvillea-covered wooden frontage—all these remind you constantly where much of the country's newer mode of life came from. Beneath this veneer, of course, the older culture of the region continues unaffected; the mosques, the markets and the unhurried social life could be on either side of the border with the Gambia's big neighbour.

Although most tourists spend little time there, it is in the dowdy little capital of Banjul that the colonial influence is most noticeable. The balding parade ground in the centre of town still serves as an occasional cricket pitch. Lunching in the Braustuble restaurant near the Law Court, you may sit at the next table to a pin-stripe suited, gowned Gambian barrister who could just as well have emerged from the Old Bailey.

Twenty minutes' drive away on the Atlantic coast, the big hotel complexes belong to a newer, more international world, with their swimming pools, water sports and evening entertainments. But they too have their own personalities.

The different nationalities who patronise them may influence their style. Germans and Scandinavians were among the earliest holidaymakers to discover the Gambia along with the British, and the French are now beginning to come down for an interesting break while visiting Senegal. Whether you want company or solitude, there's plenty of room on the pale sandy beaches and in the Atlantic rollers to make the Gambian Coast a great holiday spot.

And finally there's the river, the long snaking watercourse whose shape is the shape of the country itself. A trip by Land-Rover or boat, or a combination of the two, will provide fascinating glimpses of the rich bird and animal life, and of the traditional bush village way of life too. For a small country, the Gambia has a lot to offer.

Preceding pages: Hanging out the washing on Gorée Island; canoes and spectators in St Louis; Bassari initiation ceremony costumes. **Left,** River Gambia, key to the country.

BANJUL

Banjul, still known on signposts up-country as Bathurst, is the Gambia's capital. Estimates of its population vary between 44,000 and 60,000. As Banjul is on **St Mary's Island**, surrounded by open sea, the mouth of the River Gambia, Oyster Creek and a network of mangrove creeks, it is hard to see how it can grow.

Wealthy Gambians and expatriates tend very largely to live and play outside Banjul on the more spacious mainland at **Bakau**, **Fajara**, **Kotu Beach** and **Kololi** areas. Less well-off Gambians and migrants from neighbouring countries tend to proliferate in **Serekunda**. Therefore the "suburban" population of Banjul is considerably larger than that of the capital itself. Firm figures are notoriously hard to come by but Serekunda has been estimated at approximately 80,000.

Banjul remains the seat of government, the headquarters of banking and commerce. To the casual observer or the sometimes rather shocked glance of the foreign new arrival, the city can seem depressed, shabby, small and dusty, and pock-marked by potholes to an epidemic extent. But equally immediately it gives an impression of relaxed liveliness. Everywhere people are on the move, at pedestrian rates of progress. They crowd about their business, trading, hoping to sell or to make a bargain, visiting. The most stationary looking sewing-machine operator or street-stall holder is somewhere else 20 minutes after first sighting.

Banjul's ethnic mix is as diverse as that of the rest of the country: Aku, Fula, Diola, Mandinka, Sarakholé, Serer, Wolof. Some are immediately recognisable by caste or feature, clothing, facial scarification, but others are less obvious. There are also Moors from Mauritania, Lebanese, Yoruba, Guineans, Guinea-Bissauans, Malians, and Europeans. Sometimes tourists are conspicuously distinguishable from local expatriates by their clothing, colouring and deportment.

Banjul's charms emerge easily from the dust and disrepair. The roads are in need of remaking but the slower careful pace of locomotion, even in rare pedestrian-free sections, means that one can quickly notice things behind the tired state of the paintwork, the crumbling walls and windows. The marvellous light picks out courtyards, arches, lattices, verandahs, flowering trees, standpipes and cooking pots and local clothing styles and headdresses, especially in the back streets.

The tendency is to look for distinctive monuments, public landmarks, but Banjul's attraction is more intimate. The real wealth of the Gambia is its people. The attractiveness of domestic living, of people going self-containedly about their affairs, of the amazingly enduring good nature and welcomingness on all sides.

Colonial architecture: There are, however, interesting historical, cultural, social and gastronomic

eft, Gambian
umbrellas
row on trees.
elow, snack
me in Banjul
market.

features. **State House** and its adjoining cluster of government offices can be glimpsed across the rather moulting expanse of **MacCarthy Square** with its iron fence, mini-bandstand, cricket pitches, occasional traders' stalls frequently moved on by the police, but rapidly returning.

The tiny **Anglican Cathedral** in **Independence Drive**, by MacCarthy Square is demure and appealing. Also nearby is the small, beautifully kept and interesting **National Museum**. It contains material of considerable interest of ethnic, archaeological, historical, and contemporary kinds. The Catholic Cathedral on the corners of **Picton Street** and **Hagan Street** is larger and glossier and more opulent-looking than the Anglican and is also of interest architecturally, particularly in its interior features: ceilings, windows. The new **Great Mosque**, on **Box Bar Road**, is rather uncompromisingly new-looking, for all its splendour.

The lasting joys of Banjul, architecturally, are the surviving bungalows and storey-buildings in what the Museum calls "Creole" style. These are similar to equally picturesque adaptations of English Georgian and early Victorian houses in Freetown in Sierra Leone with balconies and shutters and dormer windows and steep roofs. Often on pillars raised above the ground, usually with weathered corrugated roofs above wooden upper floors, they might better be called Krio-style or Aku-style houses. Whatever they are called, once really observed behind their surface decrepitude and paint-fatigue, they are enchanting.

Banjul is a low-lying city as well as a small one. Modern buildings are rather anonymous and undistinguished. There is not much of the panache of Dakar's public buildings and villas. Even the buttressed pyramidal building of the **Banque Internationale de Commerce et Industrie** in **Wellington Street** cuddles so closely to its neighbours that it has no chance to shine and startle as its cousins do in Ziguinchor and Kaolack in Senegal.

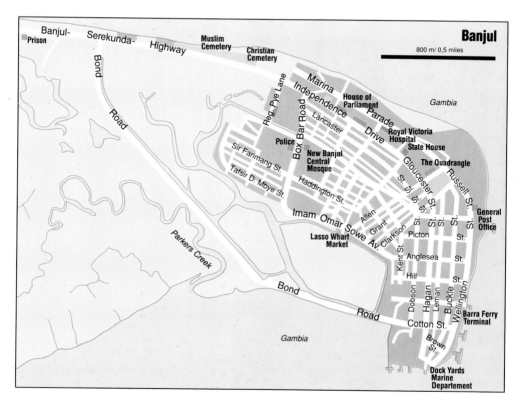

The vibrant focus of market life in Banjul spreads behind the new façade put up by Chinese constructors along **Russell Street** for the famous, colourful, inexhaustible **Albert Market**. This was destroyed by fire in 1988 and the new frontage promises a lasting elegance which the makeshift lanes of local and imported produce behind successfully dispute. Clothes and beads and kola nuts and tresses to plait into hair and skin lighteners and tea and fruit, and many other things can be found in their place. The market has been going strong since the middle of the 19th century and it takes more than total combustion to stop it.

The Lebanese cloth stalls along **Russell Street**, **Cameron Street** and **Wellington Street**, are full of bolts and rolls and odds and ends of gloriously varied lengths of cloth which ride marvellously on African skins but need great discrimination to suit European ones. Excellent cloth for men's lightweight suits, summer shirts and shorts abounds inexpensively. Local tailors wait to run up little numbers for Madame or Sir at a third of European prices with great competence, like lightning. Bargaining is essential.

The Gambian cloth and clothes sellers concentrate on tie-dyed dresses and shirts and hand-painted T-shirts ("Gambia—No Problem" is a constant seller) and "bush hats", which are seldom worn except by Europeans. The National Library has a fetching red and white *ashwebi* (matching outfit) for its staff, and one sees the occasional non-Gambian African or Afro-American in local tie die robes.

Watering holes: Thirsty or hungry after sight-seeing and shopping? The popular nourishment places for visitors are the Braustuble restaurant-bar in Leman Street, the African Heritage on the first floor of the arcaded building just beyond the CFAO supermarket in Wellington Street and the Atlantic Hotel on Marina Parade.

The **Braustuble** is German-Lebanese run and has an inside restaurant and bar, air-conditioned in

The President's residence, Banjul.

season, and an outside area with scrubbed tables and benches under thatch covers overs and a circular bar. There are also examples on the walls of the stylishly grotesque, mannered, engraved wood pictures of Tonton, as he signs himself, whose work is also prominent at Le Relais restaurant at M'Bour in Senegal.

The **African Heritage** is imaginative and attractive. It has a long first-floor pillared balcony, with one side open above the stalls and activity of **Wellington Street**, where most of the restaurant tables are placed. There are also tables in the lofty cool of the main rooms, including one magnificent refectory table and benches which have somehow ended up here from Kenya. It is run by a Danish-African couple who mix selling art objects with feeding people. The clothes, jewels, carvings and pictures on sale are quite individual, which is reflected in their prices.

Specialist visitors often photograph the art at the African Heritage, as it is the most permanent and accessible collection in Banjul. In season, there is also the view beyond the Shell petrol station opposite of the dolphins jumping in pairs or families or alone in the estuary. In and out of season, the ferries to and from **Barra** and canoes and ships pass by.

The **Atlantic Hotel** has three restaurants and is more grandiose in architecture and in scale than the others. It is approached along **Marina Parade**, past the **UN Building**, the guarded gates of State House, Victoria Hospital, and several battered and attractive colonial-style woodfaced bungalows raised on concrete pillars for pre-airconditioned cool, which for all their age are gracious, set in dilapidated gardens that must once have been lovely.

The gardens and buildings of the Atlantic are well maintained. On the right as you enter, British Airways has an office and further along the large Tesito rooms occasionally have exhibitions of the work of local or visiting artists.

For the more adventurous traveller,

A family compound in Banjul.

just off the beaten track, there are two Lebanese *shawarma* houses in **Cameron Street**, where hamburgers and Lebanese pitta-bread sandwiches stuffed with spicy mixtures are cheaply available. Further off the beaten track, there are *tangana* or chop bars or casual eating tables at odd corners (in Albert Market, for example) where *benachin* or *domoda* are very cheap.

Established visitors, and residents, can plug themselves into informal "bowling" networks for delicious and varied eating. "Bowling" is a local system by which a cook, normally a Gambian woman, supplies bowls of food at agreed times on agreed dates at agreed prices to an agreed place. For example, a friendly Lebanese store can turn into a temporary dining room over a bowl of spanking hot curried stew and rice and roasted groundnuts, for less than £1, with lots of spicy gossip and commentaries on current affairs, business and scandal tossed in.

Magical mudflats: One other thing that is invariably of visual interest is the mudflat area on the outskirts of Banjul on the **Bond Road**. The open stretch before the mangroves close in can be magical at high and low tide. Hulks, wrecks, little ships, surprise plants on the islets of abandoned vessels and bits of vessels, wading birds, pelicans, herons, plovers, gulls, emerge out of the shining water or the glistering smooth dark mud.

The best approach in Banjul is a slow perambulation of the backstreets, off **Lasso Wharf** and **Box Bar Road**, not snapping away too obtrusively in order not to antagonise local sensibilities, but savouring visually the sun-drenched vistas and above all the details of prettiness and oddity that come out of the dust and shabbiness from every corner, every direction.

Banjul is small but, like Mrs Blain's haberdashery store off Albion Place, it is chock full of vivid surprises. Choose a taxi-driver who is in no hurry. Perceptions always need training to appreciate the nuances of a new place, but Banjul is worth the extra effort.

Left, locally made furniture. **Right**, waiting for the Barra ferry.

THE GAMBIA COAST

Like everyone's idea of paradise, the coast of the Gambia sports brilliant, white coral sands and feathery coconut palms curving towards a sea of peacock blue. Giant breakers crashing on the shore invite the swimmer but beware, a steep inshore drop-off and a wicked undertow make bathing, except for the most experienced, hazardous. It was these dramatic features which kept settlers at bay as the huge waves would have made matchwood of small craft—only the fishermen of the coast know the secret of riding the Atlantic rollers.

The warm Guinea Current washes the coast and the north-east trade winds cool the tropical vegetation which edges Gambia's 40-mile (64-km) curving beaches, some of Africa's most westerly Atlantic shores. Beating down with following winds, early mariners sought out river mouths and backwaters in which to retreat from autumn squalls. With an estuary over three miles (five km) in width, it was no wonder early navigators soon made use of the Gambia River's sheltering arm and established trading posts around the tidal waters of one of West Africa's most important waterways.

On the south bank of the Gambia River the coast from **Banjul** extends west for more than five miles (eight km) before curving off to the south from **Cape Point**. Great scallops of silver-sanded beach extend as far as the eye can see, often fringed with palms, edged by lagoons, mangroves or village compounds and broken here and there by creeks and small waterways. Strolling along almost deserted beaches the only sign of life appears when the fishing fleets take to the boiling waves of the Atlantic or return laden with the fruits of the sea and when the herdsmen bring their big-horned, white Zebu cattle down to the water's edge to lick the salt from the rocks.

Beach-hopping: For spectacular views there are several points, or headlands, along the west-facing coastline from where enviable photographs can be shot. Taking a tour southwards from the city outskirts each headland opens up new vistas.

After the salt flats encircling Banjul, and wide **Denton Bridge** across **Oyster Creek**, the district of **Bakau** is a broad, built-up area behind several attractive, cliff-bound bays. Translated as "big place", Bakau consists of large groups of residential compounds, a supermarket, the **Gamtel** communications centre and local markets on the landward side of **Atlantic Boulevard**, and hotels, élite residences and fishing beaches on the seaward side.

While Bakau is the location of the British and American Embassies, the **New Town** houses an industrial centre, the Chinese-built stadium and the **West African Tours** company. There are a variety of restaurants located along the coastal road between six major tourist hotels: **Cham's African and International Fare at the Romana Hotel**, the **Chinese Rice Bowl**, **Marie's Pub** and the **Sambou Restaurant**.

Preceding pages: a Gambian riverboat skipper. **Left**, the peanut vendor. **Right**, Gambian tannery.

Out on Cape Point, between the **Cape St Mary** restaurant and the residence of the British High Commissioner, are the whitewashed chalets of a new complex (with names like "Hibiscus" and "Jacaranda"), the **Cape Point Hotel** and the luxurious **Sunwing Hotel**. Further south along the Bakau strand is tiny **St Peter's Church** overlooking the village fishing bay. Past the marketplace and Romana's on the left are the beachtop **African Village** and **Tropic Gardens** with traditional thatched bungalow rooms. Next door to the Tropic Gardens is the **Atlantic Guest House** on the very top of the Bakau cliffs.

Take a stroll down Atlantic Boulevard, past batik stalls, women selling peanuts, boys vending kola nuts and beautiful displays of hand-carved African masks, or hire a bicycle to tour the town and visit the sacred crocodile pool at **Katchikali**, located in the centre of Bakau's huddled native compounds.

Past Bakau, the beach curves to a point called **Fajara**. Sir Dawda Jawara's Presidential residence is lo-

cated on Fajara Point as is the popular **Fajara Hotel** with its Golf Club. Almost opposite is the **Two Jays** restaurant and the **Fajara Club.**

The Fajara Club, for which temporary membership is available for short visits, is charming and dowdy, or depressing and dowdy, depending on your viewpoint. The bar and entrance hall feature glass cases of sports trophies and photographs of RAF aircraft and their crews on visits to the Gambia. The atmosphere is a mixture of old colonial club house and village hall. It is well worth bearing in mind for a change from the bars of the international hotels.

Along a dirt-track extension of the metalled Atlantic Boulevard are two beach bars near the **Bungalow Beach Hotel** with its two-storey modern accommodation. The tourist market here is a big attraction and features on most tours of the area.

The large **Kombo Beach Hotel** building is part of the Novotel chain. and behind the **Kotu Beach** area is the **Bakotu Hotel and Restaurant**, near

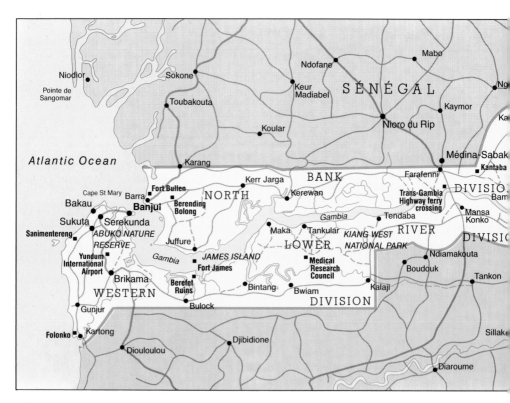

148

the headquarters of the Tourist Police. **Francisco's** delightful hotel should not be missed, with its pretty tropical garden containing a relaxed and sophisticated bar and restaurant.

Between Kotu Beach and **Kotu Point**—scheduled for several large hotel developments—is the **Kotu Stream**, a trickle in the dry season, a torrent in the rains. Around Kotu Point is the erratically seasonal casino. Nearby, a little compound tucked behind the dunes offers bargains in batiks, carvings and definitely un-local "Cartier" watches.

A long road running between scrub and pasture leads to the country's largest and most prestigious hotel—the **Senegambia**. A futuristically-designed main block embraces pool and stage area leading to tasteful chalets in mature tropical gardens and a rather small private beach.

A change from the Senegambia's hotel bars is the beautifully designed and located **Dolphin Restaurant** and **Bar**. Just across the approach road to the Senegambia, the Dolphin offers authentic African fare, and the British proprietors will also provide English breakfast or continental cuisine. In the same area is a small craft market, a local African restaurant and a bar known as **Uncle Dembo's**. Dotted around the Senegambia Beach are several quaint little local beach-bar/restaurants such as the **Chat'n'take**, or **Rose's**. Excellent lobster is served at a couple of the more recent establishments.

Mopeds, bicycles and dune scooters can be rented by the hour or day, giving the opportunity to explore further down the beach past the **Kololi Beach** time-share complex, the **Bijilo Beach Forest Reserve** where monkeys and giant hornbills can be seen, and on the Bijilo Beach. A birdwatcher's paradise, the Bijilo region offers not only the myriad birdlife of virgin Gambian forest, but a host of seabird varieties and flocks of variegated waders.

Rounding the great, sandy curve which is the extension of Bijilo and its beach one reaches **Bald Cape**, opposite

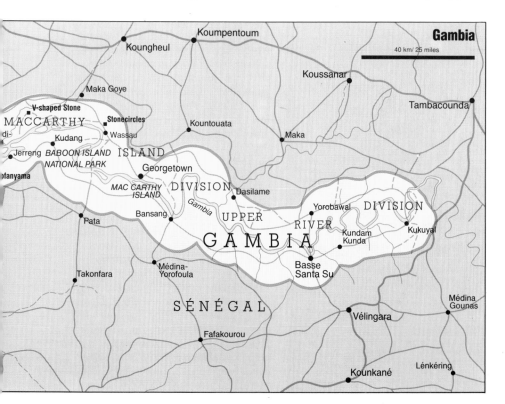

the **Bijilo Islands**. From this vantage, look along the massive sweep of fine coral sand with only the fishing boats of **Brufut**, scattered palm-thatched shelters and the green line of coco palms which interrupt the blue of the sea, the blue of the sky and the almost indistinguishable line where wave crests break on glistening shores. A little further south is **Salitor Point**, another good angle from where one can include a lagoon in the beach scene. There is a tourist camp for beach and bush parties here and the chance of refreshment.

Bush and beach parties are among the most popular excursions on offer at most tourist hotels and through the main four operators. West African Tours, Black and White Tours and Gamtours all provide four-or six-wheel trucks and Land-Rovers which take parties through the typical wooded bushland lying behind the coast. As a full day's excursion the Bush and Beach trip includes a good morning's drive into grass and savanna land, possibly visiting palm-wine tappers' encampments,

and culminating in midday arrival on the beach. Often the tour, which does not keep to a rigid itinerary, selects a beach near a fishing village. This gives the opportunity to see catches—often including turtle and shark—being hauled in with the native *pirogues*, or fishing boats.

Drinks, food and equipment for a beach-side barbecue are carried on the trucks, enabling the party to enjoy a full lunch of freshly caught fish or even lobster. After a tour around the village and its smoking-huts, the party returns before dusk.

Sea and shore: Village life along the coast is entirely dominated by the sea. Each community has access to a strip of beach and keeps its own *pirogues*. For a more detailed description of these graceful craft and their multiple uses — they are raced in addition to performing the mundane daily tasks of fishing — see the chapter on the **Thiès** region under **Senegal**.

Not only are the *pirogues* a colourful sight when drawn up on the white sand under cocoa palms, the catch itself is an insight into the teeming life offshore. Brilliant in their last natural tints, wrasse, flying fish, yellowtail, snapper, catfish, rock hind, mullet and sea bream all come tumbling out of the boats' gunwales, jumping and sparkling in the late sunlight. This is the time to buy a few fresh samples for a beach barbecue, or follow the fishermen's women up to the smoke houses to find fillets of home-cured dorado or mackerel tuna.

A road follows the coast for part of its length, turning inland as it heads south in order to pass through the main fishing villages of **Ghanatown**, **Brufut**, **Tanje**, **Tujereng**, **Sanyang**, **Gunjur** and **Kartong**. Gunjur is the Gambia's main fishing village and lies around 30 miles (48 km) south of Banjul.

During the 1800s Gunjur was a centre for *marabouts*, or holy men, and even today a small clifftop mosque still draws the devout from miles around. The great arc of sand and ideal conditions for launching boats drew fishermen from Senegal and other fishing centres, such as Brufut and Ghanatown.

Fresh shark steak tonight.

Initially the fisherfolk set up simple huts alongside the *marabouts'* shelters but, with the advent of modern technology and sponsorship from government agencies, the fishermen established a profitable commercial township. Traditional palm-thatched mud huts have now been replaced by brick-built compounds, shops and schools. Today *marabouts* still receive pilgrims in rough dwellings now almost obscured by the lines of fish-smoking huts and row upon row of brightly-coloured fishing *pirogues*.

The modernisation of facilities at Gunjur denies the village the charm of more traditional fishing villages on other parts of the coast. Motorisation has altered the face of coastal fishing with outboards instead of sails and oars, lorries and pickups instead of lines of bananabas, or women with fish baskets on their heads. Even the methods of fishing are changing and the government is supporting numerous projects to streamline the industry. Smoking ovens, fish freezers and a small fleet of custom-built fishing boats trawl the Atlantic waters off the Gambian coast, said to be among the best stocked in West Africa.

Many smaller hamlets along the coast fish directly for the pot, supplementing the onions, cassava, beans, tomatoes and root vegetables grown on the neat, sheltered plots around the fringes of the clustered houses and the staple rice. In addition, fishermen also participate in tourism nowadays.

Tourists are often delighted by the beach barbecue, a regular entertainment held at dusk when, out of the dark sea, a torchlit *pirogue* slices through the phosphorescent foam disgorging a troupe of dancers from the national folkloric group for the night's cabaret.

Rites, sports and rituals: Celebrations and festivals are something which all Gambians are involved in and sport is very close to their hearts. Torchlight processions are held on special occasions when youngsters carry carefully modelled boats called *fanals* through the streets, illuminated with lanterns

Simple,
effective toy
lorries.

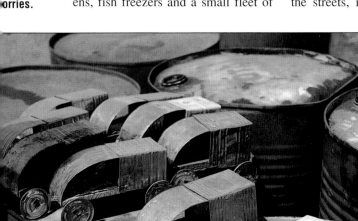

and decorated with flags. On the beach, one can often see the Gambia's top athletes running, practising on the makeshift track in preference to the Banjul Stadium's dirt track. Gambians are also keen swimmers and the nation has representation at Olympic standard.

Several of the villages to the south of the Gambian coast have particular significance as religious centres and, near **Kartong**, between sea and swamp, the compound known as **Folonko** is held as a sacred place.

Pilgrims visit Folonko to bathe in the holy water and the celebrated Gambian wrestlers insist that washing at Folonko will ensure them victory in combat. Barren women also believe that the magical waters of the region will render them fertile. This compound is similar to others around the coastal part of the country in that it plays host to a pool of crocodiles.

Further up the coast, a little way from Brufut, is the religious centre of **Sanimentereng**. A mud-built prayer house, an ancient baobab tree, a sacred pool and an altar on which locals and pilgrims place gifts to the gods make up this enclave of ancient worship mingled with Islam. Ghanatown nearby is named for the number of Ghanaian fish merchants who purchase dried and smoked fish from the Gambian stalls.

Much nearer Banjul is another religious location. The village of **Bakau Kachikally**, about eight miles (13 km) from the capital, has a crocodile pool and offers healing ritual baths and water with magical properties.

It is not uncommon to be invited to a local compound, or group of houses, to join a feast or festival. Child-naming, weddings, chief-appointments or Islamic festivals like Tabaski are all rites which may be witnessed by invited visitors. It is best to make these visits in small groups, or in organised parties such as Gamtours' "Village Festival" where the range of "masks" performed include acrobatics and dances from different tribes. One of Gambia's most famous dance troupes, often seen on the hotel circuits, is known as the **Damel**

Hibiscus in bloom.

152

and their most spectacular performance is the Dagga dance.

Inland from the fishing village of Gunjur, along a semi-made up road, is the most important town in this part of the coastal region. Most tours south to Casamance, or east along the Gambia River's south bank, pass through **Brikama**. An essential stop-over for tourist trips, Brikama is famous for its local market and large craft market.

Behind the mask: Brikama is a noted centre for wood carvers who produce the most excellent workmanship in the shape of masks or gazelle groups, which, after jovial bargaining, can be purchased at very reasonable prices. Brikama also has an historic heritage as Muslim raids in 1854 and 1874 destroyed the town twice.

Back on the coastline at Gunjur, the road south becomes less and less defined. Just five miles (eight km) further on is **Sanyang Point** from where one can see almost as far as Senegal's Casamance and back to the fishing area of **Tanje** where the bongafish is smoked

and then cured in small factory huts.

Watching the seemingly effortless launching of the fishing *pirogues* into foaming surf and milky-blue seas, tracing the passage of the lateen triangles of sail as the fleet skims way beyond the thunderous surf makes one want to participate. This is a possibility if local fishermen have the time and are financially induced to provide a short private sea trip. It is better, however, to take a more organised excursion in either native *pirogue* or motor boat along the short coastline.

At **Denton Bridge**, three miles outside Banjul, excursions can be made either along the coast or into the maze of creeklands and mangrove swamps backing the sandy beaches. Fishing boats can be hired from here and often a hotel can arrange a day's outing on the ocean or along the creeks.

Fishing excursions can be quite modestly priced. From Denton Bridge **Sportfishing Ltd.** operates half, full day and period charters for barracuda, ladyfish, kujeli, grouper, cassava fish,

Rastafarian shop and bar.

jacks, cobia, rays and several varieties of shark. Crew, tackle and petrol are provided with a small launch, or groups can hire their 20-ft (six-metre) Orkney fishing boat, fully equipped for deep sea sportsfishing. Game fishing records have been broken off this coast.

Paddle your own canoe: To experience the life of the mangrove region and view some of its astounding wildlife one can take any of a number of boat trips into the swamps and creeks behind the coast or up river.

Again from Denton Bridge, a selection of craft offers tours into the **Oyster Creek** river tributaries. Daily excursions in motor boats or native *pirogues* take visitors deep into the bolongs and creeks to view and film birdlife. Many of the larger tourist hotels offer similar excursions. **West African Tours** organise a creek barbecue trip in an authentic *pirogue* culminating in an "African Evening" with local food and entertainment, including fire-eating.

Similar tours can be made with **Black and White Tours** and **Gamtours**, or a luxury version is offered by **Graham Rainey** in one of his two sailing boats— *Spirit of Galicia* or *Spirit of Africa*. **Andy** and **Janet Macintosh**, in their river cruiser *Paunic* offer a selection of creek and bolong trips from Denton Bridge, as does the German-owned motor boat *Joven Antonia*. The same organisation has established a bolong-based restaurant and jetty-side stopover point at **Lamin Lodge**, just near **Mandinari** village. Whether taking an organised tour on a motor craft or pottering about in a hired *pirogue*, with or without a boatman, it is quite safe to swim in the salty waters.

Back to the beach: Across the peninsula from the bolongs of **Lamin**, and the mangrove-clogged waterways of the Gambia estuary, the long, sandy beaches of the Atlantic represent home to many holiday visitors. After a long day's excursion on the tidal waters, a bumpy safari trek ending in a beachside picnic or a fishing trip out on the ocean, the comfort of the modern hotels brings one back to the modern world.

Left, rice fields near the coast. **Right**, impenetrable mangrove roots on the Gambia River.

MANGROVE: THE FRIENDLESS TREE

"No-one likes the mangrove," John Steinbeck wrote. He was right: the ungainly tree with its roots buried deep in stinking mud, its gaunt branches and leathery leaves, has few sympathisers among the human population but is attended by a veritable zoo, aquarium and aviary of wildlife. However, not only do the mangrove swamps provide shelter for a wide range of creatures, but man also feeds, either directly or indirectly, off the curious tree.

Extending for almost 80 miles (130 km) up the Gambia River, the mangrove is a tropical evergreen which clings to salty tidal mud flats spurned by other life. Over 2,000 miles (5,000 km) of the Gambia's coastline and inland waterways are covered and the area is growing because of the mangrove's habit of "creating" land. Small lagoons and creeks along the coast, often in places where the sea breaks over the coastal sandbar, are typical habitats of the dense vegetation and stilt-like root systems of the mangrove.

There are four varieties of the tree: the red, most common on the west coast of Africa; the black, or honey, mangrove; the white; and the button mangrove. Each is salt-loving and among the few plants which can cope with water of a high salinity. The mangrove may grow to 80 ft (24 metres) in height and prefers regions with high rainfall. The trees grow in clumps between the low and high water marks and produce a particularly large quantity of vegetation and dead matter which decays into a very nutritious mire.

The roots, characteristically angled out of the mud, breathe in their oxygen requirement and almost leapfrog across the new banks of litter formed as the trees mature. The red mangrove sheds more than three tons of leaves per acre per year. In this way the mangrove adds to the coastal land and its special seed design and germination habits ensure that the "colony" grows.

Producing more than 300 seeds per year, the mangrove is a quick coloniser. The quill-like seeds germinate while still on the tree from the large, yellow, fleshy blooms. Between six and 12 inches long (15 cm), the germinating seed falls into the water surrounding the mother tree and inverts gradually because of its buoyancy. The sprouts touch land and the tiny plant takes hold and roots.

Should the seed be caught in a current, it will drift, alive, for up to a year until it is washed against suitable soil or further mud flats. Roots and debris along the coast break the force of the ocean waves and the seagrass, which grows in profusion beneath the stilt-lined waters, collects more vegetable matter increasing the banks on which the mangrove are embedded.

From the seaward side man takes his canoes into the backwaters and creeks of the mangrove's mysterious domain. One knows neither when one is on new dry land nor a mile out in the Atlantic; the forest of semi-floating, knee-deep trunks and thick, green canopy all looks the same. On this side of the mangrove reaches, the fishermen take an astounding variety of marine produce from shrimps and lobsters to sea bass, electric eel, catfish and yellowtail snapper. Snook, tarpon and other game fish can be hooked in the mangrove margins. It is also an ideal location for the hunter: a myriad species of duck and wildfowl either roost in or migrate through this part of the Gambia's coast and river estuary. To the landward, man harvests oysters and mussels, crabs and other crustaceans. The mangrove wood also makes excellent firewood for charcoal and it can be fashioned into carved implements and used as building material. However, indiscriminate felling has, in some areas of the West African coast, dangerously depleted the mangrove and upset the ecological balance. This is not yet the case in Senegal, or in the Gambia.

Indirectly, the mangrove helps the human population by creating a "buffer zone" between the relentlessly buffeting waves of the Atlantic Ocean and the vulnerable, sandy-rocked shoreline. The plant also serves as a filter as it breaks down a good deal of waste which otherwise would pollute the shoreline. Finally, as the treeline marches into the sea creating more land area, the rich soil behind it is eagerly tilled by local farmers. Unlovable maybe, but very useful.

THE GAMBIA RIVER ROUTE

If the ancient inhabitants of what is now the Gambia paid homage to their deity Sene, god of rock, responsible for the sky and weather, then today's prayers should be offered to the **Gambia River**, source of the country's life and livelihood. Flowing through both Guinea and Senegal before blessing the long, narrow strip of the Gambia with its waters, the river is one of West Africa's major features.

Meandering for most of its 400-mile (640-km) journey through the nation's parched countryside, the waters of this important river give the country both its varied scenery and its name. Almost 180 miles (290 km) inland from its estuary the river widens considerably. Several islands have been created by the river's winding route, which widens even more after the ferry crossing near **Farafenni**, 70 miles (112 km) up-river. The estuary is one of Africa's largest at just over 12 miles (19 km) wide.

To most visitors, the first sight of the Gambia River is not particularly exciting as one can hardly distinguish its silt-filled waters from the sea's. The river is salty as far upstream as the town of **Kuntaur**, 125 miles (200 km) inland. From the air the muddy flow of the river can be seen arching far out into the Atlantic Ocean, creating vast sand bars which shift position in the estuary. These are a constant hazard to the ferry which plies across the river mouth from Banjul to **Barra**.

Almost every visitor to the country takes the ferry at least once from the wharf on Wellington Street in Banjul to the rickety pier on the north bank. Automobiles and animals vie for position on this sturdy, German-built craft which brings the government a considerable income in fares from the 200 passengers and the constant flow of lorries and cars. The ferry's seven daily crossings take 30 minutes each; rates vary from two dalassis for foot passengers to 345 dalassis for large lorries.

Leaving the dockside, the ferry provides an excellent view over the water to the city of Banjul, and the beach leading down to the Atlantic Hotel. Many of the ocean-going steamers loading with peanuts or delivering containers of consumer goods and machinery in Banjul could ply the river as far as **Kau-Ur** 100 miles (160 km) upstream, but the shifting sandbanks and lack of adequate dredging equipment make navigation hazardous.

Port facilities in Banjul are very limited and most large vessels anchor off the port and exchange cargoes by means of lighters and small boats. Once, 30,000-ton ships could navigate up-river from the port to loading stations along three-quarters of the river's 300 navigable miles (480 km); but, with the deterioration of existing dredging and charting facilities, the silt has won in the war to maintain a good steamship passage.

In former times, steamers used to ply the river almost to the Senegalese border in the east. Many of the fondly-remembered craft such as the *Prince of*

Preceding pages: a backwater of the River Gambia. **Left**, upriver village chiefs. **Right**, an old cannon on James Island.

Wales, the *Lady Denham*, the *Sir Dawda Jawara* and the *Lady Chilel Jawara* ferry are now, sadly, casualties of the sand-bars. The *Lady Chilel*, one of the world's last floating Post Office-*cum*-ferries, succumbed to the treacherous waters of the river in the mid-1980s after having been launched in 1978. The hulk now lies near the Transgambia Highway crossing at Farafenni, a £1.5 million reminder of the river's unpredictable currents.

The North Bank: Barra Point, from halfway across the estuary, looks like any nondescript landing stage but it is an important terminal for the incessant traffic from Banjul, up-river, or into Senegal just 20 miles (32 km) to the north. The giant groundnut facility, with its covered conveyor and huge storage depots, dominates the small pier. A small restaurant, bustling market, large lorry and bus park and a tiny, fly-blown "hotel" are its main features, but Barra also has historic points of interest.

The 200-year-old **Fort Bullen**, constructed to defend Banjul from the French, lies on the point. The fort can be visited with an official guide if one follows the signpost to the left of the landing stage coming off the ferry. A variety of rusting cannon, lying where they were toppled, a few turrets and battlements are all that can be seen on the wave-lashed headland.

To the right from the Barra ferry, the road runs a short way to the junction with the north bank road which continues the length of the country as far as **Koina Tenda**, the Gambia's easternmost village. It is arguable that the north bank offers a more exciting trip than the better-kept south bank route; it is certainly more arduous, yet there are numerous places worth seeing.

Among the most interesting of Gambia's historical sites are the old British and French slave "factories", or trading posts. **Juffure**, the most famous, has received world exposure through Alex Haley's book *Roots*, which traces the author's ancestry from the tiny village, through the days of the

Alex Haley was here.

slave trade, to modern America. Juffure and a reconstructed slave compound are a short walk from the ruins of another slaving post, **Albreda**.

Little now remains from those harsh days but the ruins of the main building. The "freedom flagpole" has long since disappeared. By reaching the old flagpole standing in the middle of Albreda's compound, a slave, it was said, could be granted his freedom. Poignant graffiti on the ancient walls read "Remember our tears." Nearby is an even older, Portuguese site, that of the trading post of **San Domingo**.

Out in the river is another British trading station dating from 1651. Fort James, on **James Island** is now a ruined shell inhabited by lizards, rats and snakes. Facing the French outpost of Albreda across the waters, the fort ensured clear passage down the river for British and American slave ships until the mid-18th century.

After slavery in the British colonies was abolished in 1807, naval ships based at James Island intercepted more than 100 French and Portuguese slave vessels off the Gambian coast. A couple of cannon, thick stone and brick walls and parts of the dungeons are all that is left of the once-impressive fort.

Motor launch excursions, like those of the *Spirit of Galicia*, the *Spirit of Africa*, and the *Joven Antonia*, regularly take visitors on a half-day tour of the more interesting sites, allowing time to wander in Fort James's overgrown ruins, or listen to tales of the slave days from village elders in Juffure.

Apart from James Island, **Dog Island** and **Pelican Island** both have historical backgrounds. Leased in 1816 by Lieutenant Colonel Alexander Grant from the King of Kombo for the princely sum of £75 a year, Dog Island was a source of the stone which was used in the building of many of Banjul's early construction.

Wrestlers and crocodiles: It was probably off Dog Island or James Island that the boundaries of the Gambia were first established. As no settled frontier divided British Gambia from French

The signature that made Juffure's name.

Senegal, it was agreed that the extent of land each side of the Gambia River which would define the country would be decided by the firing range of a gunboat lying in the mainstream of the river. It can be deduced that, in the 1890s, gunboats had a firing range of around 10 miles, the average width of the country each side of the river.

A shot fired inland from Dog Island would probably have landed somewhere near another interesting site. **Berending** is a small settlement north of Dog Island. A sacred crocodile pool in Berending attracts visitors who care to make the detour off the road from Barra to Senegal. Gambian wrestlers and pilgrims bathe in the pool in the hope of superiority in the ring or the healing of their ailments.

A number of similar sacred pools exist along the banks of the river, mostly dried up or shallowly filled with damp mud in which a few crocodiles wallow. All have a reputation for magical healing qualities and the devout have been known to walk for several days in order to reach a particular sacred pool.

Pot-holed and covered with red laterite dust, which gets into every nook and cranny, the road east runs through deep brush. Scrub, thorn trees, baobabs and silk cotton trees dot the dry landscape on the landward side. On the river banks, mangrove swamp and winding *bolongs*, or backwaters, form an impenetrable jumble. Buzzards, crows, pin-tailed weavers and Wydah birds add life to the vista and small clumps of thatched roofs indicate the presence of village compounds.

From hamlets of conical-topped *rondavels*, or huts, surrounded by walled vegetable gardens, children peer out to watch the few vehicles which use this route. Often they will chase the Land-Rovers—the most common vehicles as four-wheel drive is essential on this road—and play in the dust churned up by the cars' struggles over pot-holes and gullies.

Often the only sight of adult life is women drawing clay pots of water from the village well. Saudi Arabia's Islamic Fund has provided many new hand pumps for isolated villages and one can see even the smallest of children pumping frantically in order to fill the long stone water trough from which goats will drink. Buckets of water for domestic use are filled from a spout or a similar trough. Where there is no running water, women often bring their washing to the well head and brightly coloured garments washed and left to dry in the sun form patchworks which are irresistible to the photographer.

The menfolk of the villages are generally out working the fields, or indoors sheltering from the sun's heat, while on Fridays lines of men can be seen in their best robes walking to the nearest mosque. As one drives through the flat countryside, the clumps of green trees against the iron-red of the landscape reveal the locations of villages and agricultural plots.

From mango groves or vegetable gardens the local produce is displayed on bright cloths by the roadside. Onions and radishes, oranges, bananas, cassava and yam are all arranged neatly for sale **James Island.**

162

or barter. In some areas the produce of the palm, oil, wine and palm nuts dominate the makeshift roadside stalls. In other regions mounds of groundnuts, shelled and unshelled, and bottles of groundnut oil are offered for sale. Old groundnut sacks are converted for all manner of ingenious applications, including in some cases clothing.

Vegetables raised in this arid soil require constant watering, as do the Zebu cattle, the few pigs and the ubiquitous goats. The frequent trips backwards and forwards from allotments to wells are kept up even under the midday sun and as the two can be some distance apart, relays of young girls with waterpots balanced on their heads are a common sight.

Transcontinental crossings: A ferry crosses the bolong at **Kerewan** where the road is a couple of miles from the river. After several little settlements like **Kinte Kunda** and **Saba**, a detour can be made to the larger village of **Salikene**, surrounded by mangrove. A visit to the rice fields is an interesting way to see how the crop is grown, harvested, winnowed and ground in much the same way as it was in the distant past.

Herons, storks, cattle egrets and other wading birds can often be seen in the water-filled paddy fields. After Salikene the settlements become more isolated and, for about 25 miles (40 km), the bumpy road runs across flat countryside to the town of **Farafenni**. Although Farafenni is almost five miles (eight km) inland from the Gambia River, it is the north bank's centre for transcontinental traffic.

Traffic from Senegal in the north down the Trans-Gambian Highway to Casamance and the south crosses the river on the two flat-bottomed ferries. Lorries and cars queue for places on the diesel-powered craft while *pirogues* and dug-out canoes offer alternative transport. Many travellers, tired of the rough condition of the north bank road, cross to the better kept south bank route for the 50 or so miles (80 km) to **Georgetown**.

Rice
cultivation
by the river.

THE SENEGAMBIAN STONE CIRCLES

Between 150 and 300 miles (240 and 480 km) up the Gambia River, across the northern border into Senegal and south as far as Guinea, lies a collection of ancient monuments which remain one of Africa's greatest riddles. An anthropological and archaeological enigma surrounds the rings of massive standing stones scattered across the barren countryside. Experts assume that the laterite megaliths indicate the earlier existence of a sophisticated African culture. Their formation, say experts, could point the way towards the discovery of an early empire whose only known remaining evidence is the stone circles. The circles are remarkably reminiscent of other megalithic tumuli such as those in Brittanny in France, which are generally held to be disposed in such a way as to indicate a connection with the sun, and therefore sun-worship. The peoples who live in the region nowadays hold the stones to be the work of an unidentified "earlier" civilization.

An ancient civilisation responsible for the mysterious burial grounds may have existed before that of the "Ghana" Empire (not to be confused with modern day Ghana). A royal city, named Cantor by the Arab chronicler El-Bakri in A.D. 1067, was considered to lie somewhere near the sites of the stone circles and its discovery could open up a new chapter in African history.

Some experts believe that the obelisks were erected as they now stand. Early skeletons have been found buried in the centre of some circles, as well as tools, pottery and miscellaneous ornaments.

Around 40 sites are dotted along the north bank of the Gambia River between **Kau-Ur** and **Wassau**. Thought to have originally been covered by laterite earth mounds, the standing stones sometimes include oddities such as the strange "lyre" or "V" stone at **Ker Batch**. Archaeologists suggest that the megaliths were made and erected more than 1,000 years ago and they have now weathered down to a smooth, knobbly rust-red surface, like solid iron ore.

Most sites contain around 10 to 20 stone circles, whose circumferences vary in size. Some stones have flat or concave tops and, in recent years, tourist guides have encouraged visitors to place small stones on top of the standing stones in order to "make a wish", which merely serves to confuse the original order of the stones.

Typical of sites abused in this way is **Wassau**, where the first of the Government rest houses and caretaker centres was erected. Several small buildings and a little display room at the end of a bumpy track are the forerunners of more sophisticated museum and reception buildings planned for the future.

Very little has really been done to unearth the origins of these "mystery sites", equalled only in sub-Saharan Africa by the ruins of Kumbi Saleh, the capital of the Ghana Empire, or those of ancient Zimbabwe. A so-called curse on those disturbing the sacred sites is related by local leaders. As early as 1931, a Captain Doke, an expedition leader called Ozanne, and the archaeologist Parker, all mysteriously died shortly after excavating some of the stone circle sites.

However, the team led by F.A. Evans, director of the Anglo-Gambian stone circles expedition in 1964-65, has so far been excluded from the legendary curse. One of the earliest known victims was Richard Jobson, who came across the sites in the 1620s and wrote his account in *The Discovery of the Land of King Solomon* in 1633. Don't be put off by ancient spells—the Senegambia stone circles are one of the wonders of the earth's "darkest" continent.

Stone sentinels guarding their secrets.

Although the north bank road cuts off a great loop in the river, it is worth a detour into this curve of the river to see **Elephant Island** and its resident families of monkeys. Its name is all that remains of the few elephants which lived in the Gambia until around the 1920s. A canoe trip around the island can disturb the occasional crocodile and flocks of heron from the dense undergrowth covering the island.

To get an idea of the full extent of birdlife ask the canoe owner to take you to the south bank rice fields—a magnet for ornithologists. Watch out for snakes—particularly green mambas—on the raised dirt tracks into the rice fields. **Bambali** is where your canoe can be hired and where one rejoins the track leading to the main north bank road.

Just off the route to the next township is the historic village of **Kantaba** where the last wars of the Badibu took place. There was once a small fortress here, built by the British in the 1840s. **Balangar** is the next village on the route

Below, waiting for the ferry.

before the important groundnut centre of **Kau-Ur**. In this area the first of the mysterious stone circles can be seen, many of which dot the countryside north of the river and into the adjacent Senegalese territory.

The road arcs around a swampy region at the headwaters of a large creek called **Nainija Bolong**, passing more stone circle sites such as **N'Jai Kunda**, **Ker Batch**, with its famous "lyre stone", and **Ker Jabel**.

After passing through numerous small villages, the road heads back to the river at **Wassau** where there is the country's largest concentration of stone circles. A ferry links **Kuntaur** via a trail to the south bank highway but the north bank route cuts across another bend in the river before **Georgetown**. A diversion at Kuntaur is the **Baboon Island National Park**.

With a sizeable bird population, this five-mile (eight-km) long group of islands is home to several hippopotamus families and a number of crocodiles. The species for which the

island is famed is the Olive Baboon. There is also a small population of chimpanzees, which are released here after "rehabilitation" at the Ape Rehabilitation Centre in Abuko Reserve, near Banjul. The main island and several smaller islets cover almost 1,500 acres (600 hectares) along this wide bend in the river.

Visitors are not encouraged on Baboon Island as the primates, which come originally from zoos and circuses in Europe, can easily be disturbed. Stella Brewer, the project's director, and her team occasionally invite specialist wildlife parties to inspect the progress of the island's orphaned animals.

For visitors arriving by yacht or *pirogue*, a warden might join the craft from Baboon Island in order to pilot the boat near to where about 20 chimpanzees congregate. If one is lucky, there is a chance to photograph the apes in their natural habitat—impossible anywhere else in the Gambia. With time to spare, one might arrange a *pirogue*

tour around the island from the village of **Kuntaur**. Usually the boatman will point out one of the river's more famous obstacles just off the river bank near the village, the wreck of the steamer *Lady Denham*.

Back on the eastbound road, after the thriving, brick-built village of Kuntaur, and the dust track leading off to **Wassau**'s stone circles, a long straight, laterite road cuts off a wide bend in the river. In this bend lies the giant island of **Kai Hai**. Locals tell stories of the "dragon" which is supposed to haunt Kai Hai Island, and the number of villagers which it is said to have devoured.

Visiting the island by canoe, one can certainly sense an ominous atmosphere, perhaps because of the overpowering foliage which casts a permanent shadow over the few paths through its untouched forest. However, approaching Kai Hai from the west one can see that part of the jungle has been cleared and there is evidence that at one time rice was grown on the "haunted" island. Opposite, on the south bank, there is a small landing stage where one can take a short track to join the Georgetown road.

Baboons and barbecues: On the north bank, although the Kuntaur road runs along a hillside, one cannot see the river until the route nears **Lamin Koto**. This village has been an important tourist facility since the creation of **Lamin Safari Lodge**. Opened in 1988, Lamin Camp, as it is also known, consists of half a dozen *rondavels* in the local style set in a clearing on the riverbank. Each circular mud and whitewash *rondavel* is adapted from the traditional African village hut with thatched roof and basic amenities for an overnight stop.

Constructed to house 10 to 15 travellers, but with plans for extension, Lamin acts as a base for wildlife excursions into the nearby rice fields, forests and creeks. The camp has a cookhouse equipped with a traditional clay oven, a tiny outdoor restaurant/bar and a mooring for yachts and the villagers' canoes. River excursions from Lamin Camp are an exciting way

Stella Brewer with gorilla Julia.

to see parts of the bush not accessible by truck or large sailing craft. Also, paddling silently deep into waterside forest, one sees much more wildlife than in a noisy truck.

Lamin Koto's 50 or so villagers are now benefiting from tourist visits to this part of the river. Not only do locals act as guides, oarsmen on the small fleet of dugouts, or staff in the camp itself, but the entire village turns out on a regular basis in the camp compound to entertain visitors.

A real African evening with authentic food and dancing, unlike those put on at the coastal resort hotels, is presented at Lamin. The German organisers of the camp pay the performers—strangely masked figures, characters dressed in leaves who whirl around like dervishes, and dancers disguised as animals or wielding lethal-looking weapons.

Prior to the evening dances, in which visitors are invited to participate, it is possible to visit the village itself. The locally brewed alcoholic beverages should be approached with some caution. However, the rice and vegetable dishes are delicious. Carvings and other handicrafts at Lamin Koto are well worth bargaining for—more original and cheaply priced than those at craft centres near the coast.

The camp at Lamin, surrounded by the forest and bordered by the river, is just a short walk from the jetty for the motorised ferry from **MacCarthy Island**. On the other side of the camp, along a rough trail, are the village rice fields. It is in these paddies and the surrounding forest that one can see the most astounding variety of birdlife. A morning expedition before breakfast, as the sun rises, is an unforgettable experience.

Local guides lead small parties through the forest. A good guide to west Africa's birdlife, a pair of binoculars and a camera are essential accessories. From time to time, paradoxically, as the hushed "crocodile" of bird spotters tiptoes through the swampy rice fields, a cacophony of rattling cans, shouting children and drum-banging women

A typical river village.

breaks the dawn silence. Every bird for miles is either petrified with fear or frightened into heading for the distant hills—the village bird scarers are shooing the buffalo weavers from their precious rice crops!

Lamin is the most easterly organised camp site, although another is planned for a location near **Basse Santa Su**. From Lamin, one can visit most of the more remote regions of the Gambia in reasonable comfort.

Mungo Park's memorial: A short truck ride east takes the traveller along a trail to the Mungo Park memorial obelisk at **Karantaba Tenda**. However, the riverside location of the concrete obelisk makes it easier to reach by boat. The stone marks the spot where Mungo Park disembarked in 1804, on his fateful second expedition in his attempt to find the source of the Niger River. The birthplace of President Sir D.K. Jawara is a short drive west at **Barajali** village. The historic **Georgetown** on MacCarthy Island is also a few minutes across the river from Lamin.

Georgetown, built on the mile-wide MacCarthy Island, is an attractive settlement with an interesting past and several relics from its slavery days. It is a trading centre for the eastern section of the country and there are several markets in the town. Two ancient forts in Georgetown now stand in ruins and nearby is an old slave house. Further out of the town a Government rest house has been provided for visitors.

Founded in 1823, the town has all the architectural hallmarks of colonialism. Wooden houses with iron roofs are slowly falling apart and one of the town's main features is the Armitage High School, located on the edge of town. In the main street the police station sports three iron posts which once offered freedom to those slaves who managed to grasp them. The capital town of **MacCarthy Island Division** has a pretty building set back from the main road. This is the Divisional Commissioner's house and office. A mosque stands in the middle of the residential quarter of the town, **Pretty in red.**

which has only one principal shop.

A ferry links MacCarthy Island with both the north and south bank roads, which rapidly deteriorate from this point onward, although the south road has undergone considerable improvement. Most travellers up-country select the south bank road from Georgetown to **Basse Santa Su**. The north bank road, however, has several more points of historic and natural significance.

The bumpy track runs through real bush and a guide is advisable—plus a four-wheel drive vehicle and cushions. From Georgetown the road hugs the unseen border with Senegal, returning to the riverside at **Karantaba Tenda**.

After Karantaba the countryside continues with sandy plains and reed swamps which surround the many bolongs. The swamps, which fill when the river floods its banks, are known locally as *banto faros*. At **Yorobawal**, a side road connects by ferry to the town of Basse Santa Su. Almost all travellers will gratefully take the detour after the wearing journey over 50 dusty miles

(80 km) of pot-holed track from Georgetown.

Another decaying colonial town, **Basse** is now no more than a large village with a few ageing Victorian buildings, a school founded in the late 1920s and two cinemas. Basse is a main depot for the area's peanut trade and a cotton industry has been established here. One huge market dominates the town and there are many roadside stalls selling all manner of goods. After enduring the north bank track in the dusty heat, the first place to make for is the little bar/café adjacent to the marketplace.

Back on the main route to **Fatoto**, the most easterly town in the Gambia, the place to watch out for next is **Sutukoba**, 40 miles (64 km) further upstream. This is the ancient site of a large settlement and trading town which thrived during the early 15th century. It lies on the edge of the Djolof Empire's territory and its old name means Great Sutuko.

Excavations are planned in this historic area, north of which are the two

Coming
home from
school.

hamlets of **Gunjur Kuta** and **Gunjur Koto**—one old and one comparatively new—located on the border with Senegal and noted for the traces found there of early civilisation. Fifteen miles (24 km) further on, the road rejoins the River Gambia at the ferry of Fatoto. To reach the Senegalese border, the traveller would need to go by canoe the last 10 miles (16 km).

The site of the border is at the **Falls of Barrakunda**. The road now crosses the river at the ferry and returns westwards along the south bank back to Basse Santa Su. One diversion off the road from the river crossing of Fatoto is the ghost town of **Perai Tenda**, where abandoned shops and colonial trading posts testify to the prosperity of early riverside trading towns.

The South Bank Route: At Banjul, the visitor preparing for the 240-mile (385-km) journey from the capital to Basse Santa Su, can make contact with the government rest houses and safari camps before leaving. Most tour operators will provide information on the up-country accommodation contacts. West African Tours, Gamtours, Black and White and some specialists cover the route to Basse with different stopover combinations.

Graham Rainey, alternatively, provides regular excursions up as far as Georgetown on his yachts, the *Spirit of Galicia* and the *Spirit of Africa*. Accommodation on these cruises is either in the established riverside camps or on board the yachts. By the well-surfaced south bank road, it is possible to cover the distance from Banjul to Georgetown in one day's drive, but only at a most exhausting pace.

The initial section of the road out of Banjul and through Serrekunda passes the **Abuko Wildlife Reserve** on the right and the Earth Satellite dish and **Yundum Airport** on the left. The first stretch of around 10 miles (16 km) is bumpy and badly maintained. Passing the outskirts of **Brikama** the metalled road surface improves and widens. To the right of the road from Banjul to Brikama, there are several side roads

A river cruise.

leading off to creeks like **Lamin** and villages like **Mandinari** which are included in tour itineraries for day visits and *bolong* excursions.

Brikama, with its colourful marketplace, is the first sizeable town on the road into Banjul from Casamance, in the southern part of Senegal. After the town, the road skirts marshes and mangrove swamps which extend inland from the river almost a mile. On the left a track leads to a ruined British trading post, located on the shore opposite James Island, at **Berefet**. This administrative area is known as the Western Division, which ends at the large tributary called the **Bintang Bolong**.

Bintang is a favourite spot for wildlife boat excursions and fishing trips. At **Bintang Gereejal** one can see the ruined walls which outline the site of a tiny church and early Portuguese trading post long since deserted. In **Bwiam** there is a sacred iron cooking pot which locals revere. The road does not cross the *bolong* for a good few miles, but continues alongside the swampy region bordering the winding creek. **Kalaji**, towards the narrowest part of the *bolong*, is the terminal for some of the pleasure craft from Banjul and colourful *pirogues* can be seen at the jettyside.

Across the Bintang Bolong is the track off to the left to **Sankandi** where two British Commissioners were massacred in 1900. Further up the winding path is the field station of the Medical Research Council at **Keneba**. At the end of the track, on the riverside, is **Tankular** where the tiny settlement treasures a 1711 Portuguese bell, recovered from the remains of the ruined trading post a short distance from the fishing village.

The path to Tankular runs around the edge of the **Kiang West National Park**, more than 10 sq. miles (26 sq. km) of forest and game reserve. By far the largest park in the Gambia, the Kiang West contains a great number of animal and bird species. A few miles up the road is the path leading to **Batelling**. Once a fortified site, now scattered

Doing the family washing.

cannon are all that is left of the 18th-century stronghold. To the left, a little further on, is the road to **Tendaba Camp** which can be seen from the highway.

Pool with a view: Tendaba Camp lies on the river bank a short distance from the main road. It was established as an overnight rest house and facilities are those of a basic safari lodge. Accommodation is in African style, in *rondavels* with pointed, thatched roofs. Showers are provided, but little else. Take your own bottled drinking water as the only water on tap is the slightly salty river water. Although Tendaba generates its own electricity, there is no telephone.

A Swedish couple, the Carlssons, have built up Tendaba Camp since 1974 into a busy safari base with accommodation for more than100 visitors. The pool, bar, and local and Scandinavian dishes served in the tiny restaurant more than compensate for the necessity of having to sleep with the smell of mosquito coils in the neat, clean huts. Excursions can be made from Tendaba

to little villages like **Duntumalang** and **Tunku**.

Fishing trips, wildlife expeditions and journeys to several of the stone circle sites across the river may also be made. Tours into the nearby game reserve almost guarantee the sighting of monkeys, baboons, a variety of wildfowl and several of the small forest animals. Overnight stays at the camp are not expensive and its isolation gives one a real feeling of roughing it in the African bush after the luxury of the beach hotels on the coast.

The next large township on the south bank road is **Soma**. It lies at the junction with the Trans-Gambian Highway, which comes south from the Farafenni ferry crossing. Just before one approaches the crossroads at **Toniataba** is the site of a great house which once belonged to a *marabout*, or holy leader. It is a round structure which is about 200 ft (60 metres) in circumference; the *marabout* is believed to be buried beneath its floor. Nearby is the site of the "King's Hill",

Give him a wide berth.

Mansa Konko in Mandinka, which is the name given to the region's largest town.

There is often a police check on the Soma road. The police station is almost opposite the town's massive market on the left side of the road. A little caution should be exercised in Soma as the highway crossroads offers good pickings to the less honest of both Gambia and Senegal.

Pottery and kola nuts: The road now follows a great curve in the Gambia River, skirting mangrove swamp in the region of Elephant Island and cutting through rice growing areas. In places rice fields stretch for miles like great, flat marshes with clumps of palm and solitary baobab trees. Before the bridge over the **Sofanyama Bolong**, a new overnight camp offers accommodation in 20 *rondavels* constructed along the same lines as Tendaba Camp. Run jointly by a German couple and the Gambian Tourist Board, **Sofanyama Camp** is located just off the main road before the village of **Pakaliba**.

All along this part of the route one will see vendors displaying ceramics, cane furniture and other local products. If you are on an organised tour, the guide might suggest that the group purchase some kola nuts before visiting a local compound, as kola nuts are a gift indicative of sincerity and goodwill.

From some parts of the road, the river and its many islands may be glimpsed. The islands have exotic names— **Dankuku**, **Pappa**, **Deer**, **Baboon**, **Bird Island** and **Kai Hai**. Before MacCarthy Island comes into view the road runs through an area of red, rocky terrain and passes by a National Rice Project on the left. A monument to the Chinese, who first introduced the rice system and the mechanical pumping devices to the region, stands, overgrown, on the left side of the road just before reaching the first of Georgetown's two ferries. Sadly, due to neglect, the efforts of the Chinese during the 1950s and 1960s have been undermined. The pumping machinery which they installed and which feeds

Exploring the bolongs. Following pages: cooling off at the coast.

river water to the rice fields is now in very poor repair.

The ferry from the south bank to MacCarthy Island is manually operated by means of a hawser stretched across the channel. All visitors to Georgetown join the ferryman in helping to haul on the heavy metal cable. On the other side of MacCarthy Island, the ferry which takes passengers and vehicles to the north bank is motorised.

Most travellers detour from the main road to cross over to Georgetown to stock up with water and food at the town's one store. Continuing east from the junction with the Georgetown road, the hilly countryside is wilder than before, with scrub and bush. A little further on is the river and the ferry crossing at **Bansang**, an important market town where one can buy the pottery for which the region is famous.

From tiny clay pots incised, painted or carved, to giant earthenware water containers, the potter's art here has a distinctive quality and the reds of the laterite hills around are echoed in the colours of the pots. Particularly prized is the pottery from the villages of **Sotuma** and **Aldhungari.**

The 19th-century trading houses are the last major buildings on the wide streets of Basse. From here, eastwards, the road turns into a dirt track leading to Fatoto. The big covered market in Basse is well worth a visit, although it is mainly for the sale of livestock and foodstuffs and there is little in the way of souvenirs. Buildings include the large peanut warehouse on the riverside, where groundnuts are loaded on to barges, a few ancient buildings, two cinemas, a church school and the Apollo Two hotel.

As one leaves Basse Santa Su and the comfort of a metalled road, the largest village before the town of Fatoto, **Garowal**, is on the left side. Fatoto itself is not more than 20 miles (32 km) from Basse but the trip is rough and dusty. The town has a groundnut collection factory and a ferry and it lies just six miles (10 km) from a major road which leads 40 miles (64 km) to **Tambacounda** in Senegal.

If the Gambia's capital seems like a small English provincial town transported to West Africa, Senegal's first city is much like a large French one which has drifted south a continent. Dakar's turn-of-the-century municipal architecture and marble war memorial would not look out of place in Clermont-Ferrand or Marseilles. You can sip a proper expresso on the terrace of a café watching the Renaults and Citroens, slightly more battered than European ones perhaps, driving by.

The French influence in the field of catering and hotel-keeping, combined with the size of the country, means that there are a reasonable number of pleasant, medium size hotels to accommodate tourists who wish to tour rather than to stay in one place. Older establishments such as the Hotel de la Poste in St Louis or the Hotel Aubert in Ziguinchor offer excellent value coupled with a great deal of atmosphere.

Modern luxury complexes in the international style are not lacking, of course. Club Mediterranée's hotels at the Pointe des Almadies and Cap Skirring and the brand new resort of Saly Portudal offer beach and leisure facilities to rival anything in Africa. If you are looking for complete relaxation, it is possible to book a package to one of these and not move outside their landscaped, totally equipped luxury village premises at all during your two-week holiday.

If you want to investigate the country, however, Senegal is notable for the great variety of its landscape, all of it within range during a 10-day tour. At the northern border near the picturesque old colonial capital of St Louis, the dry sandy wastes of the Sahel stretch up round the edge of the Sahara to the Atlas mountains, Morocco and the Mediterranean. In the south, the lush green mangrove creeks and forests of Casamance herald the mysterious depths of Central Africa beyond.

In between lie hundreds of miles of sandy Atlantic beaches, the bird-thronged delta of the Sine-Saloum, the great religious centres of Touba and Tivaouane, the bustling avenues and nightclubs of Dakar and hundreds of simple villages where a stop will bring crowds of giggling children asking for Bic pens and, if you choose to introduce yourself, a glass of tea and a chat under a tree with the older generation.

Though it has pressing problems—the encroachment of the desert in the northeast, the overcrowding and unemployment of Dakar-Senegal remains a peaceful and friendly country, and its richness of scenery, flora and fauna is highly accessible.

Not for nothing is the Wolof word *Teranga* much used in the naming of hotels and other facilities—it means Welcome.

Preceding pages: in the dry north; forest initiation ceremony; Dakar sunset. Left, mounted drummer of the Republican Guard.

THE DAKAR REGION

Dakar, Senegal's capital city, is a meeting point of African and European civilisations and a staging post on the route between tradition and modernity. And yet its creation, and the European occupation of the area of Cap Vert where it now stands, occurred late in the region's history. The first Europeans to arrive were the Portuguese, who landed on the Pointe des Almadies in 1444 but did not settle.

The native inhabitants of the region, who would have in all probability sailed out to meet the strangers in their expertly handled canoes, were Lébou tribesmen. There are a number of theories about the origins of the Lébou. One has it that the name comes from a Greek word meaning "black", and that the Lébou originated among the early black kingdoms of Ancient Egypt, where they came into contact with the Greeks who named them.

Another is that they came from much nearer, from the region of the River Senegal, and their migration southwards was punctuated by unsuccessful attempts to settle in other kingdoms along the way. Whatever the principal explanation, it seems clear that a number of waves of settlement occurred and that the Lébou are a composite of groups originating from other races. Lébou surnames are closely linked with the villages they come from: the M'Bengues and the Sambs are from **Ngor**, the N'Doyes and the Gueyes are from **Ouakam**, and so on.

The Lébou were among the first populations on the continent to set up a system of government akin to a modern republic. This happened early in the 19th century, when the state so constituted was recognised as sovereign by the French Crown.

The Dakar region therefore has managed to retain a high level of independence from protectorate or colonial status. The mini-government of the Lébou still exists and is recognised by the modern state of Senegal. Elections are held to nominate the *Serigne Ndakaru*, or head of state, and the representatives of the 12 Lébou constituencies known as *pinthie*.

France's power base: Of course, the original Lébou have long since been outnumbered as new inhabitants of all races moved to the growing capital. Dakar, with its sheltered deep sea port, took over from the island of **Gorée**, formerly a much more important colonial outpost, in the 1850s as the volume of trade and modern communications such as the trains began to make the little island impractical.

As the French began to build up Dakar, it grew to represent French power and influence over the whole of West Africa. Thus, the architectural legacy of colonisation is particularly impressive in Dakar.

This is not to say that Dakar, like St Louis for example, retains its colonial atmosphere largely intact. Dakar is now a large modern city. Although at the turn of the century its population was still under 20,000, its post-World War II

Left, secretary bird by the Presidential Palace. Below, downtown Dakar.

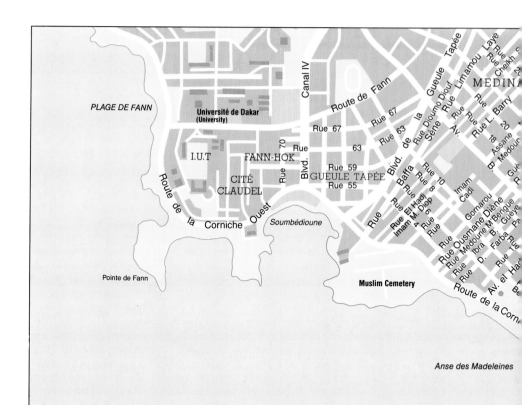

PLAGE DE FANN

Université de Dakar
(University)

Canal IV

Route de Fann

Rue 67

Rue 67

Rue 63

Rue 67

Rue 63

Rue 70

Rue

Blvd.

Blvd. de la Gueule Tapée

Rue Diouma Diouf

Rue Sène

Rue Limamou Laye

Av.

Rue

Rue L. Barry

Cheikh s

MEDINA

I.U.T

FANN-HOK

CITÉ
CLAUDEL

63

Rue 59

Rue 55

GUEULE TAPÉE

20

18

Assane

B. Medoun

Rue

Rue 10

Baffa

Rue 8

Rue

Gue

R.

Imam
Cadi

Route de la

Corniche Ouest

Soumbédioune

Rue

Rue El Hadj
Imam M. Diop

Rue 4 Rue

Rue

Gornarou

Rue Ousmane Diène

Rue Medoune M'Bengue

Rue Ibra B. Gueye

Rue D. Farba Pa

Rue Gueye

Pointe de Fann

Muslim Cemetery

Av. el Hadj

Be

Route de la Corn

Anse des Madeleines

Atlantic Ocean

Dakar

800 m/ 0,5 miles

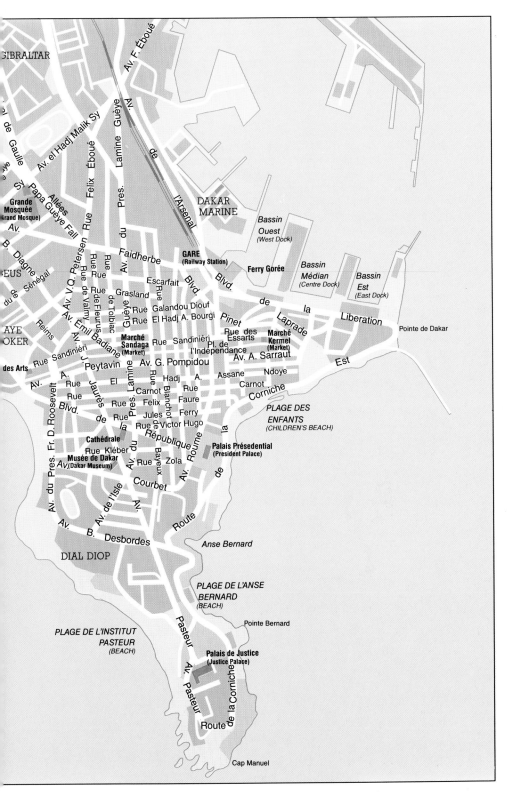

GIBRALTAR

Av. F. Éboué

DAKAR MARINE

Bassin Ouest *(West Dock)*

Grande Mosquée *(Grand Mosque)*

Av. el Hadj Malik Sy

Av. Lamine Guèye

Av. du Pres. de l'Arsenal

GARE *(Railway Station)*

Ferry Gorée

Bassin Médian *(Centre Dock)*

Bassin Est *(East Dock)*

Av. B. Diagne

EUS

Allées Papa Guèye Fall

Sy

Rue Félix Éboué

Av. Faidherbe

Blvd.

Blvd. de la Liberation

Pointe de Dakar

du Sénégal

Rue Escarfait

Rue Grasland

Rue Galandou Diouf

Rue El Hadj A. Bourgi

Pinet

Laprade

AYE OKER

Av. V.Q. Petersen

Rue de Valmy

Rue de Tolbiac

Rue de Fleurus

Av. Émil Badiane

Marché Sandaga *(Market)*

Rue Sandiniéri

Pl. de l'Indépendance

Rue des Essarts

Marché Kermel *(Market)*

Est

Reims

Av. A. J.

des Arts

Rue Sandiniéri

Peytavin

A.

Av. G. Pompidou

Av. A. Sarraut

Assane Ndoye

Av. Rue

El

Rue Hadj A.

Carnot

Carnot

Corniche

Jaurès

Rue

Felix

Rue Faure

PLAGE DES ENFANTS *(CHILDREN'S BEACH)*

Blvd.

de la République

Rue Pres. Lamine

Rue Blanchot

Rue Jules Ferry

Rue Victor Hugo

Av. du Pres. Fr. D. Roosevelt

Cathédrale

Rue Kléber

Musée de Dakar *(Dakar Museum)*

Av.

Av. du la

Rue Bayeux

Zola

Courbet

Av. Roume

de la

Palais Présedential *(President Palace)*

Av. B. Desbordes

Av. de l'Isle

Av.

DIAL DIOP

Route

Anse Bernard

PLAGE DE L'ANSE BERNARD *(BEACH)*

Pointe Bernard

PLAGE DE L'INSTITUT PASTEUR *(BEACH)*

Av. Pasteur

Pasteur

Palais de Justice *(Justice Palace)*

Route de la Corniche

Cap Manuel

boom increased the figure to 300,000 by 1960 and almost a million by 1980. Overcrowding, as in other African capitals, is becoming a problem as unemployed country people migrate into the city.

The origin of the name Dakar is unclear. The favourite theory is that it comes from the Wolof *daxaar*, the name of the tamarind tree. Early Europeans, it is said, mistook the word, which they heard from the local people, to be the name of the original settlement. It is also possible, however, that another word meaning "refuge" is the root, and that the Lébou used the term to refer to the terrain they had finally settled after their lengthy migration from the North.

Central Dakar: The obvious place to begin a tour of Dakar is in the large oblong **Place de L'Indépendance**, which has been the central point of the city ever since it was a village 150 years ago. Most of the banks and airline offices are located in or near this square. Contrasting with modern multi-storey blocks such as the Hotel Indépendance in one corner and the Sofitel in another are traditional French structures such as the marble War Memorial, the Chamber of Commerce and the Foreign Ministry (in colonial times a lawcourt).

To the east of the Place de L'Indépendance, the leaf-shaded **Avenue Albert Sarraut** leads down towards the sea at the **Pointe de Dakar**. The end of the Avenue is marked by the tall ochre and brown bank building designed by the celebrated architect Goudiaby. Beside it, set back from the avenue, is the large modern Novotel, which enjoys panoramic views over the sea to the island of Gorée.

In the late afternoon the Avenue Sarraut buzzes with life as housewives do their shopping at the supermarkets or at the circular **Marché Kermel** a block to the north. The cool, dark bar of the **Hotel de la Croix du Sud** or the pleasant little French-run **Brasserie Sarraut** a little further along are good places to stop for refreshment.

To the north of the Place de

Sandanga market ready for a shower.

188

L'Indépendance, the **Avenue Georges Pompidou** (formerly the Avenue Ponty, and sometimes still referred to by this name) runs up to the crossroads by the big neo-Sudanese style **Sandanga Market**. Formerly the heart of the French colonial shopping and business district, the Avenue Pompidou is rather run down nowadays. It is still a hive of activity, however, with street vendors selling everything from kola nuts to digital watches, beggars, the occasional hustler or pick-pocket, and many shops and cafés.

Around the Avenue Pompidou, mainly to the south, is a grid pattern of side streets containing many pleasant stuccoed colonial buildings with balconies or interior courtyards, bougainvillea draped over the walls and so on. Good visitable examples of faded colonial buildings with great charm are the **Hotel St Louis** in the **Rue Felix-Faure**, and the **Auberge Rouge**, on the **Rue Blanchot**, both of which have good, modestly priced restaurants—though neither is luxurious.

At the end of the afternoon, many Dakarois take a stroll along the Avenue Pompidou window-shopping, stopping to chat with acquaintances or have a drink in one of the French-style café-bars with terraces opening on to the pavement. The **Avenue du President Lamine Gueye**, which leads from Sandanga Market to the **Place Soweto** is similarly used, and on this street one may also find kneeling worshippers spilling over from the small mosque on the corner of the **Rue El Hadj Assane N'Diaye**.

Continuing west past the Sandanga Market junction, the Avenue Pompidou becomes the **Avenue André Peytavin**, and passes a large compound containing two-storey colonial buildings with wide shaded balconies running all the way round the four sides of the first floor. These are now occupied by various Government departments. The avenue ends at the cliff-edge overlooking the wide bay of the **Anse des Madeleines**. Turning right, one enters the long sweeping **Route de la**

Dakar Railway Station.

Corniche Ouest which leads to the University quarter and Soumbédioune Beach. Turning left, one enters the Boulevard de la République which runs back, not quite parallel with the Avenue Pompidou, towards the east of the peninsula near the Place de L'Indépendance. The Boulevard contains the Théâtre National Daniel Sorano, Senegal's major centre for the performing arts, where music and drama are presented throughout the year. Opposite the theatre is the white block housing the national radio and television company (ORTS) which is not open to the public.

Further east along the boulevard is the Roman Catholic Cathédrale du Souvenir Africain. An imposing edifice holding 2,000 worshippers, the cathedral has within its precincts a large garden and an elementary school. It was built in 1929 in a mixture of styles, with two towers reminiscent of minarets, a great pseudo-Byzantine dome and a massive monumental façade. Continuing down the Boulevard de la Répub-

lique one comes upon the great wrought iron gates of the Presidential Palace on the Avenue Roume at the end of the boulevard. The gates are guarded by the spectacularly red-uniformed Presidential Guards, who do not object to being photographed. The palace itself is a majestic white mansion, green-tiled and built in 1907, set in a lovely garden with the ocean as a backdrop.

The Plateau and South: Having walked the above circuit of the **Plateau**—the central and oldest part of Dakar—you will have noted that walking is quite practicable around the area and that this part of the city, laid out simply to a grid pattern, is easy to get to know your way around. Almost opposite the Presidential Palace is a massive 10-storey block housing a considerable number of Government functions. This edifice, known universally as *le building*, commands a wonderful view of the peninsula and the surrounding sea from its roof terrace, and it is possible to obtain permission to go up to take advantage of this fact.

To the north, the Avenue Roume rejoins the Place de L'Independance. Proceeding south from the Presidential Palace, however, you first pass the main hospital and following west as the road becomes the **Avenue Courbet**, you enter the Place Soweto (formerly Place Tascher). Overlooking this large circular place is the modern building of the National Assembly and beside it the Dakar Museum, a building in neo-Sudanese style which houses the **Institut Fondamental d'Afrique Noire** (IFAN).

Facing the museum is the **Avenue Pasteur** which passes the Le Dantec Hospital, the Institut Pasteur and the British Embassy as it heads south towards the tip of **Cape Manuel** with its powerful lighthouse (which may be visited—another splendid view).

Returning north towards the Place de L'Indépendance by the sea-front route, you go along the winding **Route de la Corniche Est**. This road, welcoming enough by day, can be lonely at night and it is wiser not to walk it alone. Passing **Pointe Bernard** and the little

Flower seller, Kermel Market.

bay of **Anse Bernard** with its good beach, you continue along the rocky ocean-front, looking across at the island of Gorée, to the futuristic low concrete buildings of the **Lagon 1** and **Lagon 2** hotels, with their excellent restaurants.

To the north of the Place de L'Indépendance, through the **Rue Canard**, also known as Allées Robert Delmas, shaded by its tall trees, one passes the 1914 colonial **Town Hall** and the **Post Office** before arriving by the port on the **Boulevard de la Libération**. To the left is the magnificent colonial railway station with its vaulted brick façade ornamented by coloured tiles and its great canopied interior. To the right, the boulevard goes past the docks to the end of **Dakar Point**, with its half-finished sea-wall protruding into the Atlantic.

The port of Dakar is the largest and best equipped between Morocco in the north and the Ivory Coast in the south. It is the first major port of West Africa and an automatic stopover for ships on the way from Europe south. Past its extensive oil, groundnut and fish depots, its great cranes, continuing along the path of the railway lines, one comes to the **Gare Routière** (or bus, coach and communal taxi station), a seething mass of travellers, drivers, vehicles in various states of dilapidation, and a thousand vendors with trays of drinks, oranges, cigarettes and virtually everything else one could possibly need.

Further out still is the big port-side industrial zone and an adjacent district of HLMs, the French-system mass low-rent housing units. Immediately northwest of the Plateau district, on the **Allées Papa Gueye Fall**, is the **Grande Mosque** of Dakar. Built in 1964 with financial assistance from King Hassan of Morocco, the building is inspired by the Mohammed V mosque in Rabat and is in the Maghreb style. It is possible to climb its tall minaret every day except Friday, when the mosque is open only to Muslims for prayer.

The Medina and the markets: In the lee of the Grande Mosque, to its northwest, lies the "African quarter", as it once was, of the **Medina**. This tightly-packed district of low plaster houses set in a square grid of streets was built in the 1920s to house the survivors of the plague epidemic of 1914-15. By day a bustle of vendors and craftsmen in little workshops, the Medina at night buzzes with Dakarois walking the darkened streets to meet, talk and visit the little blue or red-lit *dibiterie* cafés or rudimentary bar/discos.

Two blocks from the Grande Mosque is the great concrete **Iba Mar Diop** stadium, where various sports take place, including the African wrestling matches which have the stands thronged at weekends and on some evenings. Further out of town up the **Avenue Blaise Diagne**, opposite the Medissa School complex, is the **Tilène Market**, which is the least Europeanised of Dakar's markets. Here it is possible to buy charms, gris-gris, magic potions to achieve success in love or bring about a rival's downfall, monkey paws, ground antelope horns, wings of owls and much more besides.

The other two markets of Dakar are

Old and new, Dakar.

somewhat less exotic, but musts to visit. The **Sandanga Market**, on the crossroads at the top of the Avenue Pompidou, is the city's largest market, a warren of cloth sellers and tailors, fishwives cutting up great silver-scaled *thiofs*, stalls selling cassettes (many pirated or bootlegged from the radio) and shoe shops. Good buys can include leather work, ready-made or made to measure, pottery, rush and basket-work, *bou-bous* or the cloth lengths to make them (known as *pagnes*).

Dakar's third market, the **Kermel Market**, situated in a beautiful circular building off the Avenue Sarraut, is the most "de-Africanised" of the three. It is heavily frequented by expatriate Europeans. Its speciality is flowers—a gloriously colourful profusion, offered by women whose dress and demeanour are often scarcely less colourful. It is also reasonably good for craft objects, although its prices will probably be slightly higher than elsewhere.

Until 1989, a feature of Dakar was its resident population of Moorish craftsmen (from Mauritania), in their distinctive bluebell coloured all-enveloping robes. Particularly skilled silversmiths, they congregated in tiny stall/workshops in a number of locations, particularly the **Cour des Maures**, near the Sandanga Market on the Avenue Blaise Diagne. Following the racial violence in Senegal and Mauritania between African and Moorish populations, however, virtually all Mauritanians were repatriated north to their country of origin.

West of the Medina, reached from the Plateau via the long curve of the Corniche Ouest, with its joggers (and occasionally muggers) is the fishermen's village of **Soumbédioune**. Every evening the beach fills at five o'clock with the returning boats and the housewives come to buy the day's catch for their evening *thie-bou-dienne*. Between the beach and the large Muslim cemetery with its hundreds of simple stone graves all pointing in the same direction, is the **Soumbédioune Craft Village**.

Checking out the latest sounds.

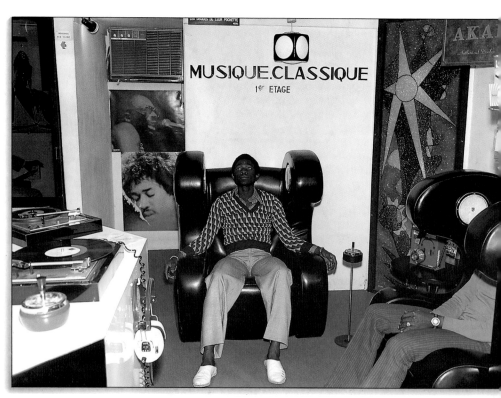

This complex, of up to 100 stands where the carvers, leatherworkers, weavers and tailors work and sell their wares, was created in 1961 and is well worth a visit. From Soumbédioune it is also possible to take a *pirogue* over the short stretch of sea to the little islands known as the **Ile de la Madeleine** and the **Ile des Serpents**. The latter, an uninhabited island, is visible from any point on the Corniche Ouest. It acquired its name (the Isle of Snakes) as a result of a mis-hearing.

It was used to detain for a period of exile one Sarpan, a French soldier convicted of some misdemeanour. Because his name rhymed with "serpent" in French, the island became identified with snakes, although none live on it. But there are a lot of interesting plants, flowers and, above all, migratory birds.

Towards the Far East: Beyond Soumbédioune is the residential suburb of **Fann-Hok**, and behind it, the extensive campus of the **University Cheikh Anta Diop** of Dakar. The institution is named after the eminent Senegalese professor whose researches into the antecedents and early social and political structures of African peoples were of such profound influence. Along the coastline in front of the University are elegant modern villas belonging to the country's social, business and political élite.

Further out of town than the University is the **Mermoz** district, named after the famous French aviator who flew the Atlantic from Senegal in the 1920s, and then the former village of **Ouakam**, now incorporated into Dakar's urban sprawl. A French military base here maintains a modest but not negligible force of around 1,000 men. Emerging into open country now, one passes **Les Mamelles**, the narrow steep hills which overlook Dakar, one of which has a powerful lighthouse (visitable) on its peak.

Continuing further, one arrives at the **Pointe des Almadies**, the most easterly point on the African continent. A large plot near the point is occupied by Club

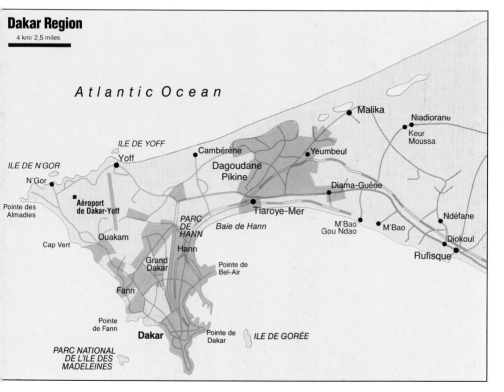

Dakar Region

4 km/ 2,5 miles

Atlantic Ocean

Malika
Niadiorane
Keur Moussa
ILE DE YOFF
Cambérène
Yeumbeul
Yoff
Dagoudane Pikine
ILE DE N'GOR
Diama-Guène
N'Gor
Pointe des Almadies
Aéroport de Dakar-Yoff
Tiaroye-Mer
Ndéfane
PARC DE HANN
Baie de Hann
M'Bao Gou Ndao
M'Bao
Cap Vert
Ouakam
Diokoul
Hann
Rufisque
Grand Dakar
Pointe de Bel-Air
Fann
Pointe de Fann
Dakar
Pointe de Dakar
ILE DE GORÉE
PARC NATIONAL DE L'ILE DES MADELEINES

Mediterranée's complex, which contains two restaurants, a large swimming pool, nightclub, theatre and the usual beach and sports facilities. Just outside the complex, a little oyster farm supplies two or three simple beach-front seafood restaurants. It is still possible to see remains of some of the wrecked ships which came to grief over the years rounding the deceptively reefed point.

Next to the Pointe des Almadies is the traditional Lébou fishing village of **N'Gor**, with its maze of houses, sandy beach with a little mosque and nearby small naval station. It is possible to be taken in a *pirogue* from the beach to the little island of N'Gor, a mile offshore. Near the village, by an extremely fine sandy beach equipped with all facilities, is the Meridien hotel complex.

Continuing northeast from N'Gor, one skirts the airport before arriving at the Lébou fishing village of **Yoff**, situated opposite the **Dakar International Conference Centre**, with its bold modern triangular buildings. Yoff,

the spiritual centre of the L'ayène Muslim brotherhood, is well worth a visit, especially on Friday afternoon when the members, who comprise the entire population of the village, all wear their distinctive white robes.

The occasional Ndeup ceremonies (see chapter on "Religion") are also fascinating to witness but unpredictable when it comes to timing. Back towards Dakar from Yoff, one enters the sprawling new housing area of the **Patte d'Oie** (Goose's Foot) before re-joining the northern suburbs of Dakar.

Along the northern coast of the peninsula are a number of new suburbs and districts which have sprung up to cater for the overspill from the burgeoning city. **Pikine**, up the road from Patte d'Oie, is the most telling example of the rapid demographic changes which have occurred. This new town, which grew out of the sand in the late 1960s, contains half a million people and is still growing.

Around the area of Pikine was the 19th-century frontier of the Lébou's

Club
Mediterranée
Pointe des
Almadies.

territory, where they had built a boundary wall of sand and clay to repel invaders. In between Patte d'Oie and Pikine are the poorer working class districts of **Parcelles Assainies** and Guédiawaye. Further north, the traditional Lébou village of **Camberène** is now surrounded by an assortment of new housing projects, the **Golf Sud**, **Golf Nord** and Hamo, financed by a mixture of public and private funds.

Cause for concern: Along the northern coastline, continuing from just outside Dakar all the way up to St Louis in the north, is a series of natural depressions, highly fertile because of their water retention, which provide much of the fruit and vegetables for the markets of Dakar. The rate of encroachment of Dakar's population is causing concern as to the long-term future of the **Niayes**, which are increasingly under pressure. In the area of **Sangalkam**, with its experimental agriculture institute, many of the small farms are owned by wealthy Dakarois.

Following the southern shore of the Cap Vert peninsula out of Dakar on the **Route de Rufisque**, one passes the **Point of Bel Air** and the village/suburb of **Hann**, with its long sweep of beach and its forested Zoological Park.

The road continues, bordered with coconut palms (wayside boys still offer you freshly-cut coconut slashed open at the top so that you can drink the milk) but also now with industrial installations. After 15 minutes the village of **M'Bao** is reached and a little further on two more Lébou fishing villages, **Bargny** and **Yen**.

The first major town outside Dakar on this coast is **Rufisque**, the former colonial port and settlement. In the 19th century, this town was an important centre for peanut-processing and it was one of the four *communes*, along with Gorée, Dakar and St Louis, which were the earliest entities represented in the French National Assembly. Today, its colonial town hall and a number of other old buildings remain, but its financial survival depends largely on one business: its cement factory.

Left, leave your shoes on the beach. **Right**, have them shined for the city.

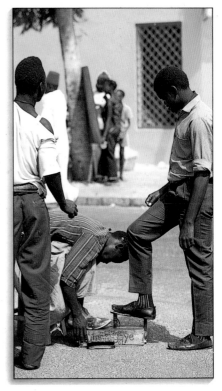

GORÉE

From the Petite Corniche of Dakar you can see **Gorée**, shining terracotta in the sun, two and a half miles (four km) out west in the Atlantic. A day or half-day trip there is a must. If the pace of the capital gets you down, and you can find a room there—accommodation is extremely scarce—a couple of days can be passed very agreeably in its slumbering ex-colonial alleys.

Access to the island is by a launch from the port of Dakar just off the Boulevard de la Libération near the Railway Station. Boats leave for the 20-minute journey approximately every 90 minutes from seven in the morning to midnight (these times should be checked—the reception clerks of most major hotels will have the information). The weekends are the busiest times, when many Dakarois go out to the island for a day on the beach; Monday is the quietest day, when the museums are

Preceding pages: Gorée, with Dakar visible behind. Left, Gorée, a study in ochre.

closed but the island is probably at its most atmospheric.

Because of its position in the lee of Cap Vert, in the largest sheltered bay of West Africa, Gorée was the first anchorage at which ships from Europe, and later transatlantic traffic, stopped.

The first Europeans to visit the then uninhabited island were the Portuguese in 1444; they named it Palma. In 1588 the Dutch took over the island and re-baptised it Goede Reede, meaning "good harbour", which was eventually corrupted into Gorée. Because of its safe moorings, convenient position off the coast of the new trading territories of West Africa, and the ease with which it could be defended, Gorée was a perfect base for the early Europeans and was hotly disputed.

Portuguese, French, Dutch and British vied with each other for control of Gorée until the Count d'Estrées took the island for France in 1677. The various European trading companies and the representatives of the French Crown built warehouses on the island to hold the guns, powder, cloth, salt, small manufactured items and other products which they bartered with the African tribal leaders for gold, hides, gum and, above all, slaves.

Black ivory: It was as a slave depot that Gorée made its sinister mark on the history of West Africa. As sugar-cane cultivation spread into the Americas and the Caribbean, more and more labour was required. First in the Senegambia region, and later further south along the coast, the slavers would barter with local chieftains for the "black ivory", which, or more properly, who, would then be transported to Gorée to be sorted and imprisoned while awaiting shipment to the plantations across the Atlantic.

In the 19th century as first the British and finally the French banned slavery, the trade died out, but Gorée had established itself as the pre-eminent port of call for vessels arriving either from Europe or the Americas. Its service industries therefore allowed it to thrive for some time. Naval forces engaged in the suppression of the slave

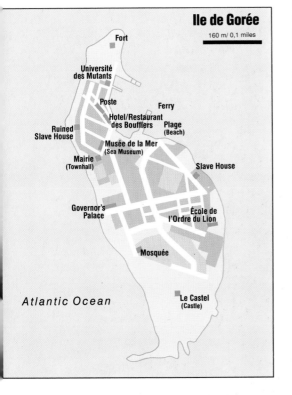

Ile de Gorée

160 m/ 0,1 miles

Fort

Université des Mutants

Poste

Ferry

Hotel/Restaurant des Boufflers

Plage (Beach)

Ruined Slave House

Musée de la Mer (Sea Museum)

Mairie (Townhall)

Slave House

Governor's Palace

École de l'Ordre du Lion

Mosquée

Atlantic Ocean

Le Castel (Castle)

trade were based there. The island was a free port and considerable commercial activity remained. In 1832, its population peaked at 5,000.

In the latter half of the 19th century, however, the population of Gorée overspilled the island and Dakar was founded on the peninsula in 1857. Commerce began to move to the mainland, where peanut cultivation had started, and the establishment of a railway made the movement of bulk loads easier. Transatlantic liners began to use the new larger port in Dakar, too. Gorée was left to the religious and educational communities which had been established there and its population declined by degrees to reach just 600 in 1931.

Gorée today: All of this history is given concrete form in the architecture of the little island. The buildings, practically none of which are more modern than the turn of the century, are dominated by either military or commercial designs, and belong to a mixture of centuries and nationalities. Many of them, and the dwellings that surround them, are crumbling, as decades of neglect followed the decline of the port.

With the launch of schemes by UNESCO and the Senegalese Government in the 1970s and 1980s, several of the more critically dilapidated structures were stabilised, and considerable will exists to restore the island, but money is of course scarce. The circumstances of the house owners and inhabitants of Gorée also complicate effective action to renovate buildings. Many of the original titles to houses have devolved to a large number of relatively impecunious descendants who are scattered around the country, uncontactable and unable or unwilling to take care of their small share in a distant property.

Other houses have been bought, or occasionally rented, by comparatively prosperous Dakarois or French who use them for weekend or holiday homes. Several of the major houses, including the beautiful walled property of the former American Consulate, have been

Staircase of the Slave House.

acquired by rich expatriates such as Mark Gilbey, of the gin fortune, and the Aga Khan. This has lead to fears that Gorée would become a semi-deserted luxury retreat, but as yet there are no signs of things becoming so extreme.

In addition to the tourists who come over on day-trips, the island's educational establishments—three schools, infant, elementary and secondary, the so-called **Université des Mutants**—and the two museums, as well as the basic services (Post Office, clinic, police station) provide jobs today. A number of civil servants from Dakar are also lodged on Gorée, in some cases in former administrative buildings. Ex-guards from the prison (now moved) which used to be housed in the Fort d'Estrées, and their families, continue to comprise a part of the population.

The arrival of the launch from Dakar is always an important event. The mid-morning boat will be bringing back Gorée housewives gone to the mainland to do their shopping. Tourists will be met by island children and youths offering, usually politely and unpersistently, to show them around. A number of private yachts may be moored inside the shelter of the mole, and usually the beach will be well-used.

Walking up from the beach into the central area around the **Place du Gouvernement**, one is struck by the visual beauty and the tranquillity. There are no cars on Gorée and most of the streets and paths are covered with sand, or sometimes paved with blocks of basalt from the island. Baobabs and palaver trees shade the public areas and bougainvillea drapes the terracotta walls or sprouts through collapsed roofs.

A fortunate gentleman: The most visible, and most luxurious, restaurant on the island is the **Hostellerie du Chevalier de Boufflers** with its charming terrace overlooking the beach and the landing jetty. The establishment has two simple bedrooms which, as they are the only two hotel rooms on the island, are extremely difficult to book. (The former **Relais de l'Espadon**, the

Beautiful old house renovated.

island's other, larger, hotel, closed down in 1981 and has failed to re-open since, in spite of constant rumours that restoration has been made possible and is under way.)

A drink or meal either on the terrace of the Hostellerie or in its cosy dining room, draped with fishing nets and hung with a mixture of African carvings and fishing objects, is highly recommended. The French owners produce excellent versions of local seafood (the sea-bass known as *thiof*, lobsters, crayfish, prawns, clams and other rarer shellfish and crustaceans) cooked in the French manner. One should also know a little about the figure after whom the hotel is named.

Jean-Stanislas de Boufflers became Governor of Senegal in 1785, and moved his residence from St Louis, which he didn't like, to Gorée. A poet and aesthete, Member of the Academie Française, he was also an appreciator of feminine beauty, and among the *signares* of Gorée found ample scope to indulge the latter taste.

The *signares* (a corruption of the Portuguese *senhora*) were women of half-European, half-African parentage who acquired great wealth and power on Gorée (as in St Louis) via liaisons with the European merchants, administrators and military men during their sojourns in Africa. These relationships were recognised as in effect temporary marriages which ended with the return of the male parties to Europe, whereupon the abandoned lady, after scooping up the sand of her beloved's footsteps and mourning briefly, would seek to replace him.

The richest *signares*, such as Anne Pépin (de Boufflers' mistress), Victoria Alberis and Cathy Louette, had large houses, and substantial entourages of slaves and women servants who would parade after their employers carrying their jewellery on display. The 18th century saw a period of lavish entertainment and considerable elegance among the small community on Gorée, with balls and banquets diverting the exiled Europeans, who were nonetheless making large sums of money from trade.

Victoria Alberis's house, with its interesting, pointed, prow-like end balcony still stands on the corner of the Rue Malavois and the Rue St Germain, where it now houses the **Historical Museum** of the **Institut Fondamental d'Afrique Noire**. The museum shows a collection of African prehistoric remains, rooms devoted to the great African empires, the European trading period and assorted other exhibits including African musical instruments.

Education and relaxation: A second museum, the **Musée de la Mer** (of the sea), situated a block away from the Hostellerie du Chevalier de Boufflers, offers a collection of 750 species of preserved fish and 700 molluscs and crustaceans. The major visit for most people, however, is the **Maison des Esclaves** (the House of Slaves), which is a strange mixture of beautiful architecture (with its famous double-crescent stairway) masking acute cruelty of purpose.

The curator, the energetic and

Warm stone and twilight at the end of the day.

fascinating Joseph N'Diaye, shows visitors the chains and shackles, the small ground-floor cells in which the slaves were locked at night while waiting to be enshipped (and the first-floor apartments, spacious and balconied, where the masters lived). He will explain how the women and children cooked and cleaned and the men were made to quarry and break the yellow marble and the basalt which were used to replace the native Bambara's wood and thatch dwellings with stone houses.

There are a number of other buildings of great architectural interest which demonstrate the typical configuration of the former slave-dealers' houses; the **Douga Dieng** house, which is to house a documentation centre on the Black Diaspora; the former **Angrand House**, in whose ruins open-air theatre is occasionally performed. All share the typical strong defensive exterior, interior courtyard with verandahed first-floor European quarters, and ground-floor cells for the slaves.

Other monuments of Gorée are the **mosque**, one of the oldest stone mosques in the country, the pretty early 19th-century **Church of St Charles Borromeo** and the earliest building in the island, the **Portuguese Church**, which dates from 1482. At either end of the island are military fortifications. At the south, on the hill which dominates the island, are the remains of the **Castel**, while at the north the old **Fort D'Estrées**, also known as the **North Battery**, awaits its conversion to an annexe of the Historical Museum.

Probably the most enjoyable way to see Gorée, though, is to stroll at random through the streets, so rich in lovely if decaying houses and in atmosphere. If you know a resident, or get to know one, you may be invited in for a leisurely tea session. If not, you may stop at one of the little cafés along the beach and the sea-front promenade of the **Quai des Boucaniers** for a drink or a meal. **Thiam's**, run by a former waiter at the Hostellerie du Chevalier de Boufflers, is good and very cheap.

The Victoria Alberis House, Gorée.

THIÈS REGION

The large town of **Thiès** is typical of many market and trading centres in Senegal which have grown up around important crossroads. As well as straddling the highways connecting **Dakar**, 60 miles (100 km) west, to towns such as **Louga**, in the north, **Djourbel** and **Kaolack**, Thiès is also a major railhead. From Dakar, the historic railway, built in 1888, divides at Thiès into two major routes linking northern Senegal with the south and east.

One of the most ancient cities of Senegal, Thiès is indicated on many early maps of West Africa. The town was originally part of the kingdom of Kayor and its Wolof leaders, from the 14th century, made their wealth from the supply of slaves to the Portugese and French traders. It was from the region of Kayor that the great leader Lat Dyor made his stand against French colonialism. When Lat Dyor died in 1896, Kayor was annexed by the French to join the colonised regions of Dakar, Gorée and St Louis.

Islam's legacy: From the 13th century, the region of Thiès had come under the influence of the Almoravid dynasty which imposed the teachings of Islam. From this period Thiès grew as an important religious centre. Today the many mosques in the city testify to the fact that it still is. The Tidjiane sect is most influential in this region as its traditional capital, **Tivaouane**, lies about 12 miles (20 km) north of Thiès.

The scenery around Thiès is far from picturesque and much of the town is a ramshackle sprawl across dusty, red, undulating sandstone. Many of the people work in the opencast phosphate mines to the north and west of the town at **Taiba** and **Pallo**, although the town's main income is from trade and its importance as a rail junction. Since the price of groundnuts dropped and the value of phosphates rose, the country's two major phosphate mines in this region have contributed vitally to Senegal's economy. For those interested, it is possible to arrange a guided tour of one or other of the phosphate mines which lie between Thiès and the coast. Most of the phosphate is converted into fertiliser, of which Senegal is the world's 10th largest producer.

It is as a transit town that most visitors see Thiès, whether travelling by road, the daily rail services from Dakar and St Louis or the twice-weekly rail link to Bamako in Mali. The station is the hub of the town and the nearest hotel to the railhead is the eight-roomed **Hôtel du Rail**, a small basic establishment usually crammed with merchants and businessmen straight off the trains. The best hotel in town, the **Hôtel Thiès**, is an oasis of calm after the bustle around the rail station and there is generally a vacancy in one of its 15 air-conditioned rooms.

The popular restaurant in the Hôtel Thiès is modern, economically decorated with the work of local artisans and serves some of the best Senegalese cuisine in the town. The menu is varied and visitors can also order international

Preceding pages: African Mass at Keur Moussa. **Left,** a venerable head of family. **Right,** Catholic church, Thiès.

dishes. As there are so many eating places nearby, the tiny **Hôtel Rex** has no restaurant but the slightly bigger **Étoile du Sud** has a small, intimate, but slow restaurant. The Étoile du Sud is just the place for a refreshing coffee after touring the stalls and workshops of the local market.

The main attraction for visitors to Thiès is its arts and crafts workshop. Founded in 1966, the workshop is located in the encampment built by Faidherbe. There are several such workshops in the country known as "*Manufactures Senegalaises des Arts Decoratifs*". In this particular workshop, under the direction of Papa Ibra Tall, the main products are the famous tapestries representing paintings by celebrated Senegalese artists such as Amadou Seck, Souley Keita, Maodo Niang and Ousmane Faye, whose most notable work is *La Forêt*. The artists produce original designs which are then woven into tapestries—some of immense size.

These unique souvenirs can be bought at the workshop, along with ceramic articles, printed cloth, paper, wood and original paintings. The tapestries, however, are quite expensive. The director, Papa Ibra Tall, is a well-known artist whose works have been exhibited internationally. His *L'heure des esprits* crops up regularly as a theme for the tapestries, embroidery and wood carvings produced in this workshop.

This part of Senegal used to be a trading centre for precious African hardwoods such as ebony, ironwood, mahogany, sapele and iroko. Today there is an acute shortage of wood as forests are cut back for firewood. Much of the exotic wood used in the workshops of Thiès and similar large towns now comes from deep in the interior, or from as far away as Casamance or Guinea. Traditional tribal masks, beautifully inlaid ornaments, statues, carved wooden African combs, bowls, plaques and dishes make excellent souvenirs, but the larger carvings are both heavy and bulky when battling through airports and Customs. Less problematic

Shaded avenue and white-washed trees.

are likely to be the handmade leather goods, gold and silver jewellery wrought in the roadside booths by Malian and Mauritanian craftsmen, and bronze castings.

Ocean rollers: From Thiès, one can reach the beautiful beaches north of Dakar by joining the coastal road at the point where Kayar is sign-posted. The Atlantic coast consists of long, straight beaches of white and golden sands, drifting dunes topped with hummocks of sea-grass and ocean rollers which would look at home on postcards of California. As one travels away from the Cap Vert peninsula, there are a number of points of interest before the Atlantic Coast beaches. It is wise to have a guide when visiting these sights, particularly if one wants to hear the background to some of the historic sites.

Sebikotane is the location of the famous William Ponty School, which has trained a number of the country's statesmen. Its imposing edifice rubs shoulders with some magnificent examples of mid-19th century architec-

ture. Nearby is **Ranch Filfill**, a Lebanese enclave created in the middle of this dry, desert-like area and planted with exotic tropical plants and flowers. A diversion off the road, to the north, leads to **Keur Moussa**, a monastery best visited on a Sunday because of the special masses sung each week to the accompaniment of traditional Senegalese instruments.

To the north of the peninsula is a string of large lakes, **Youi**, **Malika**, **Mbeubeusse** and **Lac Retba**. Between the lakes and the coast large areas of afforestation have been created. **Lac Retba** is significant as it was on the lake that the famous aviator, Mermoz, who created the first airmail service to South America in 1930, landed his seaplanes before the development of Yoff airport.

Near the lake is the settlement of **Bambylor**, close by the tourist camp on the coastal dunes. Run by a group of Peuls, the camp, known as **Ndiaga Peul**, is set in delightful surroundings with an endless white beach fringed by cocoa palms. The accommodation is

Tidjiane Muslims greeting a dignitary, Tivaouane.

rather basic, but the scenery and the succulent seafood make up for the spartan conditions. A crossroads is reached at the village of **Mbayak** where one can either return to Dakar, divert down to Rufisque or continue up the coast to the main attraction north of Dakar, **Kayar**.

Kayar and canoes: A "canoe", on the formerly French West African coast, means a *pirogue*, a long, narrow, double-prowed dugout which plies the rivers and creeks. They are generally carved in one piece from the buoyant wood of the baobab tree. The larger *pirogues,* drawn up on the beaches as one travels along the coastal road north of Dakar, are carvel-built. Almost every beach and bay from Cap Vert to St Louis sports fleets of these colourfully-decorated boats lining the high-water mark.

These elegant boats are the product of generations of craftsmanship and design. Constructed from an easily carved red wood similar to teak, the main frame consists of planks warped to a flat centre board which defines the *pirogue's* narrow, high-sided profile. In length, the traditional *pirogue* can vary from two to 20 metres and its width generally accommodates side-by-side paddlers with a central well for net and catch. At each end of the craft a curious prow gives the *pirogue* its knife-like shape and the entire construction is fashioned by a team working with hand adzes and finished by bringing up to smooth surface ready for paintwork.

To watch the laborious work of the boatbuilders on the Senegal coast is like watching the progress of a hand-built car. Working under an awning of woven palm thatch, the foreman directs the precise measurements and guides each adze stroke until the form is perfect. Often broken glass is used to prepare the surface for its final coat of paint.

Blues, black, patriotic greens, yellows and reds are applied in layers to a stylised pattern. The craft may be dedicated to saints, either Christian or Muslim. Crescents, stars, diamonds, hearts and flowers exquisitely painted, bedeck *pirogues* with names such as *Malik Sy* or *Mahmood Gadafi*. Some-

On the beach at Kayar.

times inscribed in Arabic and with intricate scrollwork, the proud beak of a bowsprit is often adorned with a Senegalese flag.

From the beaches of Kayar, hundreds of these *pirogues* brave the ocean far out from the coast in order to follow the shoals of migrating fish such as sea bass, tunny, hake, swordfish, barracuda and shark. On shore, in the maze of smoke-houses and cabins, net huts and food booths there are taxidermists who specialise in preparing shark's heads and sailfish trophies for the sporting souvenir collector.

Huge drying frames and long fish-smoking huts are crammed onto the shore at Kayar with little alleyways in between. On the beach, as soon as the fishermen return with their catches, the prime fish are sold off fresh from the *pirogues*. Brightly dressed women with enamel bowls on their heads haggle for squid, octopus, red mullet and choice cuts from the larger fish. Everyone on the beach is busy and each appears to have his own role in the process from the netting of the fish to the loading of large, gaily-painted lorries.

There is a hierarchy among the fishermen and the catch is carefully portioned out down to the last entrail. Even the small boys who organised the palm log rollers on which the great fishing boats are manoeuvered to and from the water are paid in fish. Between July and October, the population of Kayar more than doubles when fishing becomes a full-scale industry. A good percentage of the catch is sent for sale abroad.

The best time to visit Kayar beach is a couple of hours before sunset in order to watch the last catches of the day being brought in and the hundreds of fires being lit along the wide beach. The most popular accommodation on the Kayar coast is the **Auberge des Cocotiers**, where the variety of fish dishes defies the imagination.

Essential stopover: To reach the next main seaside village, **M'boro**, one should return to the crossroads at Mbayak taking the road which passes between the lake and the shore. M'boro

A kid having a corking time by the sea.

lies about 30 miles (50 km) north of Kayar and is very similar as it is also a fishing centre. Near the village of M'boro, the **Rose Lake**, or **Lac Rose**, is a spectacle not to be missed. The lake has its own peculiar movement in the form of the thousands of birds which throng its opaque pink mineral waters. Flamingo, spoonbill, pelican, heron, tern, waders of all kinds and a variety of seabirds congregate on the placid waters, making this an essential wildlife photographer's stopover when touring the West African coast.

Although one could travel even further up the coast to the more isolated villages of **Fas Boye** and **Lompoul**, these remote villages are only reached by long diversions off the main Dakar to St Louis highway. The recommended tourist circuit is to take the road from M'boro, east and inland to the religious centre of **Tivaouane**, the capital of the Tidjiane sect. This strict religious order was founded by Malik Sy and its leaders still reside at Tivaouane. The principal feast of the Tidjiane sect is *Gamou*.

North of Tivaouane, the minor towns of **Mekhé** and **Kébémer** provide stopping points on the main road to St Louis, and finally the larger town, **Louga**, is notable as a major depot for the collection and processing of groundnuts, but for little else.

Folklore festival: There are a number of traditional feasts and celebrations in this region. Entertainment managers of hotels and tourist complexes have added their own, Hollywood-style variations and costumes. This makes it difficult for the visitor to ascertain how much of the spectacle presented is authentic and how much is choreographed for tourists.

One of the more popular dances performed traditionally during the month of May is known as *syniaka*. The dance is performed by girls who are coming of age in the villages of the Thiès region. In early times, the ritual of week-long seclusion also included the practice of female circumcision. Today, the formidable surgery has been all but stamped out, but the ceremony at the culmination of *Syniaka* remains a favourite tourist attraction.

Towards the beginning of June, the rituals of female fertility and of witchdoctors' forecasts for newly-born children are celebrated with exhortations to gods and with colourful dances. This period is known as *Kunyalen* and preceeds the *Fil*, another ceremony observed during June-July.

Fil involves songs, poems and stories, coincidentally offered up just before the annual rainy season. The dances and incantations of *Fil* usually predict good crops and a healthy future for the village. Women feature as the main performers in most of the rituals of the Thiès region and another of their ceremonies, *Ebunaay*, is enacted only by women and includes the exotic and erotic dances known as *bugereb*. These rites generally last for about a week and culminate with the selection of the village's beauty queen. Today, on the stages of tourist hotels, these once important, long-drawn-out ceremonies are condensed into performances which can take as little as 20 minutes.

Left, collecting salt in the Pink Lake. Right, playing in the cotton.

ST LOUIS

The regional capital of north Senegal, **St Louis**, is the country's third largest city and its second largest seaport. The city is 165 miles (265 km) north of Dakar and is connected to the capital by a well-maintained highway. To the north of St Louis the border with Mauritania is less than six miles (10 km) away. For this reason the 95,000 inhabitants are of a wide variety of races.

Located on an island at the mouth of the Senegal River and named after King Louis XIII, St Louis was founded by French colonists in 1659—the earliest French settlement in Senegal. Before the French built an outpost on the site, early Dieppois expeditions had discovered this part of the coast and the Portugese explorer Lancarote landed near the site of the city in 1445. Thomas Lambert and the Dieppois Jeannequin set up a camp on the island in 1638, but it was Louis Caullier who started constructing the first permanent buildings 21 years later.

With its fine harbour and easily defended position, the port flourished and became one of the most important centres of the slave trade. By the end of the 18th century, the population had reached 10,000 and there were many inter-marriages between freed slave girls and French merchants. As on the island of Gorée, the half-caste ladies born of these unions, known as *signares*, came to constitute a wealthy and privileged élite. St Louis became the leading French settlement on the West African coast and, in 1816 and again in 1824, René Caillé used the port as a base from which to explore deep into the interior of Senegal.

Two Governors had considerable influence on the development of St Louis. Baron Roger, Governor from 1822 to 1827, was responsible for the building of the Maurel et Prom trading house, one of the most important buildings of its time in Senegal, and for the erection of the cathedral on the site of an earlier wooden church. When Louis Faidherbe became Governor in 1854, he began extensive improvements. As the city was expanding beyond the main island, Faidherbe built a bridge, the **Pont Servatius**, to link the settlements. In 1880 the town hall was built and, three years later St Louis was linked to Dakar by rail.

Because of its prime location as a sea port and its command of the long Senegal River, St Louis was a centre for trade both from Europe and from the Sahara region. The town is situated in the middle of the Senegal River and spreads east to the area known as **Sor** on the continent side and west to a long spit of land on its Atlantic side. The **Faidherbe Bridge** links Sor with the island where the city's main buildings are located and two bridges, the Pont Servatius and **Pont de la Géôle** give access to the suburbs known as **Guet N'Dar** and **N'Dar Tout**.

St Louis has some of the finest examples of French colonial buildings in Africa and many of its structures date from the 1700s when the city was at its

Preceding pages: market scene in St Louis. Left, Mauritanian merchants talking business.

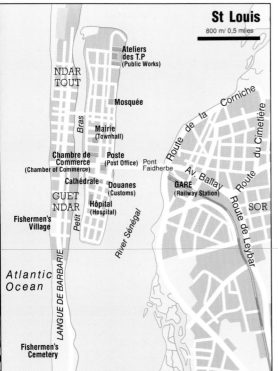

St Louis
800 m / 0,5 miles

NDAR TOUT

Ateliers des T.P (Public Works)

Mosquée

Bras

Mairie (Townhall)

Chambre de Commerce (Chamber of Commerce)

Poste (Post Office)

Pont Faidherbe

Route de la Corniche

du Cimetière

Cathédrale

Douanes (Customs)

GUET NDAR

Hôpital (Hospital)

Av. Ballay

GARE (Railway Station)

Route

Fishermen's Village

Petit

River Sénegal

Route de Leybar

SOR

Atlantic Ocean

LANGUE DE BARBARIE

Fishermen's Cemetery

most prosperous. Typical of those are the town houses with wooden balconies on the first floor, constructed around a cool patio. The *signares* instigated the building of the **Cathedral**, one of the oldest public structures in St Louis.

Now the residence of the Governor of the River District, the **Hotel de l'Administration**, opposite the cathedral, is another fine example of early 19th-century architecture. The **Place Faidherbe** (known locally as "La Savane"), in the same sector of N'Dar Island, is an oasis of greenery surrounded by town houses of the Louis-Philippe period.

This is one of the oldest parts of the city and the area of the square was originally a 17th-century cemetery. The famous botanist Adamson created a botanical garden here and there is a museum which bears his name at the southernmost tip of the island. The **Centre de Recherches et Documentation du Senegal** contains a unique collection of books, documents and artifacts from St Louis' history.

Atmospheric accommodation: The **Quai Henri Jay** leads back to the centre of the island, to Faidherbe Bridge and the **Post Office** on the left-hand side. Just beside the bridge is the three-storey waterfront **Hotel de la Poste**. The red-tiled balconied hotel with its white-painted frontage, colourful awnings and verandah looks out over the **Place de l'Indépendance**. The Hotel de la Poste has 45 air-conditioned rooms and an attractive, cool restaurant and bar. From the river the hotel and its neighbouring mansions in various shades of pastel present a picturesque vista reflected in the water.

The hotel is worth lingering on, as it represents rather more than just a comfortable elderly source of accommodation. It manages remarkably successfully—and perhaps almost a little self-consciously—to embody all the qualities one associates with an overblown, seedy but romantic late period colonial outpost. The bar is furnished in mock leopardskin and there are animal heads mounted on the pink walls. Appropri-

St Louis from the air, the mainland to the rear.

ately it played host to the cast and crew involved in the shooting of the Bertrand Tavernier film *Coup de Torchon*, which concerned shady goings-on among a group of run-down French colonial administrators in the 1930s.

The Hotel de la Poste, while typical of the colonial architecture of St Louis, is not, however, the most luxurious hotel in the city. The **Mame Coumba Bang** with 40 air-conditioned rooms, is the most modern hotel. It is furnished in classical French style and has a popular restaurant, an intimate bar and the city's only swimming pool. **La Résidence** is a comfortable, family hotel much like the Hotel de la Poste but smaller, with only 30 air-conditioned rooms, a tradition-ally decorated restaurant and bar fre-quented by office workers.

Built on a grid pattern, St Louis is easily seen on foot. At one time, no building was allowed to be higher than the **Grande Mosque**, just along the **Quai Roume** from the Hotel de la Poste. Located on the **Avenue du Gen-eral Villiers**, at the north of N'Dar

Island, the Grande Mosque is a spec-tacular structure set in the grounds of an ancient fortified mansion. Right at the end of the island is the **Public Works** building and **Radio St Louis**.

It takes a couple of hours to walk around the main island comfortably, especially if one stops to appreciate the fine architectural details of some of the larger buildings, the iron fretwork bal-conies, wooden shutters and elegant arcades and colonnades. Many of the streets bear the names of famous French writers and were laid out around 1873.

Crossing over the Pont Servatius one is immediately in the main marketplace. Wolof tribesmen in loose, embroidered shirts guide their jewellery-bedecked wives around the maze of booths and Peul women commandeer odd corners of the bazaar in which to set out their dried fish or red and green chillies.

Turning south from the market along **Avenue Lamothe**, running down the centre of Guet N'Dar, one comes to a very different part of St Louis. The white walls and red-tiled roofs give way

Faidherbe Bridge in the mist.

to a more randomly constructed sector, only metres from the elegant 18th-century quarter and its tree-lined avenues. Here the Wolof fishermen have set up their village. Amidst their huts and *pirogues*, one can observe nets being mended or drying, smoke-houses, fish being dried on racks and a constant bustle of people. On the river side of the narrow spit there are little patches of vegetable gardens. It is worth noting that the inhabitants of the fishing village, while peaceful and law-abiding, do not always take kindly to strangers peering curiously at their extremely basic accommodation and visitors may not be made to feel particularly welcome.

Pressing on briskly through the village, a kilometre south of the market is the strange and impressive **fisherman's cemetery** where rough tombs covered with fishing nets lend a weird and uncanny air to the vista of sea, sand and low huts. At the southernmost point of the spit is the **Hydrobase**, once the location of the famous airman Mermoz's airmail service. The buildings are now derelict and the whole area has an aura of decay. The huge sand dunes running along the shore attract picnic and bathing parties. As the Hydrobase and the beach are quite a way from the centre one might hire a carriage for the journey. Opposite the fishermen's quarter, one can see the **College Blanchot** and the **Research Centre** on the tip of N'Dar Island.

A little further on, the **West Quay** of N'Dar runs the length of the island up to Servatius Bridge. The large building behind West Quay is the city hospital.

There are daily trains from Dakar to St Louis taking about seven hours to cover the 165 miles (265 km). Carriages are usually packed and therefore it is wise to arrive at the station well before the train departs in order to secure a seat. There are weekly flights between Dakar and St Louis.

Outside St Louis: There are two major excursions which may be made from St Louis. Both of these are described more fully in the **Senegal River Region** chapter. The first is the riverboat *Bou el Mogdad,* which makes weekly trips up the Senegal River between November and May, leaving from the quayside at St Louis. The second is to the world famous bird sanctuary of the Parc National des Oiseaux du Djoudj, which is 38 miles (60 km) from St Louis by road. Djoudj, which is the third most important bird sanctuary in the world, is unmissable if wildlife is a major part of your interest in West Africa.

South from St Louis is the **Langue de Barbarie** (Barbary Tongue) coast. Consisting of a long spit of sand dunes and exposed, flat islets, this peninsula is also a national nature reserve protecting the hundreds of sea turtles which have adopted the lonely coastline as a nesting ground. The presence of these turtle colonies makes the park of the Langue de Barbarie an internationally important reserve. The sandy coastline also attracts birdwatchers for the variety of migratory wildfowl which come here both from Europe and southern Africa. Just 100 metres wide and 15 miles (24 km) long, the Langue de Barbarie cov-

St Louis' Catholic cathedral.

ers about 4,200 acres (1,700 hectares).

The two villages of **Patou** and **Gandiol** are generally included in the itinerary of *pirogue* tours to this small reserve in the early morning. These trips are not run to a set schedule and must be arranged with individual *pirogue* owners. Sometimes parties of ornithologists advertise in St Louis hotels for passengers to join their pre-arranged visits to the reserve. Nouvelles Frontières, Jet Tours and Air Afrique also organise excursions to the Langue de Barbarie.

The year's finale: Most spectacular of all the festivals in Senegal are the St Louis *Fanals*. Likened by some to the carnivals of the Americas and possibly having the same origin, the *Fanals* occur from 21 December to 1 January.

As the predominant religion of St Louis in colonial times was Roman Catholicism, Christmas Eve Mass was an important social occasion where ladies born of mixed race competed with each other to display the most sumptuous dress or the richest finery.

Every year the gowns became more extravagant. The rich half-castes, often mistresses of the merchant élite, employed pages to support their trains and carry lighted lanterns in their path. While the ladies attended the service, the lantern carriers held their own competition outside the church to see whose paper lantern was most artistically constructed. Coloured paper, cloth and tinsel were fashioned into fabulous shapes lit from inside by candles.

Today the *Fanals* are real works of art sponsored by local businessmen and paraded through the streets of St Louis in a whirl of excitement and a carnival air. Paper and cardboard, silver foil, gilt, tinsel and coloured cloth are employed to create spectacular designs. Ships, aeroplanes, buildings and monuments, masks—even mosques—are displayed in a great procession. A prize and the honour of best exhibit is awarded to the company with the most attractive lantern.

Visitors flock to St Louis to witness this spectacle, reminiscent to some of the carnivals of the Caribbean or Brazil.

Pirogue by old trading houses.

THE SENEGAL RIVER REGION

receding
ages:
elicans at
Djoudj Bird
anctuary.
eft,
heerfully
oing the
washing.
elow,
ringing
ome the
ish supper.

More than 1,000 miles (1,600km) in length, the Senegal River is still less than half the length of the Niger, West Africa's longest river. Rising in the Fouta Djalon mountains in Guinea, the river creates a large curve embracing both the Gambia and Senegal itself, of which it forms in effect the northern boundary. Its wide arc flows around great plains of near-desert, such as the Fouta and the Ferlo.

Unlike Senegal's other major rivers, the Ferlo, Siné, Saloum and Casamance, the Senegal flows constantly throughout the year. However, during the October–May dry season, it is quite shallow and its waters reveal large mudbanks and sandbars. These obstacles to navigating craft make the river treacherous as they move during the heavy rainy season.

Several government schemes are in hand to control the flow of the river and improve conditions, not only for boats but also for the farmers who rely on the river waters for cultivation. Vast fields of millet, rice, maize, sorghum, tobacco, sweet potatoes and vegetables, such as onions and tomatoes, are grown along the fertile plain of the Senegal.

Little pasture on the river banks is sufficient to support grazing but many villagers live from fishing in the teeming waters. The river bursts its banks every rainy season creating fertile areas and, nearer the coast, new irrigation schemes have made large-scale rice cultivation possible.

In 1947 the Delta Irrigation Scheme was opened at the head of the river increasing rice production to its present level. Another interesting product from the Senegal River Region, which used to support thousands of workers, is gum arabic, taken from the acacia tree and sold in large quantities still for use in the textile and pharmaceutical industries.

Up a lazy river: Meandering through a huge region of arid and unproductive land, the River Senegal and its banks support thousands of people. Apart from the numerous villages which survive from cultivating millet, the entire length of the Senegal supports a great number of fisherfolk. The river is tidal for almost the first 300 miles (500km) of its length. Fishing is not restricted to such freshwater catches as carp, catfish, eel and bass, as the saline waters of lakes, marshes and creeks formed by the Senegal produce fish like snook, sea bass, lady fish, wrasse and even some of the larger marine fish. Spears, rods, all types of net and even basketwork traps are employed, as are all manner of dugout canoes, from one-man skiffs to six or eight-paddle craft.

Larger boats are constructed from traditionally designed planks, shaped into double-prowed fishing boats similar to those used on the ocean. Along the riverside these craft can be seen in construction under palm-thatch shelters which protect the carpenters and boatwrights from the sun's heat.

Larger boats also ply the waters of the river which are navigable as far as Kayes in Mali. However, this is only possible in the high water season and really large craft can only navigate as far as **Podor**, 180 miles (280km) from the sea. Cruise boats sometimes make expeditions up-river as far as **Richard Toll** and occasionally Podor.

The river boat *Bou el Mogdad* makes regular trips up the Senegal as far as Podor from its base at St Louis. Georges Console, owner/operator of the large riverboat, takes passengers on a week-long cruise, beginning each Friday from the St Louis quay. These excursions continue through the months of November to May and the itinerary includes the options of fishing, hunting or just browning on the wide sundeck.

Console, one of St Louis' best-known characters, offers a choice of hunting trips from the moored *Bou el Mogdad* in either the **Maka Diama** hunting reserve, or in the **Keur Massene** reserve along the Mauritanian banks of the river. Between St Louis, at the mouth of the river, and **Rosso**, where a ferry conveys traffic across the Senegal into Mauritania, are the hunting reserve

of Maka Diama and the famous bird sanctuary of **Djoudj**.

Flamingoes galore: Senegal's third smallest national park is located far in the north of the country, tucked under the Senegal River 40 miles (60km) from St Louis. The park is on an island created by the Gorom Stream and is known as the **Parc National des Oiseaux du Djoudj**. Created in 1971, the park is 150,000 acres (60,000 hectares) in size and is one of Senegal's two World Heritage sites registered with UNESCO.

Djoudj, the world's ninth most important ornithological site, attracts thousands of birdwatchers each year. Winter is the time to see the park; then the marshy region becomes a seething mass of migratory fowl. The park is open from 1 November to 30 April and closes each day at 12 noon. This means a very early start if one is taking a *pirogue* excursion to Djoudj from St Louis or driving the 90-minute ride to the reserve.

Most itineraries include a visit to

Tigue Lake, which marks the boundary between Djoudj bird sanctuary in the north and the Maka Diama hunting reserve. The entire area between the crook of the Senegal River and the St Louis to Rosso road is known as the Djoudj basin.

More than three million birds are said to fill the Djoudj basin at any one time. Statistics read like a birdwatcher's paradise—more than 500,000 migratory ducks of varying species are estimated to visit the lakes and marshes during the winter season and over 12,000 white pelicans flock to the region. Many thousands of brilliant pink greater flamingoes enjoy the rich source of shrimp and crustaceans here. Spoonbill, a great variety of heron, stork and bustard can be watched from the numerous hides throughout the park.

Northern hunting grounds: In the Maka Diama hunting reserve there is a specially designed lodge from which guides conduct visits into the reserve. Well equipped accommodation includes 16 bungalows, a bar and restaurant with panoramic views across the low-lying Djoudj basin. Expeditions can be pre-booked in Dakar at most travel agents' offices or through the hotel receptions in most of St Louis' hotels. George Console can also advise on procedures for joining hunting parties.

To obtain one of the three categories of hunting permits, three passport photos are needed, together with a valid firearm certificate and regulation insurance and dues. On both the Maka Diama and the Keur Massene reserves, only a small game hunting permit is needed unless the hunter is after warthog or gazelle.

Official lists record a variety of game which includes francolins, guinea fowl, partridge, pheasant, bustard, rail, snipe and a variety of species of duck. Larger game consists of jackals, hyenas, African wild cats, hares, wart-hogs, white-fronted or dorcas gazelles and monkeys, although many of these are protected species. In the creeks and

marshlands snakes, crocodiles and hippopotami are not uncommon and one is advised to keep to the tracks and paths outlined between the hides.

The nearest accommodation for visitors is either at Richard Toll to the east, or St Louis on the coast. Not far from the Maka Diama hunting lodge there's a recently-constructed dam built to expand the rice fields which, paradoxically, attract many of the migrating species of wildfowl from the National Park of Djoudj across the Gorom Stream. At the southernmost point of the hunting reserve the river widens as it nears St Louis and the sea.

The delta region of the Senegal River, as it flows between the long spits of land before the island city of St Louis, is wide and fertile. Downstream from Rosso the river delta has silted up over many years, making even the port of St Louis ineffectual as a major ocean-going port. (This was one reason for the capital of Senegal to be transferred to Dakar, further down the coast.)

Rice and some vegetables are grown

on the low, marshy stretches of land alongside the river which, at this point, runs parallel to the coastline just a few metres across a sandy spit. From the river mouth the tidal waters run almost 300 miles (500km) upstream as the land is so low and flat. About 15 miles (25km) up-river is the city of St Louis, most of it concentrated on a long, narrow island running alongside the spit dividing the river from the sea.

Borders and gardens: After Rosso the scenery changes as the presence of the Sahel begins to make the northern bank look parched. Palms edge the sandy banks and red rock cliffs. From Rosso it is 120 miles (200km) to **Nouakchott**, the Mauritanian capital and a small ferry links the bitumen road on the Senegalese side of the river with a sand track on the Mauritanian side.

This highway is most important as it is Nouakchott's only land link with St Louis, Dakar and the rest of the West African coast. Many Mauritanian traders made use of this route in search of work in the richer country of Senegal until 1989's inter-racial bloodletting temporarily closed the border. The little settlement of Rosso is a crossroads and it is also used as a base from which to visit the hunting park of Keur Massene. Although no accommodation is available at Rosso, there is a hunting lodge with 17 rooms at Richard Toll, a little further upstream.

Richard Toll is a pretty, medium-sized township on the south bank of the Senegal River, about halfway between Podor and the Atlantic coast. Its name comes from the French horticulturist, Richard, who founded an agricultural irrigation project there in 1830, and from *toll* which means "garden" in the Wolof language.

Since the experiment began, the scheme has grown progressively and, by 1957, around 14,000 acres (5,700 hectares) were under irrigation and the project was producing cotton textiles, paint, liquid gas, refined sugar, chocolate, biscuits, chemicals, rope and sacking.

The expanded irrigation programme at Richard Toll is evident in the surrounding countryside by the number of rice fields—like little squares of bright green carpet when the rice is young. Rice is grown throughout the year but the main harvest, when the grain is picked by hand, is during November. The main sugar-growing area is to the east of the town and the farmers produce more than 12,000 tonnes of sugar a year.

Richard Toll is an excellent base from which to visit hunting areas and make fishing trips either on the river or the nearby lakes. There are two hotels; the Hôtel de la Poste, a well-maintained hotel with a fine, clean restaurant and a nightclub, and the Hôtel Massaada which also has a restaurant and nightclub but only two air-conditioned rooms to let. Although the hunting and fishing mainly attract visitors to stay in Richard Toll, the town has an interesting historical background.

A baron's folly: Set on the high riverbank, overlooking the river, stands a building which is as incongruous in this part of Africa as an African compound would be in the Bois de Boulogne. A huge colonial mansion set in beautiful botanical gardens is a breathtaking sight after a long river trip with little to break the landscape but baobab trees.

This magnificent building was constructed by the eccentric Baron Roger, Governor of Senegal from 1822 to 1827. Roger was an avid horticulturalist who imported trees and plants from France, cultivating them in a setting of cocoa palms and date groves. European flowers and shrubs now flourish alongside tropical trees and exotic African blossoms.

Today the gardens are overgrown and untended. The great house itself, with its monumental façade, columns, grand stairway and numerous terracotta statues, has been the subject of several plans for conversion into an hotel. So far no such scheme has come to fruition.

The parklands around the folly extend as far as **Taouey**, a weir on the river above the **Lac de Guiers**. At Taouey, a cleverly designed dam

Mauritanians and camels crossing at Rosso.

divides the saline river water from the sweet water of the lake and once irrigated 2,800 acres (7,000 hectares) of surrounding land. Today only a few of the remaining dykes and canals are in operation and only half the area is now farmed for rice and sugar cane. A recent project is now reviving the original water system here and production is expected to increase.

The "frontier" settlement of **Dagana** is 15 miles (24 km) further upstream from Richard Toll and marks the division of the territory of the Wolof from that of the Tukulors. An ancient rivalry over land between two half-brothers established Dagana as the acceptable dividing point and the town's name derives from the Wolof word *deugna*, meaning "it is truly".

From Dagana, one can detour down to the Lac de Guiers, crossing to the fishing centre of **Mbane** by ferry. Many visitors come to Dagana because it is near the lake. The town itself has little of special interest except the ancient French fort awaiting restoration, the jetty where the *Bou el Mogdad* ties up and the old part of town with its typical houses. The region's main attraction is the lake and the fishing settlements around it.

Around Lac de Guiers: The Lac de Guiers, formed by the waters of the Ferlo River running towards Richard Toll, attracts visitors for its wealth of birdlife. There is also a hunting reserve to the east of the lake which is popular with weekenders from St Louis. A particular attraction is the fishing season during the rise of the Ferlo and Senegal Rivers from November to January each year. Huge nets are cast from the banks of the lake and drawn in by fishermen in *pirogues*.

However, since the recurrent droughts of recent years, the catches have diminished and fishing is now not enough to support the population of the lakeside. To the south of the lake is the small settlement of **Merinaghen**, reached over 50 miles (80 km) of practically impassable road. This is a pastoral region and the people here

An alley in Rosso.

concentrate mainly on rice production.

Tour companies offer several circuits of the countryside from Richard Toll. The lakeside trip follows a route through **Ndiago**, Mbane and **Syer**, deep into the Ferlo Valley, terminating at Merinaghen. Around the area of Mbane many small lakes stretch out along the Ferlo River, surrounded by numerous tiny fishing villages. Two notable settlements where fishing co-operatives can be observed are the villages of **Mal** and Syer.

Many of these lakes and villages can be easily reached as the main **Gnith** to **Louga** tarmac road follows the line of the Ferlo Valley and the region is criss-crossed by small tracks. Tours can be booked in Dakar or at St Louis and groups of birdwatchers and hunters regularly visit the more easily reached lakes. Few visitors venture far up the Ferlo River but one could follow its wide course as far as **Linguère**.

Riverside life near Podor.

Much of the countryside on both banks of the river is desert and one difficult circuit, trekking into arid regions, is that which follows a trail to **Diagle**, east to the oasis of **Niassante**, to isolated **Tatki** and thence back to Richard Toll via Dagana. This tour is sometimes made by weekend hunters from St Louis or those arriving by air from Dakar at nearby Podor. The region east of Lac de Guiers is an officially designated hunting region.

Although the native population are Peul, there are a number of Chinese here on a technical assistance programme experimenting with new varieties of rice. The Chinese have also contributed to the recent development of irrigation schemes at Merinaghen.

Driving is not recommended in the desert or in terrain where no tracks have been established. Even on those routes already indicated, the surface can vary from deep pot-holes to mini-ravines, from axle-high dust to wheel-deep mud. Four-wheel drive vehicles are therefore desirable. Bush taxis, converted from an array of pick-ups, negotiate the roads frequently but their arrival is never guaranteed; breakdowns are common.

100-Mile Island: About 110 miles (185km) up the Senegal River the wide stream divides into channels forming one of the largest inland islands in West Africa. The **Ile à Morphyl** is a marshy, low-lying, narrow island around 50 miles (80 km) long. At its northernmost tip, **Podor**, with a population of around 6,000, is one of Senegal's oldest cities. Historians say that the region of Podor has been inhabited since the third century A.D. Both the Kingdom of Tekrour and the great Ghana Empire left their mark on the area.

By the time of the conversion of the Fouta Toro Kingdom to Islam in 1776, the English had already reached that part of the country and, in 1745, had constructed a fort at Podor. The regular confrontations with the Peul tribes eventually destroyed the British fort but, in the mid-19th century Louis Faidherbe rebuilt the battlements, which can still be visited.

It is well worth spending some time looking around the town of Podor as, apart from the old fort, the architecture of the houses and ancient warehouses which line the riverside is of particular interest. The housing in this area is constructed of dry earth in the style of Mali, known locally as *banco*. Industry in Podor is restricted to river transport, the movement of fertilisers and the recovery of aggregates from the bed of the river. In the town's Dieri region, there is a little port with a jetty where the *Bou el Mogdad* rivercraft moors.

The Ile à Morphyl has an interesting history. Legend has it that many hundreds of elephants used to live on the long island and became isolated by the deep arms of the Senegal River. Cut off, the elephant eventually died out and the island became known as the site of the mysterious "elephants' graveyard". Mud-bricked mosques are among the scenic attractions of the region and trips can be made to see some fine examples at the surrounding villages of **Guede**, **Ndioum**, **Kaskas**, **Salde** and **Tielao**.

A small gite is located on the edge of Podor and adventurous hunters use this as a base from which to hunt the

Podor post office.

crocodiles which are prevalent in the marshy areas surrounding the island.

Access is from the main highway which follows the course of the Senegal River. A branch of the road leads to a small jetty where the ferry boat will take you across to the island. There is an airfield at Podor served by the River Airline.

The main road to the next large town, **Matam**, is reached either by the bridge or the ferry. Before leaving Podor, most visitors like to browse in the town's small market where beautiful and inexpensive pottery can be purchased. Once this town used to be a centre for the gold trade—Podor is thought to derive from *pot d'or*, "golden jar"—and some exquisite jewellery can still be bought at the market.

Forts and dams: The road from Podor continues on the south bank of the river, almost 140 miles (220 km) to Matam, a large town of 9,000 people. Matam is famous for its craftsmanship in metalwork, jewellery and pottery, but its name originates in tribal history.

Once, during the regular skirmishes between the tribes, a small town known as **Tiade** developed as a staging post along the slave routes. The Peul drove their captured slaves through the town, stopping to make the most of the Tukulor hospitality and paying for their needs in the currency of their trade: slaves.

The story goes that the Peul then came back at nightfall and stole back the slaves whilst the Tukulor slept. Other stories relate that the Tukulor themselves collected slaves to trade with the Peul but found the Peul were not creditworthy. Whatever the true background, the Tukulor of Tiade began demanding cash from the Peul tribesmen for any service which they afforded the merchants. *Matama* in the Tukolor language, means "pay cash"— hence the name of Tiade became **Matam**.

The oldest colonial remains of Faidherbe's fort, in Matam are to be seen on the banks of the river where a flood carried the battlements away early

Young cowherd by the river.

this century. Louis Faidherbe built the original structure as one of his defending chain of forts in 1857. Downstream from the town is another crumbling structure, again on the riverbank, known as the Residence de Djourbivol. Both this colonial mansion and the fort are in dire need of restoration but little has been done to save these relics from the ravages of time, weather and the indiscriminate removal of building stones and bricks from the sites.

The only other building of any significance in Matam is its attractive mud-bricked mosque which has two tall minarets. A dam, similar to that on the river delta north of St Louis, has been constructed at Matam in order to develop the rice-growing potential of the area. This region is also known as the "granary of millet" as a result of the many acres of millet fields surrounding the town.

Accommodation in Matam is limited and the Hôtel Fadel, or Hôtel du Fleuve, is the only reasonable place to stay. The hotel has five rooms with showers but no air conditioning and is run by a Lebanese proprietor, Mohammed Fadel. Although the hotel is in a sorry state of repair, the restaurant has a surprisingly good selection of local and Lebanese dishes and M. Fadel runs the only cinema in the region.

Matam, which is just over 300 miles (500 km) from St Louis, has its own airfield, served by the River Airline. The main Podor to Bakel road is reached by an unmade track which crosses the bitumen highway and continues on to the town of Linguère on the Ferlo River. Joining the main highway and continuing upstream, the road follows the course of the Senegal River another 100 miles (160 km) to the town of **Bakel**.

The far east: Bakel is an historic town and lies near the junction of the borders of Senegal, Mauritania and Mali in the far east. Originally the inhabitants formed part of the vast Ghana Empire which spread across a major part of West Africa. Later, the invasions of **River Region mosque.**

Malinké tribes into the southern Casamance region originated in the area of Bakel. This left the township rather depleted until reoccupied by a mixture of Sarakholé and Bambara peoples.

From 1690 the entire region came under the rule of the Boundou branch of Islam. University towns were set up throughout the area linked to those of Fez and the Grand Mosque city of Tlemcen in Morocco and Algeria. These included Bakel and towns in what is now western Mali. Despite the great military strength of the Islamic rulers, the French were able to take the town of Bakel in 1819 and establish an outpost under a treaty with the local chief.

The French forces began to organise a system of commercial traffic with barges on the river, building a fort overlooking the waterway in 1847. Louis Faidherbe, who became Governor of the French West African territories in 1854, visited the town three years later and organised the construction of much more substantial fortifications, including the installation of a gunboat to protect shipping and ward off an attack by Omar Saidou. The great *marabout* of the Sarakholé ethnic group, Mamadou Lamin, in 1885 laid siege to Bakel but was shot outside the fort. Retreating to Kayes, in Mali, Lamin died of his wounds and the town returned to rule under the French for another five years.

Strategically located at the head of the Senegal River, not far from its confluence with the Falémé, Bakel represents the terminus for commerical river traffic. This historic town has a number of colonial houses worth a visit and several attractive mosques. Still well-preserved after Faidherbe expanded the original structure, the fortress is an impressive building on the bluffs overlooking the river.

Bakel fort is the third most important of Senegal's ancient fortresses. One cannot, however, look around the old fort as it is now occupied by the Prefect of Bakel. One splendid relic which can be viewed is that of the grand pavilion

Two generations on the river. Following pages: *pirogue* **crossing in front of Bakel fort.**

built by the explorer René Caillé. Constructed on a spur of rock dominating the river similar to the location of the fort, the 1819 pavilion became the stopping-over point for the military commanders Dupont and Dusseault.

The major expedition through Bakel was the first attempt by Caillé to reach legendary Timbuktu. Travellers will never forget the imposing sight of the fort and pavilion outlined against a Saharan sunset but they will have to make do with the very basic accommodation provided by the administration for visitors.

At the fort, which dates from about 1820, enquire about temporary accommodation from the Préfecture should there be no room in the *campement* nearby. There is no hotel in Bakel. Before leaving the town, if one is travelling by road, make sure to fill up with petrol at the station near the marketplace as the next town, **Kidira**, is 40 miles (64 km) away on a rough unsurfaced road. There is an airport at Bakel, served by the River Airline.

Kidira, around 400 miles (640 km) upstream from St Louis, is a crossroads which few travellers reach. Many adventurous travellers drive up the bitumen highway from St Louis only as far as Bakel where the tarmac road ends. The condition of the road from Bakel to Kidira is unpredictable and varies at different times of the year.

The only reason that Kidira survives is that it is built on the Dakar to Bamako railway. It is therefore the easternmost railway station in Senegal and the first stop for traders and visitors entering the country from Kayes, in Mali, or from further east.

Although Kidira is an important crossroads it offers no accommodation to travellers. The nearest hotel is almost 120 miles (200 km) west, in **Tambacounda**. Kidira and **Naye** are about 400 miles (640 km) east of Dakar and there are two trains a week. For faster access to the capital, it is easier to take the train from Kidira to Tambacounda and fly on the weekly plane to Dakar.

DJOURBEL AND FERLO REGIONS

This area lies between the Atlantic coast and the northern section of the Senegal River. Mainly arid with sparse vegetation, the **Djourbel** region forms the heart of Senegal's groundnut producing zone. The **Ferlo**, named after the **Ferlo River**, a tributary of the Senegal, is a belt of desert bisected by the river which runs through its valley and links with the string of lakes which include the Lac de Guiers.

The district known as the Djourbel includes part of the Ferlo desert and extends to within 45 miles (70 km) of both Dakar to the west and St Louis in the north. Locals call the western part of the Djourbel region **Baol**, as the area was once an ancient kingdom of that name. Today Baol, on the edge of the Sahel, is the country's richest source of peanuts and its flat, sandy plains support a variety of wildlife—hyena, gazelle, pheasant and partridge—and several towns, including the region's capital, **Djourbel**.

The Ferlo desert covers one-third of the total area of Senegal, around 27,000 sq. miles (70,000 sq km). The more productive part of the Ferlo is around the lakes and the River Ferlo, which is dry along half of its 300-mile (500-km) length during the winter season. The surrounding desert consists of a vast plain covered in dunes, scattered rocky outcrops and occasional small depressions of clay where waterholes form.

Between the Atlantic shores and the Ferlo Valley is the district of **Louga**, named after its main town. It is from Louga that most visitors travel into the Ferlo region, as an important highway and a railway links St Louis to **Linguère**, the Ferlo's main township, through Louga. Another major road and rail route links the town with Dakar. Louga is also a major producer of groundnuts, generating 10 percent of the nation's total income from the crop. Apart from the Grande Côte area of the region, Djourbel and the Ferlo are completely land-locked.

The peanut capital: The major town of Djourbel has a population of 50,000, of mainly Wolof origin, and is located 90 miles (145 km) east of Dakar on the northern banks of the **Siné River**. An important crossroads, Djourbel is located on the main railway and highway which links Dakar with Tambacounda in eastern Senegal and ultimately with Bamako in the Republic of Mali.

Apart from being the hub of the peanut production district and thus having the nickname of "Senegal's groundnut capital", the town is a major marketplace. Food production and processing are supplementary industries to groundnut collection while the local craftsmen draw customers from as far away as Dakar.

Outstanding among the craft workers is the local celebrity Sheikh Diop, a master of the art of bronze sculpting. Diop's favourite subjects, the ancient kings of Senegal, are among the most sought-after souvenirs of the country.

Preceding
pages:
Sahelian
sunset with
baobabs.
Left,
climbing the
groundnut
mountain.
Below, Peul
woman on
mobile
home.

They are created by the old method of "lost wax" moulding and the resulting casts are hand-finished, producing a unique artefact each time.

The wood carving booths in Djourbel's marketplace and its Centre Artisanale are favourite attractions with visitors and souvenir hunters, as are the stalls selling exquisite local embroidery. Leatherwork and gold and silver jewellery are also produced in the market and paintings with the common theme of the exploits of the national hero Lat Dyor make decorative, if bulky, reminders of a visit to Senegal.

As Djourbel is an important religious centre, the main mosque is one of the town's most spectacular structures. Its pinkish dome makes an impressive sight set in groves of deep green palm trees and from the balcony which surrounds the minaret one can get a fine view of the town and its surroundings. Pilgrims converge on Djourbel during the annual pilgrimage to nearby **Touba**, when the town's population doubles. The date of the pilgrimage, or *Grand Magal*, is around the 10th day of the 11th month of the Islamic calendar and devotees of the Mouride sect cling to every form of transport possible in order to travel to Djourbel and thence to the sacred town of Touba.

In the months apart from *Grand Magal*, accommodation can be found at the Hotel Le Baobab. Set in parkland and with its own swimming pool, the hotel and its spacious, traditionally decorated restaurant, is a haven from the bustling streets. Sixteen rooms with air-conditioning, five without, a discothèque and shops make this a welcome stopover for the visitor who has experienced the twice-a-week train ride from Dakar.

The trip takes around three hours and leaves Dakar mid-morning. Traders carrying market wares can cram the train hours before it departs. The journey, once a seat has been secured, is comfortable, with a dining car—provided the train is Senegalese. As the railway connects Dakar with Bamako, Malian trains, which are much less

Groundnut sorting by hand.

242

comfortable, also use the line. The Senegalese train generally leaves Dakar on Wednesdays, but nothing is guaranteed and it is always best to check with station staff a day in advance.

The best way to reach Djourbel is by train as the route from Dakar, although a bitumen road, is busy, dusty and a tiring six-hour drive. A regular bush-taxi service links Djourbel with the capital, but there is no air service.

There is little to visit in the immediate vicinity of Djourbel. One possibility is the agricultural research establishment at **Banbey**, 14 miles (23 km) west, on the Dakar highway. Experiments are conducted here to develop new hardier species of vegetables and fruit suitable for the increasingly arid conditions. The encroachment of the sands of the Sahel has demanded technical advances in irrigation and crop management, which the centre is also researching.

Touba, desert shrine: In the centre of the ancient kingdom of Baol and just 30 miles (50km) north of Djourbel, **Touba** can be reached by road or rail. Both routes run through the town of M'Backé which has the only accommodation along the way. Touba has a large campsite, run by the Mourides, which is only opened during the period of the pilgrimage. Also during the religious celebration one may find that the local people open their houses to visitors. In M'Backé, three miles (five km) before Touba on the main highway, there is a permanent campsite.

During the pilgrimage, both towns celebrate through the night. In Touba the ceremonies are more reserved and religious and most strangers therefore tend to stay in M'Backé, making the short trip to Touba during the day. Touba is also an important crossroads and a rail terminal, around which a large marketplace has grown. Most important by far of Touba's functions, though, is its role as the Mourides' religious centre. The Great Mosque's towering minaret is the tallest in the country—87 metres high.

If a foreigner desires to visit the town during pilgrimage, it is advisable to

Northern cattle traders.

DESERT DRIVING

More than a third of Senegal is desert and a good part of the rest of the terrain is laterite rock and sandstone through which tracks have been carved. At times these routes can be impassable because of rain which has created gorges and pot-holes—and sometimes landslides which have obliterated the tracks completely.

Not all of Senegal is so daunting to the motorist. In fact, the country has an excellent network of good, surfaced roadways between its major urban centres. Nearly 2,000 miles (3,200 km) of asphalt roads link all the main towns and more than 10,000 laterite roads support the network. However, it is in the outlying regions of open desert and the sandy central plateau where one is likely to run into some difficulties.

This is not to discourage drivers from touring Senegal by car, merely to remind the inexperienced that care and planning are necessary. Plenty of intrepid travellers nowadays take the trans-Sahara route from North Africa, including an increasing number of organised trips and of smaller amateur versions of the Paris-Dakar Rally.

In terms of choice of vehicle, you will presumably be limited either by the fact that you already have a car or by the choice of hire vehicle available. The best cars are obviously the most rugged. Peugeots are very popular in Africa and so spares are relatively easily obtained, but a number of Japanese marques are well established. Hot climate specifications—which usually comprise extra air filters, reinforced suspension and steering, and sump guards for the engine—are desirable, as is four-wheel drive, though the latter is not vital.

The list of equipment needed for desert driving is a long one: an oil temperature gauge, towing cable, lock on the petrol cap. laminated windscreen and replacement kit, car compass, jump leads, a full set of tools, an extra spare wheel, corrugated metal track lengths for sand-driving, a powerful hand lamp for night-driving, footpump, first-aid kit, a jack (particularly one with a wide base plate), puncture repair kit and tyre levers,

replacement spark plugs, fan belt and extra filters.

Petrol, water and oil are life-savers in desert driving. Make sure all petrol tanks, plus a reserve, are topped up at every available opportunity. Petrol may not be available even if the map indicates so; garages and petrol stations listed may have gone out of business or even have run out of stock. Water will be needed both for the radiator and for human consumption. In desert conditions the human body consumes eight to nine pints (five litres) of water a day, without any strenuous activity.

A larger than normal quantity of oil should be carried and, because of the climatic conditions in which the engine is being asked to perform, regular cooling-off stops should be taken. Make sure to identify the locations of all water and petrol stops by means of a good map and try to confirm this information by asking along the road. The best maps are those produced by the Institut Géographique National, Michelin, or Esso.

On the road, the heat of the day should be taken into account, as should the fact the darkness falls quickly. Dehydration is a common hazard and can occur stealthily. The head and neck should be protected from the direct rays of the sun. Large quantities of fluid and increased salt intake is the best way to avoid, or to cure, heat exhaustion. Rest is also important and therefore it is best to judge distances and driving stamina carefully. A second driver is desirable when covering long distances. Most people prefer to travel in a convoy of at least two vehicles.

If possible, it is wise to take a local guide. In the event of a breakdown, stay with the vehicle, flag down passing assistance but be watchful over possessions when it is being rendered. Sound your horn when approaching an oncoming vehicle, or flash your lights repeatedly in night conditions to warn other drivers.

When driving in sand, the trick is to maintain sufficient speed to get through loose patches without becoming bogged down. If you do, however, either reduce the air pressure in the tyres to increase traction or, better still, lay metal sand tracks (which you should include in your equipment list) in front of the driven wheels, having first dug the sand away from around them.

seek the permission of the Grand Caliph. A small gift is customary when introduced to the Caliph; once his blessing has been received, one is free to wander at leisure through the sacred city. Remember that one must remove one's shoes before entering any mosque and that smoking or drinking in Touba during Magal will not be tolerated.

The nearest accommodation east of Touba is at **Ranch de Doli**, a hunting/birdwatching lodge in the centre of the Ferlo desert region and almost 60 miles (100km) from the town. To get to Doli, one takes the main, surfaced road north towards **Dara**, turning off after about three miles on to a wide, dusty track. Sufficient water, food and petrol should be procured before venturing on to the desert roads and the best place to buy such supplies is at M'Backé. The rest houses at Doli are clean but basic.

From the ranch, trips can be made out into the wilderness where the parched, barren landscape supports gazelles, partridges, guinea fowl, buzzards and vultures. The thorn scrub, drifting

dunes and odd baobab tree allow few settlements to survive, but the ranch guides make a detour in the day's itinerary to visit one of the isolated villages, **Velingara**, which makes a meagre living from the desert and is situated on the Siné River headwaters.

In the opposite direction to Ranch de Doli, a bitumen road links Touba to the main Dakar-St Louis rail and road route at **Mekhé**. This road runs through acres of groundnut fields, baobab and palm groves and several small villages. Great piles of groundnuts can be seen at the village collecting station of **Darou-Mousti**, a typical Wolof village on the crossroads with the road to the railway station and market town of **Kébémer**.

Most villages of this plateau region are similar in design; just a short distance north, excursions can be made to the villages of **Bodé** or **Darou Ndiaye**. At either of these villages it may be possible to witness traditional Wolof dancing or a colourful and exuberant marriage ceremony.

Wilderness and lakes: Crossing the

Left, desert driving can be lonely. *Below*, take-away mutton kebab.

edge of the Ferlo desert by driving due north from Touba, the groundnut fields soon give way to sandy wasteland and rocky outcrops through which the well-surfaced road cuts a dark band.

This is the N3 highway which runs almost 150 miles (250km) from Dakar to Linguère on the banks of the Ferlo River. About 45 miles (70km) north of Touba the road joins another large highway and the railway at **Dara**, an important centre for the cattle herders who eke a nomadic existence from the Ferlo region.

Linguère, 30 miles (50km) further east, is a larger town as it is not only at the end of the metalled road from Dakar and St Louis, but is also the terminus for the rail routes from both cities. The town's layout is interesting in that the residential district is set up high on craggy rocks, the administrative and commercial centres are located in the middle of the town and its popular quarter is positioned right at the bottom, near the river. There is a very well-run *campement*-hotel at Linguère which is

used as a base for hunting and wildlife-watching.

In passing through Dara, the traveller might have noticed the Zoological Research Station which specialises in wildlife conservation. Individuals from this establishment sometimes act as guides for wildlife safari parties visiting the Ferlo from Linguère. Set tours out of the town take in a number of local villages which are particularly interesting as this is the region of the nomadic Peuls who build tiny, round mud huts miles from any visible source of water or vegetation. Typical of these villages are **Barkedji**, **Dioumanan**, **Yonoféré**, and **Fourdou**, and the town of **Ranérou**, about 90 miles (150km) east on the Linguère-Matam road.

Gaunt cattle: As one travels progressively further into the Ferlo region, the occasional villages appear more and more poverty-stricken and the advancing sands of the Sahara dominate the skyline. Little herds of gaunt, humped cattle with huge horns wander great distances in search of fodder in the dusty Ferlo valley as the Ferlo River, east of Linguère, disappears underground for many months of the year during the dry season.

Hunting trips from the town frequent the scrubland around **Yang Yang** village along the **Bounoum River** north of Linguère or the watercourse of the **Suré River** to the east. North of Linguère the waters of the Ferlo River meander to the west along a well-established valley towards the long string of lakes which link with the great Lac de Guiers and which eventually flow into the Senegal River near Richard Toll.

Scant tracks follow the course of the Ferlo. But, if one wants to explore further down river from Linguère, the best thing to do is to hire one of the little *pirogues* which ply the river from the town's small jetty. The easiest way to see the lakes of the Ferlo basin, however, is by taking a tour either from Louga or Richard Toll. Most of the regular excursions follow routes as far south as the lakeshore village townships of **Merinaghen.**

Left, horseman in the Ferlo. Right, ancient but elegant Ferlo door.

THE LITTLE COAST

Lying an hour's drive from Dakar in the shelter of Cap Vert, the scenic beaches of the **Petite Côte** stretch southwards for 75 miles (120 km). With a stunning coastline, idyllic climate and a number of good modern hotels, the "Little Coast" is a magnet for sun lovers with a hankering for little adventure.

With calmer waters than its counterpart, the "Grande Côte", to the north of Dakar, the Petite Côte draws thousands of visitors. Shimmering white beaches along the foam-edged Atlantic coastline are cooled by constant tradewinds and shaded by towering cocoa palms and lofty kapok trees. A short distance from the spectacular shore, excursions can be made into typically African forest. Boat trips can be made out into the ocean, where deep blue waters teem with a bewildering variety of fish.

Most of the Petite Côte's inhabitants live along the shore and are fisherfolk—a fact indicated by the hundreds of *pirogues* which line the wide sandy beaches. The majority of the population lives in the coast's five main towns, **La Somone**, **Saly Portudal**, **M'Bour**, **Nianing** and **Joal**. The people are mainly from the Serer or Lébou tribes and this area is predominantly Christian. Portuguese and French influence can be seen everywhere in the form of Catholic churches, missions and schools. Léopold Senghor, who was born on the Petite Côte, is a Catholic, a member of the Serer tribe and was educated at the Catholic mission school in Joal.

Crags and beach clubs: Access to the beaches is via the N1 road south through **Rufisque**. A regular coach service operates to most of the townships along the coast. The N1 is a major highway as it connects the capital with both the Transgambia Highway and the main route east to Mali. Just over 25 miles (40 km) from Dakar, at Bounga, there is easy access to the cliff-encircled beaches of **Yenne**, **Niangol** and

Nougouna. For a day's excursion these beaches make an excellent diversion from the bustle of Dakar but, at the weekends, most of the capital's inhabitants seem to be of the same mind.

There are a couple of villages nearby although both are approached by separate roads. The first, **Toubab Dialao**, is noted for its spectacular setting. In contrast to the rest of the Petite Côte, Toubab Dialao's beaches are bounded by steep cliffs of red rock. At sunset these craggy backdrops reflect a range of colours from bright orange to deep crimson and bathe the little fishing beach in shades of red.

One has to return to the highway to reach **Popenguine**, just a few kilometres along the coast. It is possible to walk along the beach from Toubab Dialao to Popenguine for a visit of a few hours. There is little to see in this village of around 1,000 people, although it does contain the first substantial hotel, the Pelican, on the coast after Dakar. Popenguine, however, is the centre of a religious pilgrimage and has also been

Preceding pages: Layène Muslims worshipping at Yoff. **Left,** the bridge of Fadiouth. **Right,** empty beaches can still be found.

chosen as one of the President's residences. Each Whit Monday, a procession sets out from the little church and makes its way towards a cleft in a nearby cliff. This is the site of the "Miraculous Grotto" where devotees pray to a statue of the Black Virgin. It is believed that, at this spot, the image of the Virgin Mary appeared to a group of fishermen.

The road from Popenguine joins the N1 at **Sindia** and one should continue to **Nguekokh** in order to visit the beaches and villages of La Somone, Ngaparou and Saly Portudal. The next permanent holiday establishment along this coastline is the **Village-Hotel of Hippocampe** at La Somone about 46 miles (75 km) south of Dakar. Somone is also a popular weekend attraction for the capital's workers. The Hippocampe has a traditionally decorated restaurant and bar and offers excursions in *pirogues* and horse riding treks along the beach or in the countryside.

Pirogue trips can be taken on the little river which runs through Somone and

comes down from the hills between the coast and Thiès. Where the river joins the sea, a blanket of mangroves around its mouth harbours a variety of wildlife from flamingo to pelicans. On a cruise upstream, the scenery changes to high-galleried forest and the river narrows as the vegetation shades its slow-moving waters.

Birds and baobabs: For ornithologists, there is an extensive bird sanctuary at Somone. Water sports enthusiasts can hire nautical equipment from the **Village du Baobab**. This 200-bed bungalow village also offers fishing excursions, rents out *pirogues* and has its own nightclub. Le Baobab has an elegant restaurant decorated to suit the traditional fishing ambience and the menu is suitably fish-oriented.

Saly Portudal, often shortened to Saly, linked to Somone by a coastal road, was one of the earliest Portuguese slave trading posts in the country. The 17th-century site is now a small town. The **Palm Beach** hotel is rated one of the most luxurious on the coast.

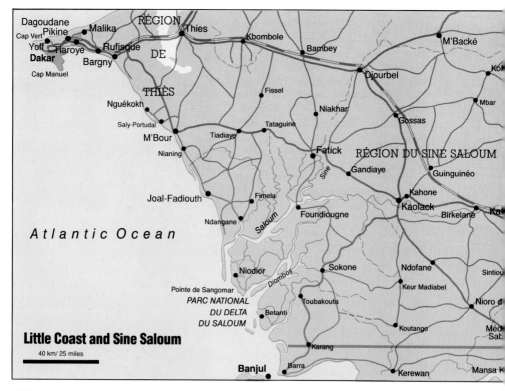

Little Coast and Sine Saloum

40 km/ 25 miles

Brilliant flowering hibiscus and oleander add splashes of colour at every corner, while cocoa palms tower over a large pool and fringe the tennis courts.

The four main hotels on the Saly Portudal beach provide horses, buggys, diving equipment and all manner of watersports. The **Novotel Club**, typical of the modern facilities, has video rooms, a theatre and a night club. The **Savana Koumba**, the second largest hotel on this beach, has an almost Olympic-size swimming pool. All the hotels organise excursions to places of interest such as the market at M'Bour a few kilometres away, or to the **Siné-Saloum** delta region in the south.

Located in the heart of the "Little Coast", **M'Bour** is the main port. This town of around 4,000 people lies just over 50 miles (80 km) south of Dakar. The township dates from the period when the French settlers began to push the Serer tribes south towards the Siné-Saloum district. The colonial leader, Pinet-Laprade, finally gained control of the entire area in 1859 and established a military zone around M'Bour which quickly evolved into a busy fishing port.

All around the port region, which is the life and soul of the town, fish-drying sheds and smoke houses for preserving the catches give the dockside a powerful aroma to which one slowly becomes accustomed. This odour is common around all the villages along the coast as the Serer people's livelihood comes from the sale of dried and smoked fish.

Fishing opportunities: Deep-sea fishing trips can be arranged through agents in Dakar or directly through most of the hotels on the coast. A day's trip usually commences at 8 a.m. and returns at 4 p.m. Where the warm Guinea current meets the cold current of the Canaries, migrating fish can be caught in large numbers. Twenty-two of the larger fish to be caught in these waters are now recognised by the Game Fishing Association of Florida and at least 30 other game fish are prevalent. Swordfish, blue marlin, tunny, sea bass, wahoo, capitaine, yellowfin, sailfish,

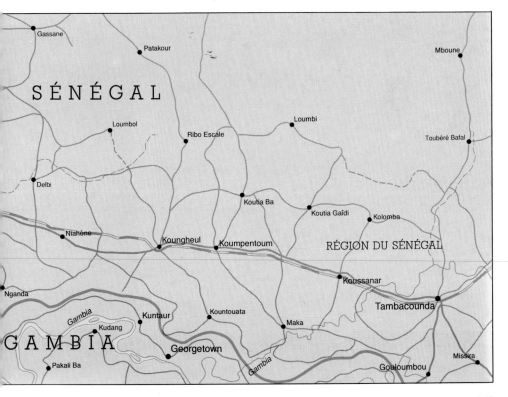

bigeye, squalus, dolphin, barracuda, sawfish, blackfin, skipjack, a number of shark including hammerhead, and rays of all sorts—even the massive sunfish—have all been caught off this coast.

The boats available carry four to six passengers and provide meals and refreshments on board. Most are well equipped with VHF radio, outriggers, downriggers, electronic depth sounders and even fish finders. With all this sophisticated equipment on board, it is an interesting comparison to meet up with a fishing *pirogue* several miles out into the Atlantic Ocean which has no more advanced technology than 20 good oarsmen.

If one is adventurous, it is possible to go out in the *pirogues* of the local fishermen or to hire a *pirogue* with crew for a private expedition. Tourism is now having its effect on the traditional occupations of M'Bour's inhabitants and many craft stalls have been recently introduced. From the hotels of Saly Portudal, visitors come on day excursions to M'Bour port and beaches and organised tours can regularly be seen wandering through the lines of fishing craft on the beach or photographing the wooden racks used for curing fish.

There are two hotels in M'Bour. The **Relais 82** has only six rooms but maintains a delightful restaurant specialising in local dishes. The **Centre Touristique de la Petite Côte** is located near the Prefecture and has 90 rooms, most with air-conditioning. It has a family atmosphere and is situated in a prime spot on the beach with simple bungalows located in a park-like area. At M'Bour the N1 highway branches away from the coast towards **Fatick**; the road that continues along the beaches is the N2.

Six miles (10 km) south of M'Bour is the delightfully isolated beach resort of Nianing, location of a large holiday village, the **Club Aldiana**, which has 300 bungalow-style rooms—all air-conditioned and with picture-book views across the beach or over the

Fish-smoking by the sea.

swimming pool. Between the Atlantic Ocean and the **Marigot de Nianing**, Club Aldiana is on the edge of an impressive forest where an amazing variety of birdlife can be observed. Set in parkland and surrounded by tall baobab trees, coconut and other palms, the **Domaine de Nianing** has 100 rooms in bungalows.

A delightful alternative to the beach is browsing in the village craft markets or those set up on the roadside near resort hotels. One can find exquisite carvings from a variety of African hardwoods, ebony, mahogany, sapele, afromosia or iroko. Basketwork from local bamboo and reeds, raffia work-woven baskets and hats made from the fibres of the raffia palm, fish baskets and even woven armchairs all make excellent purchases which are light to carry home.

Crocodile, snake or monitor skin belts and handbags should be purchased with caution as these skins come under strict regulations both for exportation and importation (into your own country). Ivory, tortoise and turtle shell items also come under strict control, but objects made from bone or horn are exempt. Pottery objects are also easily transported home, as are the delicately-wrought items of gold and silver. Cast bronze objects may also be found in the specialist markets.

The joy of Joal: South of M'Bour, about 70 miles (115 km) from Dakar, is the small town of **Joal**. The tarmac road ends here and if one travels further it is on a new road constructed from the shells of oysters, mussels and cockles. Joal has a history which goes back to the Portuguese occupation of the 15th century. The port was one of several which Portuguese traders used after acquiring them from the Dutch. A wide main street dominates the town with its population of around 5,000 and its rows of mouldering colonial houses which date from the middle of the 19th century. A house of particular interest is the one in which Léopold Sédar Senghor was born in 1906.

The setting of Joal, across the water

One-humped beach buggies.

from **Fadiouth Island**, is picturesque and there are also interesting sights in the surrounding countryside. Around Joal the great mounds of dry earth known as *tanns* are used as defences against the sea, bolstered by huge banks of sun-bleached shells some eight metres wide. Giving the scene a somewhat desolate look, hundreds of ancient gaunt baobabs are the only life to survive on the heaped shells and arid soil. These barren areas give the region a ghostly atmosphere which is even more pronounced around the fishermen's graveyards.

Accommodation is limited in Joal but **Le Finio**, which is thought to be an Africanisation of the French word for "the end", has 10 rooms, and its traditional restaurant serves high quality Senegalese dishes. Specialities include grilled mutton, lobster, giant shrimps, spicy chicken and the region's famous oysters—available from November to June. On the outskirts of Joal, where the bridge links the mainland with Fadiouth Island, there is a tiny Catholic mission run by nuns.

The village of **Fadiouth** is of considerable interest and most visitors cross the narrow stretch of water to it via the footbridge, although one can take a little *pirogue*. Constructed on an island made entirely of sea shells accumulated over many centuries Fadiouth is unusual for the lifestyle of its inhabitants and the isolation of the settlement. Held together by the roots of mangroves, reeds and the giant baobabs, Fadiouth Island is picturesque even though the environment and setting is a little grotesque. The houses are made of the same discarded shells and pounded shells make a kind of cement from which the fishermen form their small round huts.

The *pirogues* which ply the narrow channel between Joal and the settlement are the same as those which take the fishermen out to sea, while smaller canoes are used by the shellfish collectors who paddle through the creeks. On the gangling roots of the mangrove the oysters can be seen

View of the cemetery, Fadiouth.

hanging in black festoons like giant barnacles and it is these that the women gather, standing almost waist-deep in the muddy waters with wicker baskets in one hand, holding their canoes by a short line. The ancient island is partly surrounded by mangrove and on the other side there are coconut palms and shallows where the settlements have been built.

Six thousand people live and work on the island. Whitened heaps of empty shells lie everywhere. And there are blackened patches on the earth where the women have burned the shells in order to make them into a powder for use as paint for daubing the palm wood beams inside their conical huts. On the side of the island where the coconuts grow, the clusters of huts which are set over the water on coco-wood piles, with pointed roofs ending in top-knots, are used as grain stores for the staple diet, millet. The reason for these millet and groundnut stores being built in such a way is to protect the crops from vermin and to economise on the acute lack of building space anywhere on the island.

From Fadiouth, the shoreline extends south for 25 miles (40 km) to the **Pointe de Sangomar**, a long, thin spit of sand and dunes without any road access. The Pointe de Sangomar acts as a barrage which protects the **Siné** and **Saloum** river deltas from the Atlantic Ocean. Instead of trying to continue south from Joal-Fadiouth, where the N2 road terminates, some visitors prefer to make a round trip to M'Bour by following the shell road on to Ndangane, turning north by **Fumela**, **Séssène** and **Tiadaiye** to the Dakar road at M'Bour. This route cuts across the western edge of the Siné-Saloum delta and offers an interesting change of scenery from the white sandy stretches of the Little Coast.

The entire circuit is more than 180 miles (300 km) and can be comfortably explored in two or three days by making stops at M'Bour, Joal, or even at **Ndangane** where there is accommodation provided in 10 basic cabins at the **Campement de Djiffer**.

All hands to the nets.

THE SINÉ-SALOUM

North of the Gambia and almost twice its size, the Siné-Saloum region is named after the two major rivers which cross this extensive area. The extreme southern part of the region, near the Gambian border, can be reached from an unreliable track inside the Gambia. Roads do run south from the Kaolack-Tambacounda Highway, but, due to the prolonged dry season and short, sharp, heavy rains, parts of these trails can double as river gorges in places. Of the most frequented region around the estuaries of the two rivers, it is the more southerly Saloum delta which is best supplied with tourist accommodation.

North of the Saloum: Arriving by *pirogue* on the **Pointe de Sangomar** at **Djiffer**, one can't help regretting the presence of a sand-processing factory in such a pleasant location. To screen the **Hôtel de Thiès** from the scenes of industry, a large number of trees—cocoa palms, eucalyptus and others—have been planted nearby.

Among the many little villages which can be visited in the area are **Diakhanor** and **Palarin**. This area is most picturesque, both for the way the villages are constructed—often on ancient banks of shells—and for the pointed-topped rice stores built on stilts away from the rising waters.

The Siné-Saloum is rich in bird and animal life. Meandering over flat areas, doubling back in creeks and bolongs and widening into lake-like estuaries, the two waterways, plus the expansive Gambia River, form one enormous delta. Hundreds of mudflats, sandbars and vast areas of mangrove have provided an ideal habitat for a rich variety of birdlife.

In the mangroves, osprey can be seen wheeling over the fish-stocked waters while, in the northern, more desert region, buzzards search for reptiles. The two areas are in complete contrast, but it is the delta region which attracts the ornithologist and wildlife enthusiast. This coast has been the subject of much

ecological study as it is feared that the coastal defences of naturally formed mud banks and the vegetation which binds the banks together are slowly being eroded both by the forces of nature and by man, who has cut down many trees for firewood.

Among the gangling roots of mangroves white storks wade in shallows, searching out frogs and swimming snakes. On higher land, further up-river, shrikes ("butcher birds") impale their catches—from grasshoppers to small rodents—on the sharp prongs of thornbush.

Sometimes dolphins can be seen surfacing in the estuarine waters of the Saloum and flocks of great white egrets vie with solitary black cormorants for small river bass, eel and gobis. Palm plantations provide perfect cover for a colourful assortment of brilliant birds such as the violet starling, golden bishop, orange-cheeked waxbill and a variety of bee-eaters.

The opportunity to sight some of the giants of the air is also available to

Preceding pages: Mouride Muslims tending groundnut fields. Left, sorting nuts from the haff. Right, a pirogue on the river.

visiting ornithologists: the palm nut vulture, a large black-and-white bird, the West African harrier hawk, Verreaux's eagle owl, the shikra, or, the greatest coup of all, the huge long-crested hawk eagle. Many visitors come across the border from the Gambia or down from Dakar to witness the flights of enormous flocks of rosy spoonbills on the wide estuaries or to photograph hordes of migrating storks and pelicans.

This is one place where a good field guide to West African birdlife, a pair of binoculars and a camera are essential. Local villagers may also be able to direct the enthusiast to some of the region's interesting bird and animal life.

No very large creatures inhabit the Siné-Saloum, apart from the three varieties of crocodile—the pygmy, the bottlenose and, largest of all, the Nile crocodile. There are said to be several families of rarely sighted hippopotami and a number of dugongs, or manatees, in the saline waters. Journeying by boat through the maze of waterways, one can sometimes see a school of dolphins join the wake of the craft or dive across the *pirogue's* bows.

On land, the largest animals are the river (or bush) hogs, which should be treated with great respect. Python here often grow to considerable size, although the forest deer which sometimes venture into the mangroves are rarely bigger than a small dog. Monkeys—green, vervet, colobus, patas, or red—are among the largest mammals. Occasionally, tribes of baboons can be seen holding council under roadside trees—a rare excitement.

The dark, pod-like appendages festooning the exposed roots of the mangroves are a variety of oyster, a delicacy in this region. Walkways constructed between settlements across shallows are usually built of mud surfaced and strengthened with the shells of oysters. On the black mudbanks, the thousands of small holes are the burrows of sand and fiddler crabs which will emerge in their hundreds if one keeps still. Mud skippers, with adapted front fins, walk across the banks from pool to pool and

Sidewater o **the Saloum.**

may even be seen climbing the mangrove roots.

Foundiougne and further: At **Foundiougne** the holiday village of **Les Piroguiers** offers good, basic accommodation and tours on the river and through its creeks, reed beds and waterways. The complex has 60 rooms in a setting on the banks of the Saloum. From here, one can visit the little fishing villages of **Dionevar** and **Niodior**, where very simple tourist accommodation is available. These villages are built on islands in the winding estuary waters facing the long sand spit of **Sangomar**.

Regular ferries, four a day, leave from Foundiougne to link with the main road into Dakar. The boat also takes in stops at the villages of Dionevar, Niodior and **Ndangane**, terminating at the town of **Kaolack**.

Opposite Foundiougne, across the wide arm of the Siné River delta, is the village of Ndangane. Not easily reached, Ndangane lies on a remote bolong towards the north built on a peninsula with good fishing grounds on both sides. Many fishing craft gather here and, apart from the tours of the small village and its surroundings, there is the opportunity to trek south along a lengthy spit of land inhabited by large numbers of waders, ducks and other wildfowl. At Ndangane, the **Pelican Hotel** provides 60 comfortable rooms in comparatively basic conditions, although the wildlife here more than compensates for the lack of luxury accommodation and one has no doubt as to why the lodge is named "Le Pélican".

South from Foundiougne is the town of **Sokone**, a petrol stop for traffic from Kaolack to Banjul. Few visitors spend long here, as there is little to see, though it is possible to take a *pirogue* trip out to the offshore islands of **Betanti**. Most travellers journey on to the town of **Toubakouta**, another major centre for wildlife enthusiasts, served by the Keur-Saloum village-hotel. A pool, restaurant, bar, air-conditioning in all the bungalows, and fishing trips for barracuda give the place extra attractions. *Pirogue* excursions and hunting

Salt-flats near Kaolack.

trips to **Sangako** and **Medine Djicoye** can be arranged at the lodge.

Another lodge, **Les Palétuviers**, has 40 beds in 20 bungalow-style cabins, a pool and similar diversions to the Keur-Saloum. Les Palétuviers was once known as the Jardin d'Allah hotel but has since been renovated. As the town is located on the **Diombos River**, Toubakouta's 300 inhabitants earn a living ferrying tourists and hunters in their *pirogues* and organising events such as Sunday afternoon wrestling matches and evening dance performances.

Both Toubakouta and Missirah are important locations in the **Parc National du Delta du Saloum** and the region has become a favourite with hunters. The variety of game includes francolin, duck, pheasant and wood pigeon in the large National Hunting Zone, which contains all types of terrain from mangrove to scrub. River transport is available for bird watchers and hunters and there are regular shuttle trips between Toubakouta and Ndangane, via Djiffer and Niodior.

Although there are no scheduled sailing times, the cruise ship *Bou El Mogdad* sometimes makes excursions in the Siné-Saloum waterways, offering the opportunity of viewing the countryside from the comfort of a well-equipped steam vessel instead of from an open *pirogue*. Enquiries about the availability of these cruises should be made through the main hotels in Toubakouta or Kaolack, where the cruises can be joined. Fishing trips on the river, walking treks into the swamplands of the delta region and tours into the inland park regions for birdwatching or hunting can be booked at the Keur-Saloum Hotel or the Hotel Les Palétuviers.

Kaolack and Kaffrine: With around 150,000 inhabitants, **Kaolack** is the largest town of the Siné-Saloum region. The town is an important centre for the exportation of the groundnuts produced throughout the region. The port of Kaolack is also an outlet for the valuable salt which is produced on the outskirts of the town and along the water margins of the Saloum River. Kaolack

Timber-cutting in the Siné-Saloum.

stands on the northern bank of the river just over 110 miles (180 km) south of Dakar. A road runs east to Tambacounda and the Transgambian Highway runs south through the town to cross the Gambia River by the Farafenni ferry.

From Bamako in Mali, trains pass through the town on their way to Dakar and there is an airport on the outskirts of town. Bush taxis make regular trips to Kaolack from Dakar through Thiès and Djourbel, although the more interesting route runs along the **Little Coast** and turns inland at **M'Bour**.

Kaolack has a history of marketing sea salt as well as groundnuts and its main point of architectural interest is its fine marketplace with Sudan-style arcades. The deep river port is now only a shadow of what it was in its colonial heyday but it still takes the large craft which transport the groundnut crop to Dakar and abroad.

The town has two main hotels. The larger and older, Le Dior, provides 35 neat and clean rooms with air-conditioning and six sizeable apartments, each with bath. The helpful receptionist can supply a mass of information on transport and points of interest. There is a small swimming pool, a simply decorated restaurant and a bar which attracts groups of local traders permanently engaged in animated conversations about business.

Le Dior is centrally located, but its competitor, Le Paris, is in a better location to catch any breeze. With only 17 air-conditioned rooms, all with bathrooms, Le Paris is a more homely, family-run hotel. The restaurant, with traditional furnishings, offers some of the best food in town. There is a little bar and a swimming pool for residents. There is another small hotel, Le Napoléon and, a little way from the town, at **Kahone**, a small Tourist Centre also provides basic, safari lodge accommodation.

Few visitors stay long in Kaolack as there are more pleasant and picturesque lodgings on the rivers or the coast. **Kaffrine**, around 36 miles (60 km) east of Kaolack, is a groundnut collection base

Two generations tilling the fields.

and has no accommodation for the visitor and little to see in the town itself. The Saloum River, which runs to the north of Kaffrine, dries up in this arid terrain during the hot months. However, two important sites can be reached by the road that runs south from the town via the village of Nganda. These are the hunting parklands just north of the Gambian border and the prehistoric stone megaliths which are dotted across the countryside between **Nganda** and **Nioro du Rip** to the west.

Nioro du Rip, 36 miles (60 km) from Kaolack, lies on the edge of an officially designated hunting region. A lodge provides safari-type accommodation for the hunters who come to this area for francolin, partridge, guineafowl and other small game. The terrain is harsh and dry with only scrub, thorn bushes and a few gaunt baobab trees giving shelter to the flocks of small birds which survive the arid conditions.

From Kaolack, the hunter can book a day's excursion in the Nioro du Rip park and visitors can take a tour of the

ancient stone circle sites. The usual trek from Kaolack takes the road south through barren, rock-strewn countryside to the large settlement of Nioro du Rip which lies on the Transgambian Highway. The prehistoric sites are to the east of the town and can also be reached from the village of Nganda or from the railway station at **Maleme-Hodar**.

Mysterious stones: Between Nioro du Rip and Nganda the landscape is hilly with red laterite mounds and dust which creates stifling driving conditions. A truck or Land-Rover is essential in this terrain with deep, rain-made gullies and rubble-covered hillocks making driving bumpy and rough. A set route has been mapped out for the explorer visiting the megalith sites of the **Siné Ngayenne**.

The circuit of more than 150 stones is about 30 miles (50 km) long and passes through 10 small villages. Starting from the village of **Firgui**, five miles (eight km) south of Nioro du Rip, the dirt track follows the line of the **Grand Bao** bolong to the first site at **Kabakoto** where there are three circles of red ironstone stele of around a dozen stones each.

Across the bolong and along its south bank on the left of the track there are the remains of a tumulus consisting of 10 stones. A little further on are two curious stones, one button-shaped and one lyre-shaped, the purpose of which continues to defy archaeologists. After the village of **Diala Kouna**, near **Kaymor**, a selection of sites include megaliths set in lines, circles and accompanied by one "button" stone and one massive pentangular stele.

Four more sites are included in the circuit, which re-joins the Transgambian highway near **Keur Katim Diama** on the **Petit Bao** bolong about six miles (10 km) north of the Gambian border. The Universities of Dakar and of Ghana have both excavated in this area and artifacts such as weapons and tools have been recovered and dated to around A.D. 1200. Other sites have been found near Toubakouta, on the **Diombos River** and near **Diouroum**.

Left, kola nut seller. **Right**, trunk of a giant kapoc tree.

THE CASAMANCE REGION

The southern region of Casamance is named after the 200-mile (320-km) river, the area's most important feature. Its many tributaries include the **Dioloulou**, running north almost to the Gambia border, the **Kamobeul Bolong** and the much larger **Soungrougrou**. The entire area is low and much of it waterlogged but it is one of the most attractive and interesting parts of West Africa. Compared with the somewhat more brusque peoples of the North, the inhabitants of Casamance are particularly relaxed, friendly and charming.

The French have likened the swampy areas of the Casamance to the Camargue region of France, where lagoons and marshes harbour spectacular bird and animal life. Certainly, the flat areas of wide waters reflecting the sky-blue heavens are reminiscent of that part of France. The further east one travels along the river, however, the more arid the landscape and the more harsh conditions become.

Temperatures in the Casamance can soar well above 100°F . For about five months of the year no rain falls. When it does, sudden tropical storms bring flooding. Rice, millet, sorghum, maize and groundnuts, together with the fruit of the palm—dates, palm oil and even palm salad—are typical fare of the villages which cling to the life-giving margins of the Casamance.

Almost all the villages along the winding banks of the Casamance rely on the river for sustenance. Perch and catfish, waterline oysters and crabs, prawns and crawfish provide a nourishing and varied diet balanced by wildfowl like goose, duck and teal. Firewood is provided by the mangrove and, further east, the Barbary fig or thorn tree. Living so much in tune with the river, the people of the Casamance are great boatmen and their pride in river skills shows in the elaborate designs of their *pirogues*, or sharp-prowed canoes.

Getting there: There is a daily one-hour flight to **Ziguinchor**, the region's capital town, from Dakar, which sometimes continues to **Cap Skirring**, the main coastal resort. The 16-hour *Casamance Express* steamship excursion departs from Dakar every Friday and returns from Ziguinchor each Monday. The boat has air-conditioned cabins and a restaurant. An eight-day cruise from Dakar to Casamance with a stop-over at **Karabane Island** off the Siné-Saloum delta, is made during the tourist high-season.

From Dakar, one can also drive to Ziguinchor via the Transgambian highway, crossing the Gambia River at the **Farafenni** ferry. This 280-mile (450-km) trip can be covered in one day, but it is more comfortable to take the road via **Kaolack** in Senegal to **Banjul** in the Gambia, crossing the Gambia River on the **Barra** ferry and breaking the journey at one of the Gambia's comfortable hotels. Bush taxis can be taken from Dakar all the way to Casamance.

Ziguinchor, the Casamance's main

Preceding pages: initiation ceremony in Casamance; village on the River Casamance. *Left*, young girl with mongoose. *Right*, church at Karabane.

town, with a population of 80,000, is a river port around 45 miles (70 km) up the Casamance River from the Atlantic Coast. Originally founded in 1560 by Portuguese traders, it was transformed from a trading fort into a prosperous marketplace by the French during the second half of the century.

Ziguinchor is now an attractive town with wide, palm-lined boulevards, elegant French colonial buildings and the bustle of a thriving market. The wide streets lead down to the harbour area from which passenger ferries once departed. Nowadays, the vicinity of the docks is given over to the loading of agricultural produce on to large cargo vessels.

The two arms of the river are crossed by bridges. It takes just an hour to walk around this pleasant town, but one could spend another hour browsing in the famous market. Many traders from Guinea Bissau, the Gambia, North Senegal and even Mauritania haggle over fish, fruit, vegetables, groundnuts, cotton, rice, spices and palm products—as well as an Aladdin's cave of manufactured and imported goods.

The best known market is the **Marché Saint Maur des Fossés,** named after the Northern French town with which Ziguinchor is twinned. The **Artisan Centre** also attracts many visitors looking for souvenirs typical of the region. The Centre's director, Adama Goudiaby, stocks handicrafts from the entire Casamance area, including beautiful Diola sculptures.

Ziguinchor takes its name from the Izguinchors, the indigenous tribe which occupied the region in ancient times. The dominant ethnicities today are the Diola, Mandingo and Tukulor. Woodland tribesmen, such as the shy Balanté, Mandjack and Mankagné from the forests of Bayottes in the south, can also been seen in the markets.

The **Hotel Le Diola**, on the Avenue R. Delmas, has 50 air-conditioned rooms, set in a square facing the swimming pool, with a good locally-decorated restaurant and bar. The less luxurious **Aubert** has 34 air-condit-

Ziguinchor street scene.

ioned rooms, a pool, which is one of the best in West Africa, and features traditional French bourgeois cuisine and African dishes expertly rendered and modified to French culinary practice. The Aubert bar is pleasant and makes good use of tropical plants and flowers to brighten the whitewashed walls and marble-tiled floors.

The **Nema Kadior**, the third top-class hotel, has 48 air-conditioned rooms, its own pool, and no restaurant, although food can be ordered at the bar or from the reception. **L'Escale,** a much smaller and less expensive hotel, is the only establishment in town with a nightclub. It's bright, clean, well-serviced and has 14 air-conditioned rooms and a restaurant where typical Diola dishes can be ordered. Another good eating place is the restaurant in the **Hotel de Tourisme** in the town centre, which has 10 air-conditioned, basically-furnished rooms.

Further out of town, on **Pointe St Georges**, is the **Hôtel-village de la Pointe St Georges**, with a fine restaurant in a rustic setting, excellent pool, tennis courts and 28 chalet-style rooms. Tours of both the northern and southern sectors of Casamance can be organised at the larger hotels and the Pointe St Georges offers it own treks and *pirogue* excursions.

Other tours can be made east up the Casamance River as far as **Kolda**, to coastal resorts such as **Cap Skirring**, in the jungle area to the southwest of Ziguinchor before the Atlantic coast.

South and west: South Casamance can be reached conveniently by bus from Ziguinchor's centre. From **Elinkine**, where the bus terminates, there are several well-trodden excursion tracks. The management at the economical camp at Elinkine will direct you to the estuary of the wide Casamance River where palm and sandy soil give way to thick mangrove, winding bolongs, or creeks, and narrow waterways alive with an extraordinary variety of sea and river birds.

A good trek from Elinkine is the island of **Karabane**, mangrove

Palm wine collector up tree, Casamance.

encircled and reached by small *pirogue* or dugout canoe. On Karabane, near the traditional hutted village, is the site of an ancient, long-deserted colonial settlement. The ruins of an old Breton church can be seen just a short walk from the crumbling remains of the early houses. Karabane has its own campement, giving one time to explore the interesting surroundings of this river village.

There are many tourist circuits through this richly wooded region and the basic lodgings known as *gîtes* are located at Pointe St Georges, **Oussouye** and **Enamporé**.

One very interesting trip, which can be accomplished quite easily in a day, is via the lovely tree-lined rice field track to the famous *impluvia* or reservoirs of Enamporé. Great circular double roofs form funnel shapes over reservoirs where rain water is collected and kept for the dry season. The water system here is unique in Africa, as is the construction of the huts whose main compounds can shelter 50 people as well as their cattle, goats, chicken and grainstore.

On the bend in the Casamance River where the estuary is at its widest is the hôtel-village of Pointe St Georges. Here one can take boat rides out to the numerous islands in the estuary. Both the largest island, Karabane, and the 2,000-strong community of **Niomoune**, have Catholic missions and the four villages on the island of **Hillol—Kanoun**, **Kaoui**, **Kouba** and **Mantat**, are worth visiting in their setting of high forest.

Cap Skirring and the coast: After the exertions of bush or forest, *pirogue* trips and visits to the islands, the fresh sea breezes of the coast are a delight. Cap Skirring is one of Senegal's most famous resorts. One hour's flight from Dakar and 45 miles (70 km) by road from Ziguinchor, the Cape lies almost on the border with Guinea Bissau.

The beautiful coastline is punctuated by sandy bays and rocky outcrops. Fishing villages are dotted from Cap Skirring itself north to **Diembering** and

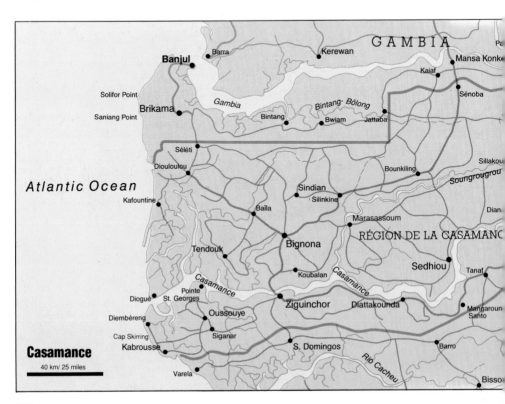

the Casamance estuary. Coconut palms fringe the white sandy beaches and behind the shoreline little tracks lead through palm forest rice fields to palm-thatched villages. The exploitation for tourism of these natural attributes has been carefully monitored by the Senegalese Government. Nonetheless, the major hotel complexes cannot help being the dominant feature of the coastline.

Club Mediterranée runs a 300-bed village-hotel on a prime site at Cap Skirring. It has 266 bungalows, a pool, restaurants, a night club and facilities for tennis and watersports and numerous excursions. **Kabrousse Mossor** is smaller—132 air-conditioned rooms with pool, restaurants, and the usual activities. **La Paillote**, managed by the Hotel Aubert in Ziguinchor, has 34 rooms in small bungalows, and the **Emitai** has just 27 rooms. The smaller hotels, as well as the Kabrousse Mossor, close from mid-May until the end of October.

Other tourist hotels on the Cap Skirring strip range from the 100-room **Savana**, and the luxurious **Kassou-may**, to a number of *gîtes* and camp-sites. Seven miles (10 km) north of Cap Skirring at **Diembering** is a less-developed beach, with palms fringing white sand and Atlantic surf. A 40-bed safari-type hotel offering basic accommodation, the **Aten-Elou**, occu-pies the prime site here and shares the beach with a campsite called **Delmas**.

Most of the activity along this coast is beach-oriented but there is the opportunity to visit local villages or the fishing town of **Kabrousse**, south from Cap Skirring, where the Diola king in 1942 declared war against the French.

The great **National Park of Basse Casamance** is a favourite day's excursion. Thirteen miles (20 km) from Cap Skirring, on the road to Ziguinchor, the Park covers 12,000 acres (5,000 hectares) but has only one overnight base, with 10 rooms and a restaurant, located near the park entrance. If one arrives at the entrance by dawn there is time to make a full tour of the park in

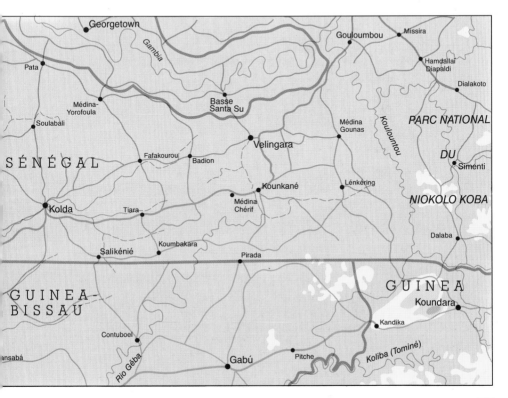

one day. The authorities insist on groups of 10 visitors at a time entering the park and prices have been known to vary. At the exit from the park, there is a Diola settlement where one can purchase souvenirs.

Up-river exploration: As one travels up the Casamance River from Ziguinchor, the waters widen dramatically, becoming almost an inland lake. Wide areas of mangrove swamp and marsh each side of the river become less deep after the junction with the **Soungrougrou**. The banks, however, still clad with almost impenetrable mangrove, become higher in places and one passes the small river villages of **Goudomp** on the south bank and **Tintinkomé** opposite. The river narrows after **Diatakound** and, after a bend in the river, the area administrative centre and town of **Sedhiou** comes into sight on the north bank.

Sedhiou can be reached faster by road from **Bignona** or even Ziguinchor, via the villages of **Diéba** and **Marasassoum**. This route cuts across the Soungrougrou tributary and some quite barren, rocky terrain, with only a few hills and palm groves to break the monotony of the scenery. Because of this, the opportunity to travel by *pirogue* really opens up the landscape and certainly the most interesting route is by river.

Although Sedhiou is more of a village than a town, it is quite one of the most impressive river settlements after Ziguinchor. Colourful *pirogues* line the banks of reddish soil and nets show that the inhabitants depend on the river for a livelihood. The river is still wide, around a mile across at this point. **Sandinière** fishing hamlet can be made out on the southern bank. Wildfowl are fewer but the inevitable cormorants and heron stab at fish from branches and roots caught in the stream.

Back from the river bank a little further on to the right is the French experimental agricultural station and, after several twists and bends, the north bank village of **Mankono** can be seen. The river narrows considerably as it

Central well of a rain-gathering house.

winds east towards **Kolda** which is a main crossroads town for trans-west African trade and has its own airstrip. Above Kolda, the river begins to disappear into the hard rock and sandy desert on the fringes of the great mountains to the southeast. Furthest east of all the settlements on the Casamance is the village of **Fafa-courou**, which is on the main Kolda-Tambacounda Highway.

After this outpost, the real desert encroaches until one reaches the hilly region near **Velingara** where the River Gambia etches its way through deeply incised banks. From one of the most spectacular estuaries on the West African coastline, with vast carpets of lush mangrove swamps brimming with life, the scenery has changed to barren, rocky outcrops jutting from arid desert sand, supporting only the hardiest of elephant grass or palm.

Northward bound: If one takes the shortest road from Dakar to Ziguinchor, via Banjul, **Sélét** is the first village inside the Casamance region. Driving

south from the Gambia, one gets a good idea of the varied landscape of this region. Desert, sparse vegetation and thorn scrub precede areas of marsh, small creeks and bolongs. **Diouloulou** is located on a *bolong* of the same name and at this point the road heads east to Baila, Bignona and Ziguinchor. From Diouloulou, one can visit a typical Diola village compound, or take the track to the coast at **Abané** where a tourist encampment has been established. If one prefers the African *rondavel* to the chalets at Abané, such accommodation can be found further south at **Kafountine**, 20 miles (32 km) from Diouloulou.

Apart from the attraction of the Atlantic coastline, the region is a magnet for ornithologists. A 13-mile (20-km) hike from Kafountine, the **Peninsula of Birds** (Presqu'île des Oiseaux) indicates by its name the importance of this area. The nearest accommodation is the overnight lodge at **Sitokoto**. There are also camping grounds at Sitokoto and Kafountine.

Casamance rice fields.

Around the Forest of Tendouk there are a number of other villages offering accommodation in *gîtes* or basic lodging-houses. **Thionk-Essyl**, a village just north of the forest has such a facility, constructed in the form of a cross of two corridors with two or four-bedroomed huts; this *gîte* is fairly typical of overnight accommodation in the region.

A *pirogue* service from Ziguinchor to **Diatok** stops at **Afiniam**, 20 miles (32 km) on from Thionk-Essyl. There are 40 beds in the Afiniam *gîte*, which is served by local villagers. Continuing along the road from Afiniam, the track returns to the main road at Bignona. This is an important stop-over, being half-way between the border with Gambia and Ziguinchor. The most substantial of the small hotels at Bignona are the **Relais Fleuri** and the **Palmier**.

In the Bignona region, there are several circuits of interest into the **Forest of Kalounayes**, or up to the fishing settlement of **Marasassoum** on

the Sougrougou River. From Marasassoum or nearby **Dieba**, one can head off into virgin countryside, a 30-mile (50-km) trek to Sedhiou on the Casamance River.

South of the Forest of Kalounayes, there is a rest house at **Koubalan**. The circuit from Bignona and along the creek of the same name includes an interesting variety of terrain and wildlife.

From Bignona, the short distance to Ziguinchor is picturesque with high roadside forest alternating with rice fields and village huts with the conical roofs typical of this part of Senegal.

Harvest time is cause for celebration everywhere and in Casamance the two-day festival of *Beweng* is extremely colourful. Sheaves of rice are offered to the gods in the hope that permission will be granted to store the crop. Feathered costumes, beaded and tassel-decked arm and leg-bands, flamboyant head-dresses and flowing garments whirl in organised chaos to the pulsating beat of drums and gourds.

The ceremonies of the Ziguinchor area vary considerably from those celebrated 30 miles (50 km) away in the area of Oussouye nearer the coast. Fire is a part of the dance of initiation occuring during the last week in April, in which the initiate's old personality is ritually burned, releasing a new, more responsible character. In May, the feast of initiation, or *Nity*, is followed by *Zulane*—the feast of the King of Oussouye.

Dances feature prominently in all celebration rituals. *Zumebel*, one of Senegal's most popular spectacles, involves a wrestling contest between young girls. It is held in July. At *Ekonkon*, a festival celebrating fertility and productivity, men and women leap about like acrobats in a spectacular display of their agility. *O Lumata*, which involves trance-inducing drugs and rhythms, occurs at the end of the year, again in the Oussouye region. The ritual dances of *O Lumata* are designed to induce acolytes to communicate with the dead and with gods related to the "great dead" and the "eternal living".

<u>Left</u>, spear-fishing in the river. <u>Right</u>, explosive dance from an initiation ceremony.

SOUTHEASTERN SENEGAL

This region, covering around a fifth of Senegambia, is quite different from the rest of Senegal. Bordered on the east by Mali and on the south by Guinea Bissau, Southeastern Senegal is mostly savanna covered with high "elephant grass". It lies in the shadow of the Futa Djalon mountains between rolling hills and mountain peaks ranging from 1,000 to 1,300 ft (300 to 400 metres) in height.

High, tropical galleried forest carpets the foothills and borders the upper reaches of the three largest rivers which cross the region. The **Falémé River** forms the border with the Republic of Mali and both the **Gambia** and **Niokolo Koba** rivers run through the national park where they are joined by many tributaries, such as the **Nieriko** and **Koulountou**. Parts of the countryside are more like equatorial Africa in their variety of trees and high bush.

To the northeast of the region, however, near the junction of the Falémé with the larger river, the Senegal, the terrain is flat and desert-like. Here, hardy trees such as baobab, shea and thorn survive the sands but nearer the southeastern borders acacia mixes with tall grasses and palms and forest trees become more prevalent. In the mountain regions teak and mahogany are common.

The wildlife of southeast Senegal is also richer than in the rest of the country because of the variety of the landscape and the luxurious vegetation. In the bamboo forests along the river sides and in the high jungle galleries a fascinating variety of bird and animal life abounds. But it is in the **Parc National du Niokolo Koba** that the visitor may find the best selection of the wildlife.

Africa's largest lions: It is in this spectacular park that Africa's biggest mammals find sanctuary. Seventy different species can be found, including elephants. Moving around in small herds, the total number of elephants in the Niokolo Koba region is estimated at 150 to 200. More than 100

lions roam the savannah and tropical grasslands; the particular sub-species living in Niokolo Koba is one of the largest varieties of lion in the continent. Leopards also haunt the plains, lurking among the acacia trees and preying on the numerous antelope. Hyenas, wild dogs and jackals complete the population of the park's carnivorous mammals.

Other smaller mammals inhabiting the wooded river sides range from the little striped ground squirrel to the crested or brush-tailed porcupine. The smaller cats, preferring woodland fringes, are difficult to spot and most evasive in their nocturnal habits; they include the civet, serval and genet.

The grasslands between rivers are a haven for a number of rare antelope including the largest known—the Lord Derby's Eland. Other quadruped species are bushbuck, roan antelope, waterbuck and kob. In total, the number of antelope, including the little duiker, black antelope and gazelle, is estimated at hundreds of thousands. Several

Preceding pages: Bassari initiation ceremony. Left, Bassari matching cap, pin, whistle and cowries. Right, lioness in Niokolo Koba.

thousand buffalo inhabit the parklands and can generally be viewed near river banks or around the numerous waterholes which attract a rich selection of wild game.

Hippopotami and wart-hogs enjoy the mud-wallows around the edge of waterholes and the rivers support many hippo families. Crocodile, particularly the large 'niloticus' which can grow to a length of 10 ft (3½ metres), are common in the rivers where 60 different varieties of fish and aquatic reptiles abound. Seven foot (2 metres) monitor lizards of two metres or so can be seen basking along riverbanks together with small turtles and terrapins, the occasional water snake and colourful butterflies.

Screaming and chattering in the riverbank vegetation and perching high in the ancient silk cotton, mahogany and kapok trees is a fine variety of monkeys. Green vervet, or grivet, monkeys leap in squadrons from tree to tree whilst red colobus perform remarkable aerial feats. Often a local guide will call to these charming creatures and entice them nearer to the camera or binoculars. The lucky observer may catch a glimpse of the few chimpanzees which have been logged among the five species of primates inhabiting the Niokolo Koba Park.

Some of Africa's most prolific birdlife either passes through, or resides in, the Niokolo Koba Park region. More than 300 species have been reported in the varied habitats of the parkland. Over three million migratory birds visit the area each year, feeding off the cross-section of vegetation from piassava palm to the giant baobab trees. Grasslands attract all manner of weaver birds such as the scarlet bishop bird, the buffalo weaver and blue-billed weaver.

The plaited nests of the weaver birds give thorn and silk cotton trees the appearance of Christmas trees. Stork and heron nests are easily spotted along any of the waterways through the parklands and spoonbill can be seen in great flocks on some of the more open expanses of water. The largest nests of **Sunset over the marshes.**

all are the massive platforms built of twigs by the comical hammerkop.

The UNESCO World Heritage Convention has selected the park as a site for conservation—one of 16 sites of natural splendour throughout Africa. The region is the nearest part of Africa to Europe and the United States where one can view such a variety of animals and birds in natural surroundings. Visits and tours to Niokolo Koba National Park are organised both from Dakar (details from the National Bureau of Tourism) and from the Gambia (contact West African Tours in Bakau, Black and White Tours, or Hornbill Tours). It is possible to enter the park independently, provided it is with an official guide but on the variety of tours offered one would generally see more. Access to the park is by truck or jeep and there are air services into the **Simenti** safari lodge.

Tambacounda's attractions: Most visitors approach the park via the region's administrative centre and its largest town, **Tambacounda**. Two trains from Dakar and a weekly flight link this town of 20,000 people with the coast and there is also a 300-mile (480-km) bitumen highway between Tambacounda and Dakar—and between Tambacounda and the Gambian capital, **Banjul**. Most organised circuits of the Park start from locations along the main **Tambacounda-Kédougou** road.

It is said that the name Tambacounda comes from the sound of the local drums. The town grew up because of its location on the colonial railway and its position on the crossroads connecting Dakar with Kidira and Bamako in Mali. There is little of interest in the bustling town except the markets, the tree-shaded avenues and the small craft shops. The history of Tambacounda dates back to the original settlement of the Wali-Wali tribe which set up camp near the railway to trade with the passengers.

Today, most visitors use the town as a base from which to make excursions into the Niokolo Koba Park or the

Tourists and animals, by painter Alpha Dio.

Bassari country in the foothills of the Futa Djalon mountain range. The tribes most commonly seen in the town are Peul, Sarakholé, Tukulor, Malinké, Bambara and Wolof. The indigenous tribes of the region are retiring and avoid towns.

The **Asta Kebe** is the best hotel in the town with 61 air-conditioned rooms, a large restaurant and a swimming pool. The noticeboards at reception are usually plastered with notes advertising tours into the National Park and the staff are very helpful in pinpointing the best excursions. Tambacounda's other hotel, the **Hôtel de la Gare**, offers basic accommodation in its 10 rooms—more for the backpacker than the tourist. There are several guesthouses, including the **Maison des Jeunes**, a type of hostel, and the Catholic Mission where overnight accommodation can be sought.

Trucks can be hired to visit the park in Tambacounda, although taxis are not allowed into the reserve. A Land-Rover is available to take visitors from the gate of the park into town, but the vehicle has to be called by radio from the park entrance as it is based in **Simenti** village, site of the airstrip.

Around Niokolo Koba: From Tambacounda one may drive down the N7 highway, through the villages of **Missira** and **Hamdalaye**. Just across the river **Nieriko**, a tributary of the River Gambia, the road enters the village of **Wassa Don**. This village overlooks a ford across the Gambia River and the road across the ford leads into one of the main entrances to the Niokolo Koba Park. Some excursions continue down the N7, 10 miles (16 km) further on. At **Dienoun Diala**, a further six miles (10 km) on, the highway enters the park and another road leads around its north boundary towards the east and the road to Mali.

Six miles (10 km) or so into the park from Dienoun Diala, a track leads into the forest from the village of **Tali N'de Boulou** and, another 20 miles (32 km) on, one comes to the park's centre, the town of **Niokolo Koba.** The town is

Track through Niokolo Koba.

little more than a large village but it does provide accommodation. The river after which the park is named runs through the town. One of the reserve's two hotels is located nearby, as is the town's service station and garage.

The **Campement-Hôtel Niokolo Koba** has 18 rooms, six of which are air-conditioned, but otherwise the level of comfort of the hotel is fairly rudimentary. The park's other hotel is more sophisticated and much larger and more popular. Easily reached by forest roads from the N7 at Dar Salam or Tali N'de Boulou, the Simenti safari lodge is exquisitely situated in the depths of the wildlife reservation and has 40 air-conditioned rooms, all modern facilities, a pool and an excellent restaurant—usually the first place the visitor will taste real African game.

From the hotel's bar, situated beside one of the most beautiful lakes in the park, guests gather to watch hippopotamus, elephant and antelope come in the evening for water. Simenti readily conforms to most people's idea of a classic African safari lodge.

All other accommodation in the Niokolo Koba reserve consists of camp-sites where conditions are primitive, though enjoyable.

At **Camp de L'Eland**, located on the ford of **Vorouli**, a great bank has been constructed to contain the frequent floods of the River Gambia. Most of the forest camps are located at river crossings and some consist of little more than clearings, such as those at **Damantan** and **Fourou**. Also located on the banks of the Gambia, the "haltes" of **Malapa** and **Badoye** are free camping places but with no water or electricity. The traveller must carry everything with him and it should be remembered therefore that an adult needs at least five litres of liquid a day in this climate.

Other official camping sites on the itineraries of guided tours include the **Camp du Lion** on the **Ba Foula Be** ford, one of the prettiest camping locations in the entire park, and **Camp du Koba**, alongside the Niokolo Koba

the biggest of Senegal's big game.

River. A little more sophisticated than the basic safari camps is the **Campement de Badi**, located off the N7 road about 60 miles (100 km) west of **Tali N'de Boulou**. Equipped with showers and WCs but with no electricity, the accommodation consists of 20 *rondavels* in local style on the ford at **Koba**.

No food or drink is provided at the Campement de Badi, so one must bring supplies. Generally, organised tours supply all the group's needs for the duration of the one or two-day safaris. One particularly favoured day trip is from Niokolo Koba, along the winding course of the Gambia River, through the ford settlements at **Vorouli**, **Banharé**, **Malapa**, **Bafoulabé** to the lodge at Simenti.

High forest gallery follows the river and this route allows for a stop-over at the campsite at **Malapa**. This trip can be made in half a day, although the circuit can also be extended to take in the river loop at **Badi**, the clearing of **Bafoulabé**, the beauty spot known as **Goose Foot** (Patte d'Oie) and the ford at **Fourou** camp, before reaching **Wassa Don** and turning back on to the main highway to Niokolo Koba.

Much shorter treks can be made on well-signposted paths like those to the ponds of **Diamouel** and **Mansa-Farak**—an afternoon's jaunt from Niokolo Koba. Such routes are well-organised; visitors are issued with a track plan and signs clearly mark the paths and the wildlife which can be seen at the different points.

The park is overlooked in the south by the Futa Djalon range of mountains, with individual peaks rising to more than 1,200 feet (400 metres). In the park, the highest mountain is **Assirik**, located along the Niokolo Koba-Vorouli road.

Bassari Country: At the southern end of the N7 highway is the crossroads township of **Kédougou**, near the border of Guinea Bissau. The town has 6,500 people, and is located on the banks of the Gambia River, south of the Niokolo Koba Park. The region around Kédou-

Bassari village dwelling.

gou is known as **Pays Bassari** after the local tribe. Developed into its current size in order to service the iron mines of the Faléméé district at **Nafadji**, the original settlement dates back to the gold trade of the Mali Empire.

About five miles (eight km) from Kédougou, through a range of picturesque hills, are the quarries of **Ibel**. It is from these quarries that the marble is taken to build the houses of the town. In striking contrast to the usual straw-roofed huts, these marble houses bear the multiple hues of the stone. Although Kédougou contains little to delay a visitor long, it is an interesting fact that the town was used as a base by many early explorers into the headwater regions of the Gambia River.

There is no accommodation in Kédougou apart from a small camping site on the outskirts. Situated in mountainous region of the Futa Djalon range, the roads are almost impassable by ordinary car and even four-wheel drive vehicles can find the going difficult.

The countryside around Kédougou is more of an attraction than the town as the Bassari people maintain a number of traditional ceremonies which fascinate anthropologists and excite photographers. In addition, experts are studying the traditional remedies and medications evolved by the Bassari, who are now mainly employed in growing cotton, fishing, hunting and, of course, making souvenirs. A favourite local souvenir is the woven rice winnower.

During April one might have the chance to take photographs of the tribal initiation ceremonies. In this region there are also branches of the Peul tribe and another local tribe, the Boin, inhabit the region west of Kédougou, especially around the villages of **Ebarak**, **Salemata** and **Etiolo**.

Etiolo, about 50 miles (80 km) west of Kédougou, is reached from the main road at **Salemata**. This village, set within a circle of mountains which provides a stunning backdrop, is a popular tourist attraction. Located in the heart of the Bassari country Etiolo is

one of the best locations to view an initiation ceremony.

The tribes of the Bassari region are less dispersed than those in the rest of the country. There are a number of smaller groups in addition to the majority Bassari. In the hills around **Bandafassi**, just west of Kédougou, live around 1,500 members of the Badik tribe, known more commonly by the Peul name "Tandanké".

Further south, in the **Fougolembi** area of the Futa Djalon mountains, live the Diallonké. These and the other tribes of the area also overspill the border into Guinea Bissau. Generally, the tribes of Guinean origin inhabit the hilly regions and those of Peul descent cultivate the low-lying areas.

East of Kédougou, it is possible to meet gold prospectors in the foothills and to visit local villages such as **Binbou**, **Saraya** and **Ilimalo**. A few kilometres from Ilimalo there is an important site for pilgrimages and a centre for traditional religious ceremonies. Called **Kouroun-**

iengouniengou, this sacred place is overlooked by a massive rock balancing on a cliff edge high above the valley floor. It is considered to be one of the most spectacular geological formations in Senegal.

Around 15 miles (24 km) from Kédougou, across the Futa-Djalon hills, is the settlement of **Fougolembi**, which makes an interesting excursion into the Senegal/Guinea Bissau border region. This is the country of the Diallonké tribe and there are several villages such as **Sintiou**, **Wallan**, **Toumanéa** and **Niagalankomé** where the traditional way of life of this tribe persists almost unmodified by the 20th century.

One of the curiosities of the region is a village named **Iwol**, near Bandafassi, which is noted for a baobab tree on its outskirts which is said to be the largest in the country. Other picturesque villages include **Ibel**, **Etchouar**, **Sangola** and **Landiéni**, all within a short distance of each other along tiny forest tracks.

The Futa Djalon mountains are the homelands of the Fulani tribe and are deeply scoured by numerous gorges and fertile valleys. Bananas and fonio (a tiny form of millet) are grown in the valleys and livestock is reared on the hillsides. Between the Niokolo Koba National Park and the Bambouk mountains is the Falémé River valley with its rolling savannah. This region is a well-loved hunting area.

To the east of Niokolo Koba lies one of the country's seven officially designated hunting grounds. It is open from December to April. For details of times and permits, contact the Direction des Eaux et Forêts in Dakar. Hunting, however, is severely restricted because the Senegalese are concerned about the preservation of wildlife. The Parc National du Niokolo Koba represents one of the last enclaves for big game in the whole of West Africa. The terrain of southeast Senegal, the Futa Djalon mountains and the arid areas to the north and east ensure that the wildlife is contained in its natural surroundings for the enjoyment and education of the park's thousands of visitors.

Left, full moon over Niokolo Koba. Right, Bassari bark, leaf and palm mask. Following page: gazing out over the Atlantic.

TRAVEL TIPS

GETTING THERE

BY AIR

To the Gambia

British Airways has two scheduled flights a week from Gatwick Airport, London direct to the little Yundum Airport, Banjul. The flight takes around six hours.

Ghana Airways and Nigeria Airways have several flights a week, coast-hopping and linking Lagos, Abidjan, Freetown, Conakry and Dakar to Banjul.

Gambia Air Shuttle links Banjul with Bamako (Mali), Guinea-Bissau, Cape Verde and Dakar with regular scheduled flights.

Air Senegal runs a service between Dakar and Banjul on the days when Gambia Air Shuttle does not operate.

Bookings on British Airways scheduled flights can be made from any travel agent in UK or Europe or the USA.

Visitors from the USA should book via BA London-Banjul or take the direct Air Afrique flight from New York to Dakar and continue by Gambia Air Shuttle or Air Senegal. Similarly, visitors from Europe can take scheduled flights by Sabena, Swissair, Air France, Air Afrique, Royal Air Maroc, Aeroflot or Iberia to Dakar and continue in the same way. A number of tour operators offer packages and some may sell seats without accommodation on a charter flight. Details from travel agents (and see Tour Operators).

To Senegal

Yoff International Airport, 10 miles (15 km) north of Dakar, is one of the largest and best equipped in Africa. There is an average of two scheduled flights daily between Dakar and Paris. Airlines operating scheduled flights into Dakar include Sabena, SwissAir, Air France, Air Afrique, Royal Air Maroc, Aeroflot, Iberia, Ghana Air-

ways, Nigeria Airways.

Certain flights from European capitals stop at intermediate European airports such as Marseilles, Bordeaux.

Several French tour operators run charter flights to Dakar. In addition, visitors from Britain could buy a charter flight into the Gambia and continue to Dakar via Gambia Air Shuttle, Air Senegal, Ghana Airways or any other link between the two cities.

BY SEA

Passengers wishing to travel by sea must allow themselves plenty of time (8-10 days) for the journey which is unpredictable and rarely used but still theoretically possible. Accommodation is on cargo boats from Liverpool, London or certain European ports, which call at other ports en route and may even leave out a port if there is no reason to stop there for cargo. Not all ships allow passengers so make your enquiries in good time. It is even rarer for ships returning to Europe to take passengers, so you cannot count on obtaining a return ticket. Lines making the journey from the UK to Banjul are West India Conference Lines, 323 India Buildings, Water Street, Liverpool L2 0RB. Tel: 051-236 1024. This company comprises Elder Dempster, Palm Line, Guinea Gulf, Nigerian National, Black Star and Hoegh Lines.

For details of European lines serving Dakar, which include Paquet, Socopao and Delmas-Vieiljeux, contact the nearest Senegalese diplomatic or tourist representative well in advance of your intended departure date.

BY RAIL

There is a train between Bamako (Mali) and Dakar which runs twice a week, stopping at Tambacounda and Kaolack. Travellers to the Gambia can get off at either Tambacounda or Kaolack and continue by taxi, minibus or public transport bus. For information, contact any travel agency in Bamako or Dakar. For comfort, travel on the express train (once a week only). You must take your own food and drink.

BY ROAD

It is possible to drive to Senegal (and therefore on to the Gambia) from North Africa and the Mediterranean, but the trip is obviously long, complex and requires considerable equipment and planning. It should be attempted only by groups in rugged four-wheel drive vehicles. The shortest route, south from Morocco through Mauritania to the border at St Louis, is virtually closed by the twin problems of civil war in the western Sahara and disputes between Senegal and Mauritania. Other routes via Algeria and Mali are open but involve crossing the Sahara.

Senegal is connected by a perfectly serviceable road with Guinea-Bissau in the South, crossing from **Fatim**, in Guinea-Bissau, into **Tanaf** (Senegal). It is also possible to enter from Guinea; the crossing point will be from **Koundara** (Guinea) into **Velingara** (Senegal).

Travelling overland via different countries obviously necessitates forward planning to ensure that visas are procured for transit areas.

Road connections between Senegal and the Gambia are reasonably efficient. There are good roads from **Dakar** via Kaolack to **Barra** (4½ hours drive) on the mouth of the River Gambia, directly opposite **Banjul** or to **Farafenni** (five hours) by the Transgambia Highway.

At **Farafenni**, a 15- to 20-minute car-ferry crossing takes you to Mansa Konko from where a tarmac road with a reasonable surface goes east to Basse, west to Banjul (three hours) or south on to Ziguinchor in Senegal by the Transgambia Highway continuation. Be prepared for a longish wait in the queue to get on the ferry. Private cars often get preferential treatment but taxis can wait hours. The Japanese have provided two new ferries for this crossing and the new slipways are in the process of being built.

If you cross the River Gambia at **Barra**, the ferry delivers you straight to Banjul. The ferry runs every two hours (last one 6 p.m.) and takes 45-50 minutes to cross and unload. Just occasionally there are two ferries which mean less waiting time. Foreign registered cars have to pay in foreign currency (CFA francs if you are coming from Senegal), Gambian registered cars pay in dalassis

(D40 for a normal saloon). Tickets are bought from an inconspicuous ticket shed on the left, about 15 minutes after the border and well before you reach Barra. Easy to miss.

Customs and Immigration controls are at **Karang** on the Senegalese side and at **Amladai** on the Gambia side. Verify that your car insurance covers you in the Gambia. Senegalese insured cars need extra cover for the Gambia. Take something to eat and drink with you in case you just miss the ferry. Cold bottled drinks are available from small boys and from the pleasant open-air Lingaire Bar by the ferry entrance.

To go to Barra from **Kaolack**, turn sharp right off the Transgambia Highway after crossing the mud/salt flats, at a tumbledown signpost marked to **Les Palétuviers** and **Karang**. No mention of Banjul and hence easy to overshoot and find yourself going to Ziguinchor.

Coming from the south, the Transgambia Highway goes from **Ziguinchor** to **Mansa Konko**. At **Bignona**, there is a left turn to the Gambia via Diouloulou which takes you to Banjul (two hours). No ferry crossing necessary. Only Customs and Immigration on both Senegalese and Gambian borders.

Taxis and minibuses ply all these routes (approximately CFA 2,000 Ziguinchor to Banjul, CFA 2,500, which is negotiable, Dakar to Barra) and the Gambia Public Transport Corporation runs a reasonably comfortable airy bus between Dakar and Barra, cost CFA 2,500 each way, leaving Dakar at 9 a.m. and 11 a.m. from Place Leclerc just below the Novotel. (Five hours traveling time with a 10-minute stop at Kaolack.) At Barra you get out and cross to Banjul as a foot passenger, then take a taxi the other side.

TRAVEL ESSENTIALS

VISAS & PASSPORTS

The Gambia

A full valid passport is needed for anyone entering the Gambia. (A British Visitor's Passport is not acceptable.) Citizens of the following countries do *not* need visas for a tourist or business visit to the Gambia for up to three months: United Kingdom, all Commonwealth countries, all West African countries, Denmark, Federal Republic of Germany, Finland, Greece, Iceland, Italy, Liechtenstein, Luxembourg, The Netherlands, Norway, Sweden, Tunisia, Turkey, Uruguay.

Citizens of all countries not mentioned above need a visa to visit the Gambia. South African and Israeli passport holders will be refused entry.

A visa is valid for 90 days as a rule, but transit visas for a period not exceeding five days are issued on condition that a visa to the continuation country has already been obtained by the applicant.

It is a good idea to get a visa for Senegal before you leave for the Gambia as day or weekend trips are easily organised from the Gambia to Senegal or you may wish to make such a trip when there.

Senegal

Full valid passports are required for anyone entering the country. Citizens of the following countries do *not* require visas: France, West Germany, Italy, Morocco, Tunisia, Algeria and all West African states bordering on Senegal.

Nationals of all other countries need visas, which may be obtained from Senegalese missions abroad or on arrival in Senegal.

Multiple-entry visas valid for three months are normally granted.

MONEY MATTERS

The Gambia

You can take as much money into the Gambia as you wish, either in travellers' cheques or in hard currency, but you may not take out more than you brought in. A currency declaration form sometimes needs to be completed on arrival. Banks will exchange both travellers' cheques and currency at the official rates posted up daily in the banks. Take your passport with you when you go to the bank. US dollars, sterling, and CFA francs (from Senegal) will sometimes be accepted by traders but black market exchange is officially discouraged. Foreign currency from Algeria, Ghana, Guinea, Mali, Morocco, Nigeria, Sierra Leone and Tunisia is neither accepted nor exchanged.

The local currency is the Dalassi, made up of 100 Bututs. Notes are in denominations of D25 (blue), D10 (green), D5 (red) and D1 (purple). Coins are in denominations of D1 (hexagonal), 50, 25, 10 and 5 Bututs. Recent exchange rates have fluctuated around £1 = D12; or US$1 = D7.

All major hotels have foreign exchange facilities at their reception desks but commissions will be greater than at banks.

Credit cards are accepted by the larger hotels and by some car hire companies. Check with your credit card company before leaving and with your bank and hotel on arrival. Restaurants usually only take cash payments. Main credit cards acceptable: American Express, Diners Club, Visa, Mastercard.

European Eurocheques supported by Eurocheque cards are accepted by some hotels.

Bank Addresses:
Standard Chartered
Buckle Street, Banjul (Head Office)
and Atlantic Road, Fajara (next to Tropic Garden Hotel)
and Basse Santa Su

International Bank for Commerce & Industry (BICI)
11 Wellington Street, Banjul (Head Office)
and Bakau (behind CFAO)
and Serekunda

Central Bank of the Gambia
Buckle Street, Banjul

Gambia Commercial & Development Bank
Buckle Street, Banjul (Head Office)
and Bakau, and Yundum Airport

Gambia Commercial Development Bank
Farafenni and Basse Santa Su

Banking Hours: Normally from 8 a.m. to 1 p.m. (Monday to Thursday) and 8 a.m. to 11 a.m. (Friday and Saturday).

In addition, some banks in Bakau open in the afternoons from 4 p.m. to 6:30 p.m. (Monday to Friday only).

Senegal

Similar currency regulations to those obtaining in the Gambia apply. In theory, you must declare the amounts of currency you bring into and take out of the country.

Senegal belongs to the CFA franc system which is common to all of France's former West African colonies. The CFA franc issued by any of these territories is accepted by all of them. The exchange rate of the CFA franc is tied to the French franc at French franc 1 = CFA francs 50. There are notes of CFA 10,000, 5,000, 1,000 and 500 and coins of CFA 100 and 50 (silver in colour) and CFA 25, 10 and 5 (copper in colour).

In addition, French francs are widely accepted as are, to a lesser extent, US dollars, but nothing else.

All major hotels have foreign exchange facilities but charge commissions.

The main credit cards (American Express, Diners Club, Visa and Mastercard) are widely accepted, except in small businesses.

European Eurocheques supported by Eurocheque cards are accepted by an increasing number of hotels and some banks.

Bank Addresses in Dakar:
Al Manar Islamic Investment Bank
Avenue Sarraut

BCEAO (Central Bank of West African States)
Avenue Abdoulaye Fadiga (ex-Barachois)

Banque Internationale pour l'Afrique de L'Ouest (BAIO)
Place de l'Indépendance

Banque Internationale pour le Commerce International du Sénégal (BICIS)
Avenue Roume

Banque Nationale pour le Développement du Sénégal
Avenue Roume

Banque Sénégalo-Koweitienne (BSK)
Rue de Thann

Banque Sénégalo-Tunisienne (BST)
Avenue Georges Pompidou

Bank of Credit and Commerce International
Place de l'Indépendance

Caisse Nationale du Crédit Agricole
Rue Huart

City Bank
Place de l'Indépendance

Société Générale des Banques du Sénégal (SGBS)
Avenue Roume

Sonabanque
Place de l'Indépendance

Union Sénégalaise de Banque (USB)
Boulevard Pinet Laprade

Banking Hours: Normally from 8 a.m. to 11:30 a.m. and 12:45 p.m. to 4 p.m. (Monday to Friday).

In addition to the major hotels, the Chamber of Commerce on the Place de l'Indépendance offers a service outside banking hours for the exchange of travellers' cheques.

HEALTH

The Gambia

A valid certificate of vaccination against **yellow fever** is the only compulsory health precaution necessary to enter or leave the Gambia for all people over the age of one year. If there are medical reasons which prevent this vaccination, a certificate of exemption from a qualified medical practitioner must be presented to the Health Authorities. Immunisation must be given at least two weeks before reaching the Gambia by a doctor or clinic authorised to issue the certificate. Check with your local doctor. Valid for 10 years.

Senegal

There is no longer a requirement for visitors to present a yellow fever vaccination certificate. A **cholera** vaccination certificate is in theory necessary for visitors arriving from affected countries, but these vary. Check with your doctor.

Immunisations advisable for both the Gambia and Senegal:

Typhoid and Paratyphoid (TAB) – a gastric fever caught from infected or dirty food. Valid three months.
Hepatitis A (jaundice) – caught from infected water or food and sometimes, regrettably, from local oysters. Valid six weeks.
Cholera – diarrhoea, vomiting, dehydration. Valid six months.
Polio – Valid two years.

These immunisations are all optional unless you are coming from an infected area but are to be recommended. Check with your doctor when to have them done. Some can be done all on the same day as the yellow fever, otherwise you may have to wait a week or two between injections and thus delay your departure on holiday.

Malaria: Anti-malarial drugs should be taken by visitors (and residents) in both countries as this disease, carried by the anopheles mosquito, is prevalent everywhere and can strike anyone at any time. The recommended prophylactic dose is 200 mg (two tablets) Paludrine (proguanol) daily with 400 mg Chloroquin/Nivaquine once a week on the same day each week. Start a week before you arrive and continue for six weeks after your return. Side effects are not noticeable although it has been said that Paludrine taken over a lengthy period can make one forgetful. If you get malaria, see a doctor immediately. Symptoms are a high temperature, wracking headache and alternate bouts of the shivers and hot fevers.

However there are fewer mosquitoes around in the dry (tourist) season (November to May) than in the wet season. Hotel rooms usually have mosquito-proofed windows and an air-conditioner and/or fan (if you have electricity) will help keep them away. Up-country, where there is little or no electricity, a mosquito net or strong anti-mosquito spray is necessary or you can burn anti-mosquito coils which give off a scented smoke obnoxious to mosquitoes but tolerable for humans. One coil lasts about eight hours. Bring a good supply of insect repellant as a back-up.

Medical insurance should be taken out before you leave your home country. Details from your travel agent, insurance company or bank.

AIDS: It is prevalent in the region, although figures, unreliable as they are, seem to be no worse than those for Europe. The percentage of the population infected is slightly worse in the Gambia than in Senegal. The virus is transmitted as much by heterosexual contact as by homosexual, and also by contaminated needles and blood transfusion equipment. Emergency medical packs containing sterilised needles and plasma are now available in the developed countries for visitors to take with them.

Although free emergency medical treatment is theoretically available in both countries, it is likely to be unreliable or non-existent (the latter obviously in remote areas) and full medical insurance to cover all eventualities is therefore necessary.

DRINKING WATER

Bottled water is widely available and should be used in both countries. The extent of other precautions to avoid stomach upsets will vary depending on how much restriction of food choice you are prepared to put up with. It is sensible to peel all fruit, whether washed or not, before eating. Some people will wish to avoid salads and other uncooked, washed foods, as well as ice-cream and ice in drinks. Others will resign themselves to the occasional bug and eat whatever is going. In general, standards of hygiene in both countries in most commercial establishments are well controlled.

WHAT TO WEAR

From November to May, the region has a very pleasant sub-tropical climate, warm, dry and sunny during the day but with an unexpectedly cool breeze in the evenings so bring a cardigan, jacket or sweatshirt as well as normal summer clothes – skirts, dresses, shorts, shirts, T-shirts, sleeveless tops and dresses, trousers – in a lightweight material. In the humid wet season, clothes should not cling to the skin. Trousers are necessary in the evenings (against mosquitoes and the chilly breeze) and on expeditions into the bush. From November to May it is not too hot to wear jeans. Tights and stockings are not usually worn. A hat is useful on the beach and on excursions. Locally-made bush hats are cheap and cool. Suits, too, are not worn. Jacket and tie are acceptable for the businessman. Man-made fabrics such as nylon are much worse at coping with the heat and humidity than natural ones such as cotton or linen. In the wet season, an umbrella, lightweight raincoat and shoes that can get wet without spoiling should be brought.

Both men and women need open sandals or flip-flops for beach, hotel and street. Roads are exceptionally sandy so shoes should be strong enough to resist the pressure and open enough to be able to shake out the sand. Stouter shoes such as trainers (with socks) are recommended for excursions into the bush. If you want to be smart in the evenings, bring appropriate shoes.

More than one swimming costume is recommended. It is perfectly acceptable for women to go topless on the beach or by the hotel pool but beyond these areas it would give considerable offence. Hotels usually request their guests to dress respectably but not formally in their indoor restaurants and bars especially in the evenings.

In public, visitors should respect Islamic customs: women should try to wear knee-length skirts, trousers or a wrap-around piece of cloth and shirt; men are tolerated in shirt and shorts.

Hotels provide laundry service at very reasonable prices and there is no problem about getting clothes dry.

WHAT TO BRING

It is best to bring everything you think you will need with you and not to rely on buying it in the region. The only town in either of the two countries with a reasonably extensive selection of consumer goods is Dakar. Even if it is available, it will be more expensive than at home.

For the beach: your own towel, as hotels do not like theirs taken onto the beach; an inflatable pillow (and lilo if you have room) is handy both on the beach and on excursions; sunglasses; suntan cream or oil; after-sun cream or other moisturising lotion (the air is very dry in January and February); lip protection.

From the chemist: plenty of insect-repellant (spray, cream, lotion); antihistamine or sting-relief cream; anti-stomach upset medicine; indigestion tablets; water-sterilising tablets (especially if you are travelling up-country); throat lozenges; anti-malaria prophylactics (see Health) and cures (ask your doctor); basic First Aid equipment including elastoplast, antiseptic cream, cotton wool; shampoo (sachets are lightweight); soap or shower gel; toothpaste; talcum powder; your own personal make-up; a small pair of scissors; prickly heat powder for the wet season (actually available in the Gambia); headache tablets; tampons; deodorants, perfumes, etc.

For men: if travelling outside major tourist hotels, a disposable or battery-operated razor for when there is no electricity; shaving cream; after-shave.

Miscellaneous: camera (in a carrying case); lenses; enough film to last your stay; plastic bags to keep these in (protection from dust and damp); money-belt with zipped pockets big enough for passport or ticket if travelling around; torch.

If you are travelling cheaply on your own: apart from some of the items mentioned above, you will also need lightweight water containers (two small rather than one large), lightweight sleeping bag, toilet paper, matches, candles, a small camping gaz ring and camping utensils e.g. for boiling water in or doing your own cooking, depending on how you feel about eating the local food.

For tips, presents, children: items which in the developed world might be considered too petty to give are often much prized, particularly in the country. Literally nothing is too small to make at the least a very welcome present for a child. Disposable ball point pens, cigarette lighters and notebooks are especially useful. For adults, cigarettes (all Western brands) are much appreciated.

ON ARRIVALS & CUSTOMS

The Gambia

Yundum Airport is situated about 20 miles (35 km) from Banjul and 12 miles (20 km) from Bakau, the main tourist area. Formalities are minimal: a passport and yellow fever certificate check and you are through to the verandah where tour representatives wait for their guests. Baggage is unloaded on to the ground outside and passengers have to make their way across to identify their cases, then carry them past the Customs officer who may well want to look inside. All this takes place in the open air (and sun).

Personal belongings (including cameras, binoculars and video cameras which are not for resale) are admitted duty-free. Also duty-free are 200 cigarettes or 250g tobacco, 1 quart spirits (just over a litre), 2 quarts (2¼ litres) wine or beer, one half pint (28 cl) perfume or *eau de toilette*.

There is a small branch of the Gambia Commercial Development Bank at the airport for currency exchange on the spot, also a Gamtel telephone office which will make international calls and a kiosk for the sale of cold drinks. For transport, see "Getting Around".

Senegal

Yoff Airport is sizeable, well-organised by African standards, and situated 10 miles (16 km) from Dakar.

Queues for passport and visa checks are usually well ordered and not too slow. Baggage is unloaded onto a carousel or stationary platform. Porters are available to carry luggage through Customs and should be paid approximately CFA 500. Luggage trolleys are theoretically available free of charge but may be difficult to find.

Senegalese duty-free allowance consists of: two cameras, a cine camera, a tape recorder, a portable radio receiver, a portable record player, a portable typewriter, personal jewellery (not more than 200g of gold), 200 cigarettes, 50 cigars, 250g of tobacco and your personal clothing.

Yoff Airport is equipped with a full range of shops, cafeterias, a *bureau de change* and telephone facilities. The opening and, especially, closing hours can be erratic however and it is unwise to rely totally on any of these facilities at night or during a slack period when no flights are arriving or departing.

There is a desk manned by hostesses of the Ministry of Tourism at the airport, but the same comments apply to its opening hours.

RESERVATIONS

The Gambia

If you have not booked any hotel accommodation before arriving, your best plan of action is to go to the Gamtel telephone exchange in Bakau and phone the various hotels for a room. Don't dally at the airport telephone: everyone leaves once the plane and passengers have left and you will be stranded. During the tourist season it may be difficult to find a room in one of the bigger hotels but there is usually room in one of the cheaper hotels in Banjul.

The Banjul Travel Agency, Buckle Street, Banjul (Tel: 28813 & 28473), or the Columbus Travel Agency, Kairaba Avenue, Fajara (Tel: 96135), may also be able to assist with hotel accommodation.

Senegal

As there should normally be no difficulty in obtaining transport into Dakar, telephoning for hotels is best done before leaving Yoff Airport, especially if the tourist hostesses are available to help.

Alternatively, go to the Ministry of Tourism in Dakar.

It is usually quite easy to make advance telephone bookings with medium-sized and large hotels within the country is you are touring.

EXTENSIONS OF STAY

The Gambia

If you want to stay in the Gambia beyond the three months on your visitor's visa, you will have to apply to the **Immigration Department, Ministry of the Interior**, Banjul (on the corner of Dobson Street and Anglesea Street) giving a good reason why you want to stay on and proving you can support yourself financially.

Senegal

The same procedure applies for Senegal, where visa extensions are dealt with by the **Ministry of the Interior**, Dakar (Place de Washington office).

ON DEPARTURE

The Gambia

Confirmation of return flight: this is not necessary for visitors on full package tours, but flight-only charter travellers should confirm 48 hours in advance with the representatives of their tour companies.

Travellers on scheduled flights should confirm with the **British Airways'** representative at the Atlantic Hotel, Banjul, with **Gambia Airways**, Wellington Street, Banjul, or with a travel agent.

An airport tax is levied on everyone leaving the country: D7 for foreigners, payable in hard currency; D35 for residents of the Gambia. Package tourists should check whether this is included in the price of their holiday.

After registering luggage in the normal way and passing through passport control, you will then have to identify your baggage again and put it on to the van yourself for loading into the aircraft.

Refreshments are not always available in the departure lounge so take something to drink in case of a long wait. Duty free items are on sale but dearer than in Banjul or Bakau supermarkets. The Gambia Commercial Development Bank will change a certain amount of dalassis for you as they are useless outside the Gambia.

Senegal

Confirmation of return flights: for scheduled flights, this should be done if possible 72 hours in advance with the airline in question or a travel agent.

There is no airport tax. It is advisable to keep ready the declaration of currencies form, which arriving visitors will have filled in, in case it is requested on departure.

Although Yoff Airport is reasonably well run and modern, it is advisable to allow double the amount of time you would calculate on at a European airport to check in

luggage, complete customs formalities, etc.

Unless the flight is very late at night or early in the morning, the normal range of shops (including duty-free), cafeterias and a *bureau de change* should be available.

GETTING ACQUAINTED

GOVERNMENT & ECONOMY

The Gambia

The Gambia has been a remarkably stable country since independence in 1965. It is an independent sovereign state headed by President Sir Dawda Jawara of the People's Progressive Party (PPP), and became a Republic in 1975. There is one house with 49 members including some from the NCP (National Convention Party) and the UP (United Party). The President is elected every five years. In 1982 the Senegambia Confederation was set up with Senegal to co-ordinate policy on matters of defence, economy, communications and transport but the Confederation was dissolved in 1989. The Gambia is also a member of the Commonwealth.

The economy of the Gambia is mainly agricultural, depending on groundnuts which account for nearly 90 percent of exports. Fishing has great potential and is being encouraged by the United Nations Development Fund. Drought has played havoc with crops in recent years so that the country cannot rely on being self-sufficient in rice, millet and sorghum and has to import rice from Thailand and the USA. Tourism is a dynamic sector of the economy and brings seasonal work to many Gambians. General policy is to try to broaden the economic base of the Gambia and many initiatives are being funded by international aid. The majority of the people make their living from agriculture, fishing and forestry.

Senegal

Senegal became independent in its own right in 1960. Its constitution remains modelled broadly on that of France, with a President and national assembly elected by universal suffrage. It has proved stable and relatively peaceful in spite of occasional student-led civic unrest. The current president, Abdou Diouf, took over peacefully according to constitutional procedures from his predecessor, the country's founding father Léopold Sédar Senghar, and has since won two reasonably fair elections. There are more than a dozen opposition parties which are legally tolerated. The short-lived Confederation of Senegambia, which attempted to co-ordinate policy in certain fields between the two countries, was dissolved in 1989.

Senegal's economy is largely agricultural, depending on subsistence crops, millet, sorghum, rice, maize, vegetables and pulses, and cash crops, groundnuts (the most important, used mainly for pressing into oil), cotton and sugar. In addition, Senegal's long Atlantic coastline means that fishing is of great importance, both for home consumption and for a substantial source of export revenue.

Tourism accounts for a smaller percentage of the country's income than in the Gambia, but is nonetheless an important and growing industry. A limited quantity of mineral resources exists, mainly phosphates and iron ore.

GEOGRAPHY

The region of Senegal and the Gambia occupies the most western part of the African continent. Senegal is bordered to the north by Mauritania, to the east by Mali, to the south by Guinea and Guinea-Bissau and to the west by the Atlantic Ocean.

The Gambia is a narrow strip of land, not more than 30 miles (48 km) at its widest, running east-west for about 300 miles (500 km) along both sides of the River Gambia into the centre of Senegal. It is bounded on the west by the Atlantic Ocean and on all other sides by Senegal. Except for a few rocky outcrops at the eastern end of the river, the country is very flat. To the north, it gives way to scrub and eventually desert in Senegal. The south gradually becomes more

tropical, with oil and coconut palms, silk cotton trees, bamboo, mahogany and tropical fruit trees in abundance. The river, which divides these two distinct regions, is tidal for about 60 miles (100 km) and is navigable as far as Basse for the groundnut-collecting lighters. Mangroves line the river banks and rice is cultivated in small fields irrigated by river flooding. In the drier, sandier areas, millet and sorghum are grown. Citrus fruits do well in this climate; grapefruit, oranges and limes particularly. Beautiful sandy beaches stretch along the Gambia's 30 miles (48 km) of coast attracting both visitors and fishermen.

The topography of Senegal follows the directions indicated by the division of terrain within its own central dividing belt, which is the Gambia.

The north, which forms part of the Sahel, is dry, sandy and scrub-patched, and has faced increasingly grave threats from drought and locusts in recent years. The terrain is generally flat; the only substantial mountains in the country are in the extreme southeast, where the Futo-Djalon range extends deep into Guinea and adjoining territories. The interior of Senegal north of the River Gambia is arid and semi-desert. The great River Senegal curves round the top of the country, irrigating a long arc of land and forming the country's effective northern border. The rivers Siné and Saloum and their many tributaries irrigate a large delta between Dakar and the Gambian border. South of the Gambia, Senegal's Casamance region is green, forested and rice-growing, while the Casamance River provides another wide area of mangrove-clogged waterways.

POPULATION

The Gambia

The population of the Gambia is about 800,000, made up of several ethnic groups. The Mandinkas are the largest ethnic unit and are spread throughout the country. The Wolofs are found mainly in Banjul. The Akus are descendants of freed Africans and formed the pillar of the Establishment in the first half of the 20th century. The Fulas are wanderers, the Sarakholés traders and the Diolas a closely-knit group in the south extending towards Senegal.

Other residents include Lebanese, Europeans, Indians and expatriate Africans from Ghana, Nigeria and Sierra Leone. Until recently, Mauritanians ran small stalls selling everything useful at street corners.

Senegal

The population of Senegal is around six million, and all of the same ethnicities as are found in the Gambia are present, with the exception of the Aku, whose numbers are insignificant. The large Peul population (Senegal equivalent of the Gambian Fula) are mainly found in the north, and the interior and east of the country. A substantial Tukulor population is mainly in the north. Dakar is situated in a primarily Wolof area, while the Cap Vert region around the capital is also the traditional home of substantial numbers of Lébou. The south is the preserve of Diolas and Mandinkas.The same non-African residents are found in Senegal as in the Gambia, although the former colonial English presence in the latter is replaced in Senegal by a French community.

LANGUAGE

In both countries, the predominant indigenous language of the major population areas is Wolof. However, each ethnic grouping has its own language, which will obviously dominate regions where the grouping is particularly concentrated.

In the Gambia, English is widely used as an official, business and social language, while in Senegal a similar role is played by French.

TIME ZONE

Both the Gambia and Senegal are in the Universal Time Zone, previously known as the Greenwich Mean Time Zone.

CLIMATE

The entire region has an agreeable subtropical climate. The dry season runs from November to April/May with sunshine, an average temperature of 72°-74°F (24°-26°C) and a cool breeze blowing off the sea. In the eastern interior of Senegal, however, temperatures can reach considerably higher, into the 30 or even 40 degrees Centigrade. Nonetheless, it can be chilly enough in the evenings for a light jacket or cardigan, or a blanket on the bed, especially inland. It will not rain, except for a freak storm. The dry Harmattan wind, coming from the desert, often blows in January and February, bringing with it thick red dust that settles everywhere very suddenly and can even prevent planes landing and taking off. Throat lozenges are a relief at this time. The dust will disappear as suddenly as it arrived. Up-river, the cool season is shorter, ending in February/March.

During the wet season (June to September), humidity rises drastically (80 percent or more) which makes the temperature (average 84°F or 28°C) seem even hotter. Rain falls in torrential downpours with high winds, lasting a few hours at most, giving way to clear skies and a brief cool respite before the sun and humidity take over again.

The hottest months are between the two seasons: May/June and October on the coast, March/June and October inland.

WEIGHTS & MEASURES

In the Gambia, both metric (metres, grammes, litres) and imperial (feet, ounces, pints) measures are used.

In Senegal, only metric measures are used.

ELECTRICITY

The Gambia

The country's mains power can be erratic, with frequent power cuts. Hotels, supermarkets, banks and restaurants usually have their own generators so food and drink are kept fresh and cold and air-conditioners working. The current is 220V but the constant fluctuation of power can damage hi-tech equipment, freezers etc. Private citizens often bring stabilisers.

Up-country towns (Basse, Mansa Konko, Farafenni, Bansang and the larger villages) normally have electricity in the evening and for some period during the day but power should not be relied on. Battery-operated radios, shavers and torches are essential and cold drinks will often be unobtainable.

Senegal

The major towns are all well supplied with reliable mains electricity. The voltage is

220V. In remote parts of the interior, generators, private supplies and battery-operated equipment may have to be relied on.

BUSINESS HOURS

The Gambia
Government offices: 8 a.m. to 4 p.m. Monday to Thursday; 8 a.m. to 1 p.m. Friday.

Other office hours can vary, some closing for lunch, some opening Friday afternoons and/or Saturday mornings.

Bank opening hours: see Money section.
Shops: see Shopping Hours.

Senegal
Most offices: 7:30 a.m. to 12 p.m. and 2:30 p.m. to 6 p.m. Monday to Friday; 7:30 a.m. to 12 p.m. Saturday.

On Friday, some offices and most shops will re-open at 3 p.m. because of Friday prayers.

HOLIDAYS

Senegal and the Gambia both celebrate the feast days of the Muslim Calendar. These are variable as they depend upon and sightings of the new moon and may not be known until very shortly beforehand. In general, they get earlier each year. *Approximate* times are as follows:

Korité (known in Arabic as Aid el Fitr, the end of the month-long fast of Ramadan): early May.

Tabaski (in Arabic, Aid el Kebir or Aid el Adha, the feast of Abraham's sacrifice of the sheep): mid-July.

Tamharit (the Islamic New Year): early August.

Maouloud (the Prophet Mohammed's birthday): mid-October.

In addition, **the Gambia** has the following public holidays:
January 1 : New Year's Day
February 18 : Independence Day
March (variable) : Good Friday
May 1 : Labour Day
August 15 : Feast of the Assumption of St Mary
December 25 : Christmas Day

Senegal celebrates the following:
January 1 : New Year's Day

March (variable) : Easter Monday
April 4 : Independence Day
May 1 : Labour Day
May 4 : The Assumption
May 15 : Whitsuntide

FESTIVALS

The Gambia
Organised festivals in public for special occasions are rare in the Gambia. There are plenty of celebrations on feast days and for marriage or baptism ceremonies but they will be in private. You may be lucky enough to get to know a Gambian whose family will be celebrating something while you are on holiday and who will take you with him. Or you may happen to be passing a compound where dancing or drumming is taking place and be able to watch. On feast days, small groups of young people will dress up as birds, animals or magicians and dance in the road to the music of whistles and drums, but not necessarily everywhere.

During the Christmas/New Year season, **Fanal** processions take place in Banjul, Bakau and Serekunda. Intricate ships made from split bamboo and cut-out paper patterns delicately glued together are constructed by clubs in honor of their patron. These are then paraded through the streets every evening in the dark, with candles lit inside them to illuminate the tracery, accompanied by drumming and dancing crowds, until they reach the patron's house. At the end of the season (just after New Year), the ship is given to the patron for him to display. Donations are accepted for the club. If you know where to go, you can watch the processions. Good examples of the ships are in the National Museum in Banjul.

Senegal
The same remarks apply to Senegal as to the Gambia (above). The most noteworthy and famous Fanals are in St Louis, where the museum contains some examples of the construction.

There are in addition a number of regional tribal festivals and ceremonies. In the Thiès region, the month of May sees a series of dance rituals known as *syniaka*, while the Fil festival brings together another set of rituals and ceremonies in June and July. In the southeast, the Bassari peoples indulge in spectacularly-costumed initiation rituals for young boys in March. In Casamance, a number of ceremonies include the **Zulane** Festival in June, the **Zumebel** in July and harvest festivals in May.

RELIGION

Islam

Although the great majority of both Gambians and Senegalese are Muslim, there is complete religious freedom, and Islam does not dictate the official days of business, which instead follow the Sunday-based weekend of the former colonial mother-countries, Britain and France.

Friday is however the Muslim holy day and working hours are modified slightly to allow for the times of prayer and mosque attendance. Men and women will be seen in their beautiful flowing robes, or just in ordinary day-wear, walking to their local mosque to attend Friday Prayers.

Muslims, in any event, pray five times a day. These are the names in Arabic (first) and Wolof (second) of the five daily prayers: Subh or Fajar (6 a.m.); Suhr or Tisbar (2 p.m.); Asr or Takusan (5 p.m.); Maghrib or Timis (7 p.m.); and Isha or Gewe (8 p.m.).

Other Religions: The Gambia

The following is a selection of the places of worship of some of the major non-Islamic religions, with details of the times of their services.

Anglican/Protestant

Cathedral of St Mary, Independence Drive, Banjul (9 a.m. Matins; 9:20 a.m. Sung Eucharist; 7:15 p.m. Evensong)

St Paul's Church, Fajara (9 a.m. Holy Communion)

Christ Church, Serekunda (9:30 a.m. Matins and Sung Eucharist)

Church of the African Martyrs, Farafenni (10 a.m. Holy Communion and Matins)

St Cuthbert's, Basse Santa Su (9 a.m. Holy Communion)

Roman Catholic

Cathedral of Our Lady of the Assumption, Hagan Street, Banjul (Mass at 7 a.m., 9:30 a.m., 7:30 p.m.)

Church of the Holy Spirit, Box Bar Road, Banjul (Mass at 7:30 a.m. and 10 a.m.)

Star of the Sea Church, Bakau (Mass at 9 a.m. and 10:15 a.m.)

Methodist

Wesley Church, Dobson Street, Banjul (9:30 a.m. and 7 p.m. on alternate Sundays)

Methodist Church, Atlantic Road, opp. BICI Bank, Bakau (10:30 a.m.)

Trinity Church, Serekunda (11 a.m.)

New Apostolic Church of the Gambia, Serekunda (10 a.m., Divine Service)

Glory Baptist Fellowship, Kanifing Road, Old Jeshwang (9:30 a.m. Bible Studies, 10:30 a.m. Worship)

Other Religions: Senegal

The following is a selection of the places of worship of the major religions in Dakar. In addition, Catholic churches will be found in all sizeable towns throughout the country.

Protestant

St Paul's Church, Rue Carnet (Services at 8:30 a.m. and 11:15 a.m., Sunday in both French and English)

Roman Catholic

Cathédrale du Souvenir Africain, Avenue de la République (Mass at 7:30 a.m. daily; also 7 p.m. on Saturday; 9 a.m. and 10 a.m. on Sunday)

Evangelical

Evangelic Church, Rue 11, Sicap Amitié 2, Dakar (9:00 a.m. Bible Studies and 10 a.m. service, both in French; Sunday)

Assembly of God

Chapel, Boulevard de Général de Gaulle (10 a.m., Sunday Service)

COMMUNICATIONS

MEDIA/BROADCAST

The Gambia

The government controls two radio stations which both follow official government policy but run their own programmes.

Radio Gambia: Situated on Bakau New Town Road, Bakau, not far from the stadium. Programmes are in all the main Gambian languages and in English, with regular news bulletins, schools' broadcasts and general programmes on education, culture, religion and music. Transmission is on 648 kHz.

Radio Syd was started in 1967 by a Swedish woman, Britt Wadner, who moved to the Gambia via Radio Caroline and the Canary Islands, when her pirate radio station, Radio Mercur, operating off the Danish coast, was threatened by the Danish authorities. The present station is on dry land at Mile 2, on the way out of Banjul. Programmes range from European and African music to news bulletins in English and Swedish (regularly listened to by Swedish tourists). Local information is advertised and requests can also be broadcast for a small fee. Transmission is on 909 kHz. (Incidentally, "Syd" is Swedish for "South" – nothing to do with anyone's name.)

Radio Senegal (1300 kHz), with programmes in Wolof, Diola, Fula and French is also regularly listened to in the Gambia.

BBC World Service is easily picked up on several short wave frequencies, depending on the time of day. 11, 13 and 19 metre bands are best during the day and evening with 25, 31 and 49 metre bands for the early morning, 5 a.m. to 9 a.m. The BBC Africa Service (African News, Focus on Africa, Arts and Africa) is available between 6:30 a.m. and 8:45 a.m. and again at intervals between 4:15 p.m. and 10 p.m. *London Calling*, their overseas programme journal, is available by post from BBC World Service (African Section), P.O. Box 76, Bush House, Strand, London WC2.

Television: Gambian television does not exist but Senegalese TV can be picked up in the Gambia by those who don't mind programmes being mostly in French.

Senegal

The **ORTS** (Office de Radiodiffusion Television du Sénégal) is the national government-controlled radio and TV network, which operates a monopoly on broadcasting in the country. Its radio broadcasts take place in Wolof, Diola and Fula but French is the official and most used language. There are news programmes in English on **Radio Senegal** (1300kHz) on Mondays to Fridays between 6:40 p.m. and 7:05 p.m. and on Saturdays between 6:45 p.m. and 7 p.m.

In addition, it is possible in Senegal to pick up **Radio Syd**, **Radio Gambia**, **BBC World Service** (see above under the Gambia for details of all three) as well as a wide range of far-flung stations if you have good short-wave equipment.

Senegalese Television: Broadcasts a mixture of current affairs, cultural and sporting programmes and occasional films from 6:15 p.m. to 11:15 p.m. daily. There is a News in English on Thursdays and Sundays from 7:50 p.m. to 8 p.m.

MEDIA/PRINT

The Gambia

The Gambia has a free press in theory, though due to scarcity of resources not much is made of this liberty. The Government publishes a weekly, *Gambia News Bulletin;* and a variety of independent publications such as *The Gambia Onward* appear from time to time, printed and designed in a rather rudimentary fashion. (This is not to say they cannot be lively if idiosyncratic reads, with the African capacity for scurrilous cartooning much in evidence.)

A limited selection of mainly British publications is available from outside the country.

Senegal

Senegal also has a free press and in this larger, more sophisticated country a reasonable selection of papers and magazines gets published.

The only national daily is *Le Soleil* which is widely available in the main towns in the morning. Other publications include: *Sud Hebdo*, a weekly devoted to politics, current affairs and business; *Walfadjiri*, a current affairs weekly; *Le Devoir*, a bimonthly also devoted to current affairs; *Le Cafard Libéré*, a satirical weekly modelled on the celebrated French Canard Enchainé.

Le Dakarois is a free monthly information pamphlet which also carries small features, recipes, many advertisements of interest to visitors and good up-to-date information on leisure activities and culture. A small English-language equivalent named *This Month in Dakar* also exists. The news kiosks of Dakar offer quite a good selection of international publications. Obviously, the French press is best represented, but British and American papers also are available, usually not many days late.

POST & TELECOMMUNICATION

The Gambia
Mail: Mail to and from UK and the Gambia is quick and cheap. Letters take about five days to reach Europe.

The main Post Office is in Russell Street, Banjul, next to the Albert Market and there are branches in Bakau (set back off the road opposite the African Village Hotel), Kairaba Avenue (opposite Mrs. Ndow's school), Serekunda and in the larger up-country towns. Hours are 8:30 a.m. to 12:15 p.m. and 2 p.m. to 4 p.m. (Monday to Friday) and 8:30 a.m. to 12 p.m. (Saturday).

Most hotels will sell you stamps provided you buy the postcard there as well. They also have their own postboxes which are regularly emptied in time to catch the flights out.

Telephone and Telex: A brand-new telephone system using satellite connections has recently been installed in the Gambia, run by GAMTEL. You can call internationally as easily as you would from home, but only from certain public international exchanges. These are in the GAMTEL offices in: **Bakau** (Atlantic Road, opposite African Village Hotel), open 8 a.m. to 11 p.m.; **Kotu Beach Complex** (next to Novotel), 8 a.m. to 10 p.m.; **Serekunda** (junction Kairaba Avenue/Serekunda Avenue), 8 a.m. to 11 p.m.; **Banjul** (Russell Street, next to Post Office),

open 24 hours; **Banjul** (Telegraph Road, near Atlantic Hotel), open 24 hours; **Yundum Airport**, 8 a.m. to 10 p.m.

International calls are monitored at the main reception desk of the GAMTEL public exchanges and you will pay for the amount of time used. Keep account of the minutes or you will be faced with an unexpectedly large bill as you leave. The ringing tone is a single longish bleep, repeated. For international calls, dial 000 then the country code followed by the number you want, omitting any 0 from the area code e.g. for London 000-44-1-number. See below under Senegal for a list of some of the most common country codes.

For local calls within the Gambia, coin-operated phone boxes have been installed in certain areas.

Telexes and Telegrams can be sent from any of the public international exchanges listed above.

Fax machines are at Russell Street and Telegraph Road branches in Banjul, as well as at a number of the large hotels in Bakau and Fajara.

Senegal
Mail: Mail between Europe and Senegal is reasonably efficient. A letter should not take longer than a week and can take as little as four days.

Dakar's main Post Office is on the Boulevard Pinet Laprade and is open 8 a.m. to 4 p.m. Monday to Thursday and 8 a.m. to 1 p.m. Friday.

All major towns have Post Offices and most medium-sized and large hotels will sell stamps and accept letters for posting.

Telephone and Telex: Senegal has an efficient French-system telephone network, operated by the national company SONATEL. International calls, using coins or pre-paid cards, may be made at the two main SONATEL offices in Dakar – Boulevard de la Republique and Rue Wagane Diouf – which are open until 1 a.m. There is a small number of less reliable public telephone booths in the street, but they are often in a state of disrepair.

For international calls, dial 00 followed by the country code, area code omitting the 0, and number e.g. for London 00-44-1-937-6316. The ringing tone is a single longish bleep, repeated; engaged is a rapidly repeated series of short bleeps.

The following is a list of some of the most common country codes:

UK 44	*USA & Canada* 1
France 33	*West Germany* 49
Norway 47	*Sweden* 46
Denmark 45	*Switzerland* 41
Austria 43	*Netherlands* 31
Belgium 32	*Ireland* 353

Telexes and telegrams may be sent from the SONATEL offices mentioned above.

Fax machines are found in all of the major hotels.

EMERGENCIES

SECURITY, CRIME & LOSS

The Gambia is one of the safest countries in West Africa for visitors. Senegal also has a low crime rate in terms of the whole sub-region, but the city of Dakar is now such a major metropolis and so overcrowded that street crime has unfortunately become a considerable problem. You are unlikely to be mugged in the streets or threatened by a souvenir vendor in Banjul because you do not want to buy his wares though the risk is greater in Dakar. All white people (and tourists more than others) are rich in comparison with the average Gambian or Senegalese, so you should not flaunt your wealth in public as there are occasional thefts everywhere.

Don't leave valuables somewhere tempting such as on the car passenger seat, on the back of your chair in a bar, or sticking visibly out of your pocket. Many of the thefts that occur happen on the spur of the moment – a quick snatch while your attention is distracted. Don't walk alone along a deserted beach especially at night when the guards have gone home. Certain areas and beaches, e.g. near the Palm Grove/Wadner Beach hotels outside Banjul and along the exposed Route de la Corniche in Dakar, are well known for thieves. If you got to markets where you are continually nudged and

jostled, leave your watch and jewellery at home, keep your handbag, fastened up, in front of you and remove your money from your back trouser pocket. If you are bird-watching in an isolated area, go in a group without money or valuables (binoculars are not what thieves are after).

If you do lose anything valuable, report it to your hotel, to the local police station and to your tour operator, but don't be surprised if not much happens. Hotels have safe deposit boxes for valuables and money. In the case of a lost passport, notify your country's High Commission, Embassy or Consulate and ask for a certificate of loss and a temporary passport. Lost travellers' cheques, credit cards or bankbooks should be reported immediately to the local banks as well as to your issuing bank at home by phone.

In the Gambia, the emergency telephone number for the police is 17 (Ambulance is 16 and Fire 18).

In Senegal, where there is a special plain clothes police unit dealing with tourists' security, the emergency police telephone number is 232323 (Fire is 18).

MEDICAL SERVICES

The Gambia

Most hotels have a nurse or doctor on call for emergencies and will treat the minor irritating infections that occur such as stomach upsets, cuts, sore throats, coughs etc. at a hotel "clinic". In emergencies, the nearest hospital will be called. If you are on your own and are taken ill, you must make your own way to the doctor or hospital; ambulances are rare although there is theoretically an emergency ambulance service (phone 16). **The Royal Victoria Hospital** in Banjul has good doctors and operating facilities, as has the **Westfield Clinic**, Kanifing.

The Medical Research Council in Atlantic Road, Fajara, is a research establishment, not a hospital, and is not equipped or obliged to deal with emergencies. Wherever you are, treatment is not free, however small the complaint, and it is best to take out medical insurance before you leave home.

Some medical practitioners in the Banjul/Bakau area:

S. J. Palmer and L. Peters (Western Clinic, Kanifing) (Tel: 92213/92142); Sheriff Ceesay (Tel: 28111); J. A. Mahoney (Tel:

95325); M. K. B. Faal (Banjul Clinic, Independence Drive) (Tel: 28832); Adama Sallah (Lamtoro Clinic, Independence Drive) (Tel: 28457).

Dentist: R. O. W. Carrol, 9 Cameron Street, Banjul. Tel: 28304.

The only hospital up-river is the Government Hospital, Bansang, run by Chinese doctors. There are government and/or mission clinics in the larger towns or villages such as Basse, Brikama, Kaur. Also at Marakissa, Bwiam, Georgetown, Fatoto, Karantaba, Kerewan, Sibanor, Somita, Kuntaur.

Senegal

As in the Gambia, all major hotels will have medical assistance on call for guests. In terms of public health, the country is one of the best equipped in Africa, with 10 major hospitals and a substantial network of clinics and dispensaries. A disproportionate amount of this infrastructure is concentrated in and around Dakar, however, and you should obviously not expect to find modern facilities (or any facilities) available in small towns and villages in the interior of the country.

There is no government ambulance service; the service of the Institut de Santé, Dakar is available (Tel: 22 62 52).

The best hospital in Dakar is the fully equipped **Hôpital Principal**, Avenue Roume. Others are the **Hôpital Aristide le Dantec**, Avenue Pasteur and the **Hôpital Fann**, Route de Ouakam.

The national daily newspaper, *Le Soleil*, publishes a list of doctors and chemists on night duty, as does the free monthly magazine *Le Dakarois* and its English language equivalent, *This Month in Dakar*.

The following is a list of some medical practitioners in the Dakar area:

L. Leblanc (Tel: 21 35 74); V. Frament (Tel: 22 47 65); J. L. Cabrol (Tel: 21 23 64); H. D'Erneville (Tel: 22 02 67); B. Diop (Tel: 22 02 59); M. Touré (Tel: 21 59 46); I. Gueye (Tel: 21 16 38).

Dentists:

G. Drouet (Tel: 21 11 58); P. Lagier (Tel: 21 11 58); A. Aidara (Tel: 21 68 47); M. H. NDiaye (Tel: 22 65 77).

GETTING AROUND

ORIENTATION

The Gambia

Signposts and street signs are fairly minimal in number in the Gambia, but then the country is tiny and possesses a small uncomplicated road system. Major directions on the few roads inland are signposted. In Banjul, roads are easy to find, but individual buildings not always so as numbering may be erratic or non-existent.

Senegal

In the interior, the same problems exist as in the Gambia i.e. few and unreliable signs. There are almost always plenty of people around to check directions with, however.

Dakar is well-endowed with French-style street signs and the central districts are very easy to negotiate.

In both countries, people will come up to visitors in the street offering to act as guides. You should be wary of such people in proportion to their demeanour and where you are. In other words, it would be extremely foolish to accompany a tough-looking man in an isolated part of Dakar, while the risk from a young boy in Banjul would be likely to be negligible. In both countries, however, professional guides are available through the major hotels and tourist facilities.

MAPS

The Gambia

A selection of maps for tourists can be found at the **Methodist Bookshop**, Buckle Street, Banjul (Tel: 28179), and also in hotel shops. The Ministry of Information produces a good Tourist Information and Guide Map for D35 and Admap, in conjunction with Enterprise Holidays, does a simplified tourist map at D15. Both are clear and informative and are on sale at the bookshop.

Senegal

The best maps of Senegal and Dakar are published by the Institut Géographique National de France (107, rue de la Boétie, 75008 Paris or P.O. Box 4016, Dakar). Michelin's sheet 953, Africa, North and West, is the best general map to the region with most important information for travellers shown.

Both are available from a number of bookshops in central Dakar.

A free Dakar city plan can be obtained from the Ministry of Tourism.

AIRPORT/CITY LINKS

The Gambia

On arrival at Yundum Airport, package tourists and those with reservations at the major hotels will have the privilege of special buses to take them to their hotels but there are no public buses. Hertz will send a chauffeur-driven car to meet you by prior arrangement with your hotel, otherwise there are no cars for hire at the airport. Taxis have a set price per vehicle for the journey to Bakau (D80) or Banjul (D100). If you cannot afford this and cannot find someone to share a taxi or car with you, you will have to walk to the main road (1 mile/ 1.6 km) and catch public transport (bus or shared bush taxi – see under **Public Transport**) to Serekunda from which point other taxis will take you to your destination. Public taxis and minibuses only ply regular main roads. If you want to be dropped at your door, you will have to pay extra.

Visitors on package tours will also have their own bus provided for departure. If you are travelling independently, you will have to make your way to the airport by private car or taxi. Public transport (bus or bush taxi) will only take you as far as the entrance to the airport, leaving you with a mile to walk, carrying your bags.

Senegal

Package tourists will be met at Yoff Airport by buses to transfer them to their destinations within the country. The major hotels of Dakar also have courtesy minibuses to meet guests with reservations.

Independent travellers have a choice of taxi or airport bus to get to the centre of Dakar. Black and yellow government-regulated taxis wait in a line outside the airport lounge. There is a fixed price which is usually displayed on a board at the head of the taxi queue. At the time of press, the journey to central Dakar was fixed at CFA 3000 for day trips and CFA 3500 at night (from midnight to 5 a.m.). If you have a lot of luggage, it is considered reasonable to leave an extra CFA 1000 as a sort of semi-tip, semi-payment. Before starting the journey, make sure the driver knows you know the fixed price and agrees to abide by it. Do not accept offers of taxis from people inside the airport building – they will almost certainly not be licensed taxi-drivers and will be looking for an exorbitant fee.

Buses run from outside the airport building into central Dakar until midnight. The service is reasonably efficient, but can get crowded. The fare into the city is approximately CFA 500 one-way.

PUBLIC TRANSPORT

The Gambia

Buses: Gambia Public Transport Corporation (GPTC) has the monopoly of the public buses. They are enormous blue and white MAN vehicles which ply in and around Banjul and Serekunda, go up-country as far as Basse and Fatoto and also run twice a day to Dakar in Senegal.

Fares are cheap (D2 Banjul-Serekunda) but timetables irregular and crowds prohibitive at rush hours (school and office closing times, mid afternoon). Buses pick up and set down only at recognised bus stops.

Long-distance buses go from **Banjul** and **Serekunda** up the south bank as far as **Fatoto** and along the north bank from Barra to **Farafenni** and **Lamin Koto** (for Georgetown). Express buses take approximately 10 hours to Basse and only stop at Soma, Georgetown, Bansang and Basse. Non-express buses stop at all villages en route. You may well have to change buses somewhere on the way.

Banjul-Dakar by bus: Buy your ticket (D60 or CFA 2500) at the ferry terminal in Banjul. Cross the ferry as a foot passenger and make your way to the bus waiting at Barra. Customs formalities at Karang (Senegal) can take some time. Allow for a five-hour journey.

Departure times daily:

8 a.m. ferry from Banjul for 9 a.m. departure from Barra.

10 a.m. ferry from Banjul for 11 a.m. departure from Barra.

Taxis: These can be hired privately for the day with a driver. Rates are displayed on the boards outside hotels and are for the whole car, irrespective of the number of passengers, and include petrol. If you want to go somewhere not mentioned on the board, negotiate a firm price with the driver before you start. Compare his prices with some of the other prices and distances on the board and perhaps with that of another taxi-driver before you agree. Pay cash on return.

Sample rates: D550 to Tendaba Camp and back for the day.

D500 per day in and around Banjul, Serekunda and environs.

D600 to Ziguinchor (Senegal) and back in one day.

D1500 to Dakar and back in one day.

Short-Distance Taxi Drives: Gambian taxis can be any make of car, any colour, any size, and are only identifiable by their yellow number plate. They have no meters and prices are fixed for tourists between hotels and certain destinations. A board outside the hotel will give you the rates. They are not cheap.

Sample rates: Bungalow Beach Hotel to Bakau, return, including one-hour wait: D75

Bungalow Beach Hotel to Banjul, return, including one-hour wait: D130.

Bungalow Beach Hotel to restaurant, including two-hour wait: D80.

However, at these prices you will have the taxi to yourself, door to door, and will not be obliged to pick up people on the road. Agree your price before you set out, whatever the board may say.

Bush taxis: These are large saloon cars or minibuses, licensed to carry passengers. They can be boarded by the side of the road (if they have any seats left) but only ply the main roads and will not drop you at your door without a fairly large extra charge (e.g. D12 on top of a D3 fare). They are often reluctant to pick up white passengers whom they expect to be able to pay for a tourist taxi.

To travel long distances by bush taxi: Go to Serekunda taxi park. Choose a taxi that is almost full, then you won't have long to wait before setting off. Again, agree your price before you get in.

Sample rates: Serekunda-Brikama, D12; Serekunda-Soma, D35; Serekunda-Ziguinchor, D45.

Bicycles: Bicycles may be hired by the hour, the half-day or the full day from outside the main hotels (Senegambia, Kotu Complex, Fajara, Tropic Garden, African Village, Sunwing, Atlantic, Palm Grove) and are a cheap way of getting around locally and seeing places off the main roads. There are no hills to contend with, only the heat and distances.

Rates, which are reasonable, vary from season to season and are written up on a board nearby. Prices should still be confirmed before you ride off. Check brakes and that you are given a lock and chain with key.

Water Transport: River excursions are organised by Gamtours, West Africa Tours and Graham Rainey, mostly during the tourist season (November to April) but with a few day-trips into the creeks at other times of the year. (See **Excursions**.)

Ferries across the River Gambia:

Banjul-Barra: every 2 hours. First one 8 a.m. Last one 6 p.m.

Barra-Banjul: every 2 hours. First one 9 a.m. Last one 7 p.m.

Crossing time: 20 to 40 minutes. Cost: D40 for Gambian registered cars; D50 for Gambian registered Land-Rovers; CFA 4500 for foreign registered cars; CFA 5000 for foreign registered Land-Rovers.

Mansa Konko-Farafenni (and vice versa) on the Transgambia Highway: No regular crossing times; as soon as the ferry is full. Anticipate a long wait to get on.

MacCarthy Island: to and from the south bank – more or less as soon as you arrive. No charge. To and from the north bank – as above.

Senegal

Buses: The Dakar region is served by the SOTRAC company (Société des Transports en Commun de Cap-Vert) which runs a substantial network of town bus routes as well as long-distance coaches to all the major cities.

Local buses are cheap and reliable, but can be extremely crowded during rush hour. Under these conditions, you should obviously watch your pockets and handbags against pick-pockets. Buses carry a number which corresponds to their route and the driver or conductor will happily advise you of your stop – if you can see him during rush hours.

Coaches depart from two main stations in Dakar, in the central **Avenue Malick Sy** and at the **Rond Point de Colobane**, near the beginning of the autoroute north. The coach to and from Banjul uses the Malick Sy terminal. The offices of SOTRAC, from which information may be obtained are in Rue A. Ndoye, Dakar (Tel: 23 23 16).

Taxis: Government-licensed and regulated taxis are painted yellow or orange-and-black and circulate in the streets of Dakar as well as waiting outside the major hotels and in ranks here and there. They operate on meters which start at CFA 60. Make sure that the taxi-driver starts his meter and beware of tricks to extract a higher than permitted fee. This includes demanding a large sum to pick up passengers late at night when they are in a vulnerable position (with no alternative means of transport available) and short-changing.

Bush Taxis: Known in French as *taxis-brousse*, they are usually Peugeot estates carrying up to seven passengers which ply the routes between towns. They leave from the bus stations (see above) when they are full. To travel to, for example, St Louis, go to the bus station in plenty of time and ask for the place where St Louis taxis leave from. It is a good idea to do this in a (town) taxi as obvious tourists can be swamped by vendors, would-be porters and other less innocent opportunists. If you choose an empty taxi, remember that you will have to wait until up to six more passengers arrive before the driver will set off. You can, of course, offer to pay for as many places as you wish up to the total potential complement of the vehicle.

There are in addition privately-owned minibuses, painted blue, named "cars rapides" which carry passengers to the suburbs, stopping by the side of their route to pick up and set down. All of these vehicles have government-regulated fares, which vary widely according to the large number of possible trips.

Bicycles: Bicycle hire is relatively rare in Senegal, although many people use bicycles as daily transport. Some of the big holiday complexes have a number of machines available, however.

Water Transport: The principal navigable or crossable rivers are the Senegal, Gambia and Casamance.

The ferry across the Senegal at **Rosso** runs to no precise timetable, crossing as and when traffic demands. Since the closing of the Senegal-Mauritania border in 1989, however, this service has been severely disrupted and in the unlikely event of visitors wishing to use this service – its sole function is to take traffic north into Mauritania – enquiries should be made in Dakar or St Louis as to the situation.

Details of the river steamer *Bou El Mogdad*, which runs a weekly trip up the River Senegal in the winter season, may be obtained from the Ministry of Tourism, tour operators in Dakar, from any of the hotels in St Louis, or directly from the proprietor Georges Console at B.P. 124 St Louis, (Tel: 71 042). For full details of the ferries crossing the major waterway cutting through the centre of the country, the River Gambia, see above.

Two boats link Dakar with the southern estuary of the Casamance. The *Casamance Express* is a cargo boat with a number of cabins and room for many passengers who sleep on deck.

The *M.S. African Queen* is a luxurious ocean-going yacht, fully equipped with sports and accommodation facilities of a high order. It is operated by the French company Africatours, 9-11 Avenue Franklin-Roosevelt, 75008 Paris (Tel: 4723 78 59).

Information about both services may be obtained from the Ministry of Tourism in Dakar.

Trains: Senegalese Railways, R.C.F.S. (Regie des Chemins de Fer Senegalais), 11 Rue Parchappe, Dakar, (Tel: 21 72 24), operates services on two lines. The first connects Dakar with St Louis in the north, with branch lines running off from Louga to Linguère. Theoretically, the St Louis train runs twice daily, taking four hours for the trip. It is advisable to check this information, however.

The second line links Dakar with Bamako in Mali, via Thiès, Djourbel and Tambacounda, with a branch line to Kaolack.

Information about times of trains may be obtained by telephoning Dakar 22 31 40. The central station is a rather beautiful turn of the century building beside the port.

PRIVATE TRANSPORT

The Gambia

A valid driving licence for your own country or an International Driving Licence is required to drive in the Gambia. Driving is on the right.

Remember that breakdown services are non-existent. If you can get access to a telephone, a call to your car hire agent will perhaps get them to come out to you. Otherwise you must have the car mended locally if at all possible and charge the firm on return.

The following is a list of car hire facilities in the country:

Hertz, The Senegambia Hotel (Tel: 93393). They hire out chauffeur-driven cars (Volvos) only. Businessmen in the Gambia for a few hours only may hire Hertz cars for up to 12 hours at an hourly fee, plus petrol. Cars can be ordered before arrival through British Airways agents or through your hotel booking agent.

Avis, Atlantic Road, Bakau (Tel: 96119, Tlx: 2303). Self-drive or chauffeur-driven cars.

Black and White Safaris Ltd., Serekunda (Tel: 93174 and 92815), have four-seat and eight-seat Land-Rovers for hire with a driver who acts as a guide.

Francisco's, on the corner of Kairaba Avenue and Atlantic Road (Tel: 95332), has Suzuki jeeps for hire, self-drive.

Fritz Enterprises Rent-a-car, 17 Kairaba Avenue, Serekunda (Tel: 91464), hires out Citroen 2CVs, self-drive.

Autogam Co. Ltd., Atlantic Road, Bakau (Tel: 96020), has Peugeot 305s and 505s, self-drive.

Senegal

A valid national driving licence or an International Driving Licence is required. Driving is on the right, and French traffic rules are followed (e.g. priority to the right).

In the interior, the same warnings about lack of availability of breakdown assistance apply as to the Gambia. In Dakar, garage facilities are not too bad.

The following is a list of car hire facilities in Dakar:

Hertz, 26 rue Jules Ferry (Tel: 22 52 87). Self-drive and chauffeur-driven, selection of vehicles. Hertz also have offices at the airport (Tel: 22 39 93), and in St Louis (Tel: 61 12 60), Nianing (Tel: 57 10 85) and Ziguinchor (Tel: 91 11 71).

Car Afrique, 100 rue J. Gomis (Tel: 21 88 67).

Dakar Auto, 7 rue Marclary (Tel: 21 55 58).

Eurocar, Boulevard de la Libération (Tel: 22 18 99).

Locatour, Avenue Lamine Gueye (Tel: 22 71 44).

Soatour, 29 rue A. A. Ndoye (Tel: 21 38 45).

Transacauto, 61 rue Felix Faure (Tel: 22 20 16).

INTERNAL FLIGHTS

The Gambia

There are no internal flights within the Gambia.

Day trips by air can be taken to **Cape Verde** (Ilha del Sal) by Gambia Air Shuttle once a week on Fridays, and to **Dakar**, daily, by Gambia Air Shuttle and Air Senegal (Air Shuttle one way, Air Senegal the other). A visa is needed for Senegal by citizens of some countries, e.g. UK (See **Visas and Passports**.) Schedules and prices are subject to changes.

Addresses: Gambia Air Shuttle, 23 Buckle Street, Banjul (Tel: 26998).

Air Senegal, c/o Gambia Airways, 69 Wellington Street, Banjul (Tel: 28207).

Banjul Travel Agency, 61 Buckle Street, Banjul (Tel: 28813 or 28473).

Senegalese High Commission, 10 Cameron Street, Banjul (Tel: 27469).

Senegal

The national airline has flights to St Louis, Ziguinchor and Tambacounda. Schedules variable.

Address: Air Senegal, 45 Avenue Albert Sarraut, Dakar (Tel: 22 72 29).

It is possible to charter light planes (eight-seater Kiger 90 or five-seater Seneca 2) from Dakar Yoff Airport.

Addresses: Senegalair, 31 Avenue Roume (Tel: 21 34 25) and Air Senegal (as above).

ON FOOT & HITCHHIKING

The heat and distances are not conducive to walking tours in the Gambia or Senegal and hitchhiking is not common. It is done by volunteers around the main population centres but not much up-country. If you try to hitch and someone stops for you, you may well be asked to pay for your ride.

WHERE TO STAY

HOTELS

The Gambia

Since the Gambia has become such a popular destination for winter holidays, hotels have sprung up at a rapid pace. Some are open all year round and others only during the tourist season (November-April). Tour operators from several European countries organize package tours at very advantageous prices. Even so, there is always room somewhere for the business person and the independent traveller. Only the larger hotels take credit cards: American Express, Diners Club, Mastercard, Visa.

Hotels catering for tourists on a large scale are little worlds on their own, set in landscaped gardens of colourful tropical trees and flowers with their own swimming pools, bars, restaurants, shops, sports facilities, entertainment and access to the beach. Numerous smaller hotels also exist at lower prices but without the same facilities. Booking for the latter is done on the spot, when you arrive, whereas the larger tourist hotels are normally booked through travel agents at home. During the tourist season it is necessary to book early. Air-conditioning is not essential during the dry (tourist) season but is recommended for comfort at other times of the year. Most hotel bedrooms have their own shower and toilet en suite. There is no system of grading in operation but the following is a list of the major hotels.

Banjul and the Coast

International Standard, Large:

African Village, Atlantic Road, Bakau (Tel: 95307, 95384). Open high season only.

Amis Beach Hotel, Cape Point (Tel: 95106, 95035). Open all year.

Atlantic Hotel, Marina Parade, Banjul (Tel: 28601). Open all year. A Copthorne Hotel. Reservations UK (0800-414741).

Bakotu Hotel, Kotu Beach Complex (Tel: 95555). Open high season only.

Bungalow Beach, Kotu Beach Complex (Tel: 95288). Self catering suites. Open all year.

Fajara Hotel, Fajara (Tel: 95351). Open all year.

Kotu Strand Village, Kotu Beach Complex (Tel: 95609). Some suites with cooker and fridge available. Open all year.

Palm Grove Hotel, Mile 2 from Banjul (Tel: 28630). Open all year.

Senegambia Beach Hotel, Kololi Point (Tel: 92717/8/9, 91838/9/40). Open all year.

Sunwing Hotel, Cape Point (Tel: 95428). Open high season only.

Tropic Garden Hotel, Atlantic Road, Bakau (Tel: 95369). Open all year.

Wadner Beach Hotel, Mile 2 from Banjul. Open high season only.

Smaller Holiday Hotels:

These hotels have no pool and fewer facilities than the larger hotels. Accommodation and meals only. Used by tour operators to house extra guests at lower prices. Still comfortable and pleasant.

Cape Point Hotel, Cape Point (Tel: 95005).

Francisco's, Atlantic Road (corner of Kairaba Avenue), Fajara (Tel: 95332).

Friendship Hotel, near the Stadium, Bakau (Tel: 95829).

Romana Hotel, Atlantic Road (behind CFAO), Bakau (Tel: 95127).

Other Hotels in the Banjul/Bakau/Serekunda Area:

These hotels are cheaper, more basic and not designed to modern standards of comfort. They do not have their own generators and are therefore subjected to electricity cuts.

Adonis Hotel, Hill Street/Wellington Street corner, Banjul (Tel: 27262)

Apollo Hotel, 33 Buckle Street, Banjul

(Tel: 28184).

Atlantic Guest House, Atlantic Road, Bakau (next to Tropic Garden Hotel). No telephone.

Carlton Hotel, Independence Drive, Banjul (Tel: 27258).

City Travellers Lodge, Dobson Street, Banjul.

Gambisara Motel, Kairaba Avenue (opposite Gamtel), Serekunda end (Tel: 93114).

Kantora Hotel, Independence Drive, Banjul (Tel: 28715).

Up-Country Hotels, Rest Houses and Camps:

Eddie's Hotel, Farafenni (Tel: 31259). Restaurant, bar and nightclub. Own generator, therefore reliable electricity.

Apollo 2 Hotel, Basse. Basic but clean.

Georgetown District Commissioner's Rest House. Prepare your own meals on your own cooker. Use of refrigerator when current is on. Running water in afternoons and evenings only.

Mansa Konko Government Rest House. Just arrive and hope there is room. Bring your own food and water.

Bansang Rest House. Get permission from Mansa Konko Divisional Office on your way up. Bring your own food.

Tendaba Camp, on the River Gambia, 100 miles from Banjul. This camp caters for tourist excursions from Bakau and Banjul but is open all year round for anyone to stay in. Accommodation is in African-style huts; showers and toilets in a separate block. Restaurant and bar. Own generator. Relax on your own or join one of the land or river excursions organised from this camp.

Peter's Camp, Lamin Koto. Newly opened camp on the north bank, opposite Georgetown. Contact Gambia River Excursions (Tel: 95526).

There are no Youth Hostels in the Gambia, as in much of Africa.

Senegal

As a much larger and more varied country than the Gambia, Senegal has a wide range of accommodation, from the most basic of overnight facilities to luxurious modern 300-room hotels exactly as you would expect to find in Europe or the United States. Unlike the Gambia, where the vast majority of hotels are recently built and designed for tourism, Senegal also contains many small hotels in towns built at any time over the last century to cater for travellers of all descriptions. The general cultural background of the hotel industry in Senegal is French and a number of small establishments run by French proprietors offer a service not dissimilar to French country inns.

It is impossible to list all hotels, hostels and travel lodges and campsites here, but a selection of the more prominent places follows. See also the text in the "Places" section for hints on accommodation. Note that, in some cases, a telephone number is unavailable; in others, a complete address is not given where a town is too small to warrant it. The Senegalese Ministry of Tourism grades hotels on a scale of 0 to 4 stars, although the actual top category is 4 stars plus the letter L for luxury. This category would be occupied by large modern air-conditioned hotels with sizeable, well-decorated rooms with bath and toilet en suite. The lowest category would be a campsite or extremely basic small hotel without any of these facilities.

Dakar, Gorée and Region

Dakar:

Teranga Sofitel (4-star L), Rue Colbert (Tel: 23 10 44, Tlx: 21634).

Novotel (4-star L), Avenue Albert Sarraut (Tel: 21 88 49 Tlx: 21831).

Savana (4-star L), Pointe Bernard (Tel: 22 60 23 Tlx: 51424).

Indépendance (4-star L), Place de l'Indépendance, (Tel: 23 10 19 Tlx: 21837).

Al Afifa (4-star), 46 rue Jules Ferry (Tel: 21 85 43, Tlx: 51424).

La Croix du Sud (4-star), 20 Avenue Albert Sarraut (Tel: 23 29 47, Tlx: 51576).

Le Lagon 2 (4-star), Route de la Corniche Est (Tel: 22 17 80, Tlx: 51214).

Al Baraka (4-star), 35 Avenue A. K. Bourgi (Tel: 22 55 32, Tlx: 1428).

Afritel (4-star), Avenue Faidherbe (Tel: 22 13 12, Tlx: 61200).

Nina (4-star), 43 rue du Dr. Thèze (Tel: 21 41 81, Tlx: 61105).

Pacha (4-star), 40 Avenue Lamine Gueye (Tel: 23 10 18, Tlx: 21 636).

Le Plateau (3-star), 62 Jules Ferry (Tel: 21 04 20, Tlx: 61252).

La Paix (3-star), 38 rue A. A. Ndoye (Tel: 22 40 52).

Atlantic (3-star), 52 Rue du Dr. Thèze (Tel: 21 63 80).

Central (2-star), 16 Avenue Georges Pompidou (Tel: 21 72 17).

Continental (2-star), 10 rue Galandou Diouf (Tel: 22 03 71).

Gorée:
L'Hostellerie du Chevalier de Boufflers (Tel: 22 53 64).

Ngor:
Les Almadies (4-star L, Club Mediterranée), Pointe des Almadies (Tel: 23 39 14, Tlx: 31526).

Complexe Meridien (4-star L), Route de Ngor (Tel: 21 01 45).

Diarrama, Reservation Meridien Paris (Tel: 47 57 15 70, Tlx: 31516).

Massata Samb (4-star), Route de Ngor (Tel: 20 05 12, Tlx: 31515).

Le Sunugal (4-star), Route de Ngor (Tel: 20 03 30, Tlx: 31514).

Le Village Club Calao (3-star), Route de Ngor (Tel: 20 05 40, Tlx: 31501).

Hotel de l'Aérogare, Aérogare de Dakar Yoff (Tel: 20 07 35).

Hotel Darkassé (1-star), Route de Ngor (Tel: 23 03 53).

Thiès, Little Coast and Siné-Saloum
Thiès:
Hotel de Thiès (2-star), Rue Faidherbe (Tel: 51 15 26).

Hotel Rex (1-star), rue Douaumont (Tel: 81081).

Little Coast:
Village/Club du Baobab (4-star), La Somone (Tel: 22 02 66).

Village, Hotel de L'Hippocampe (2-star), La Somone (Tel: 26814).

Le Club Aldiana (4-star), Nianing (Tel: 57 10 84, Tlx: 77106).

Domaine de Nianing (3-star), Nianing (Tel: 57 10 85, Tlx: 77125).

Le Finio, Joal (Tel: 57 61 12).

Centre Touristique de la Petit Côte, M'Bour (Tel: 57 10 04, Tlx: 51683).

Savana Koumba (4-star), M'Bour (Tel: 57 11 12, Tlx: 77128).

Saly Hotel (4-star), M'Bour (Tel: 57 11 31/57 11 25, Tlx: 77124).

Royam (4-star), M'Bour (Tel: 57 10 79, Tlx: 77118).

Le Palm Beach (4-star), Saly Portudal (Tel: 22 03 81, Tlx: 77105). Reservation France (Tel: 42 96 37 70).

Novotel Saly (4-star), Saly Portudal (Tel: 57 11 91, Tlx: 77111).

Savana Saly (4-star), Saly Portudal (Tel: 57 11 12, Tlx: 77128).

Le Dior (3-star), Rue de la Gare, Kaolack (Tel: 41 15 13/41 18 45, Tlx: 51479).

Le Paris (2-star), Kaolack (Tel: 41 10 19, Tlx: 21512).

Keur Saloum (2-star), Toubakouta (Tel: 41 10 10, Tlx: 74063).

Les Palétuviers, Toubakouta (Tel: 21 87 73, Tlx: 51475).

Les Piroguiers (3-star), Foundiougne (Tel: 45 11 34, Tlx: 74068).

Le Pelican du Saloum (3-star), Ndangane (Tel: 23 54 46).

Centre Touristique (2-star), Kahone (Tel: 41 11 16).

Campement Hotel Djiffer, (Tel: 51 15 26).

St Louis, Senegal River, Djourbel and Ferlo
Mame Coumba Bang (4-star), Route Nationale 2, St Louis (Tel: 61 19 53, Tlx: 75111).

La Residence (3-star), Rue Blaise Diagne, St Louis (Tel: 61 12 60, Tlx: 75119).

Hotel de la Poste (2-star), St Louis (Tel: 61 11 18, Tlx: 75122).

Gite d'étape du Fleuve, Richard Toll (Tel: 63 32 40).

Hotel de la Poste Rest House at Richard Toll (contact Hotel in St Louis).

Campement Hotel, Maka Diama (Tel: 21 97 68, Tlx: 51432).

Le Baobab (3-star), Djourbel (Tel: 71 10 07).

Casamance and Southeast Senegal
Club Mediterranée (4-star L), Cap Skirring (Tel: 91 10 43).

Savana (4-star), Cap Skirring (Tel: 91 15 52, Tlx: 61331).

Kabrousse Mossor (4-star), Cap Skirring (Tel: 91 14 26, Tlx: 73020).

La Paillote (3-star), Cap Skirring (Tel: 91 13 79, Tlx: 73021).

Emitaï (3-star), Cap Skirring (Tel: 94 11 26, Tlx: 7301).

Hotel-Village de la Pointe Saint Georges (2-star), (Tel: 91 12 27, Tlx: 73012).

Le Diola (4-star), Route de Kandé,

Ziguinchor (Tel: 91 12 62, Tlx: 73026).

Le Nema Kadior (4-star), Route de Kandé, Ziguinchor (Tel: 91 10 52).

Aubert (3-star), Ziguinchor (Tel: 91 13 79, Tlx: 73012).

Le Tourisme (2-star), Ziguinchor (Tel: 91 12 27).

L'Escale (1-star), Ziguinchor (Tel: 91 204).

Le Relais Fleuri (2-star), Bignona (Tel: 94 12 02).

Campement Hotel "Le Hobe", Kolda (Tel: 96 11 70).

Village Hotel La Palmeraie, Sedhiou.

Asta Kebe (3-star), Tambacounda (Tel: 81 10 28).

Niji Hotel (1-star), Tambacounda (Tel: 81 12 50).

Hotel de la Gare, Tambacounda (Tel: 98 015).

Relais de Simenti (2-star), Niokolo Koba (Tel: 32 804).

Campement-Hotel du Niokolo Koba (Tel: 23 10 55).

In addition, the Casamance Region is the centre for the project of village *campements*, a way of offering low-rent accommodation to travellers who are interested in experiencing village life at close quarters. The *campements* are run cooperatively by villagers and consist of huts exactly like the others in the village, furnished with between two and four simple beds equipped with foam mattresses and mosquito nets. Lighting is usually by paraffin lamp and there will be simple separate WCs and showers. Basic meals will be offered, as well as the chance to participate in any activities, ceremonies, etc. that may be scheduled. *Campements* are situated in the following villages in the region: Elinkine, Enamporé, Baila, Koubalan, Thionck Essyl, Affiniam, Abané, Oussouye, Palmarin.

Information on how to book, what ceremonies may be taking place, etc., may be obtained from Mr. Adama Goudiaby, Director of the Centre Artisanal of Ziguinchor.

FOOD DIGEST

WHAT TO EAT

The general gastronomic background of the region of Senegambia is fairly simple. The staples are millet in the north and rice in the south, with rice making inroads generally. A great deal of fish is eaten – from the sea all along the Atlantic coast, and from the rivers throughout their hinterlands. There is less meat, although it is freely available everywhere.

In many cases, meat could do with more expert butchering before it reaches the kitchen. Steaks, stews, minced meat balls and kebabs are the most popular ways of serving meat dishes in almost every restaurant. Chicken, freshly grilled or roasted, can be tender and tasty.

A wide range of vegetables is available, so that a typical cooked dish might consist of a meat or fish and vegetable braise served with rice or millet. Peppercorns and chillies often add a touch of heat to the recipe.

Visitors should take advantage of the abundance of fresh fruit available: mangoes, pineapples, bananas, oranges (local ones are green, not orange, when ripe), water melons, pawpaws. All are sold outside tourist hotels and along the roadsides and supply ready-made refreshing desserts at all times of the day. Wash them well, peel, eat and enjoy.

Try also the groundnuts, dry-roasted in their skins and sold by the market women. Although most groundnuts (a.k.a. peanuts) are crushed into oil, they are also available freshly roasted everywhere at negligible cost, and find their way also into tasty sauces and soups.

Onto this African background has been grafted, in the case of the Gambia, the English culinary practices of the country's former colonisers, while Senegal has local adaptations of French cuisine. This can be extremely good.

Both Senegal and the Gambia share a taste for Arabic-style tea, sometimes with mint, served after meals according to an immutable ritual. Three little glasses – the first strong, bitter and frothy, the second sweeter and a little weaker, the last very sweet and quite pale.

The Gambia

Most hotels and restaurants serve both European and Gambian food but there are ample opportunities to try a wide range of other cuisines: Chinese, Malaysian, Vietnamese, Swedish, Lebanese and "international". "Fast food" snack bars are springing up everywhere too, especially Lebanese *shawarmas* – grilled meat slices served in pitta bread.

Fish is the obvious food to ask for in a country which lies along both sea coast and river. There is a disappointing lack of variety in the methods of serving fish dishes but garlic prawns, prawns Gambian-style and freshly fried or grilled ladyfish, barracuda, mullet, butterfish or sole are excellent. Local lobsters are fortunately quite safe to eat (whereas local oysters from the creeks, with their risk of hepatitis, are not) and are delicious served either as soup (bisque) or grilled with herbs over an open fire.

Gambian specialities which should definitely be tried include: *benachin* (fish stewed with a variety of vegetables and served with rice), *domoda* (groundnut stew with meat and vegetable, *chicken yassa* (*sissay yassa*, chicken smothered in fried onions), *sissay nyebe* (chicken with black-eyed beans), *akara bean fritters* (ground black-eyed bean fritters), *oleleh* (steamed bean cakes with palm oil). At all markets, women sit with large bowls of different types of cooked dishes which they serve to you in a piece of fresh bread, should you wish to be a bit more adventurous: D5, or less, for a palm oil and *nyebe* sandwich which is very satisfying.

Most hotels have *à la carte* and *table d'hôte* restaurants open to the general public and serving both European and African food. Some hotels have specialities of their own: Sunwing for Swedish fish dishes, Le Rive Gauche (Novotel) for French cuisine, Bungalow Beach for seafood buffet (Scandinavian style) on Saturday evenings, Tropic Garden for Japanese table, Senegambia for pizzas.

The following is a list of interesting restaurants in the country. Except in the big hotels, the Gambia entirely lacks any particularly up-market restaurants, so do not expect *haute cuisine* or luxurious and smart decor in any of these establishments. A pleasant meal in quite jolly surroundings may be had, however.

Banjul

African Heritage Gallery, Wellington Street (Tel: 26906). Light lunches, Danish-style. Good selection of meat and fish main dishes.

Braustuble, Leman Street (Tel: 28371). Indoor or outdoor seating. German-Lebanese run restaurant. Snacks, freshly grilled barbecued fish, good main dishes.

Oasis Bar and Restaurant, Clarkson Street (Tel: 26996). Gambian and other dishes.

Express Fish and Chips, Leman Street. Fish and chips. Cleanish and friendly.

Samburger Fast Food, Cameron Street. Shawarmas and cold drinks.

Carlton Hotel, Independence Drive (Tel: 27258). Lunches, suppers and drinks in cool, shady courtyard.

Hawa's Bar, Russell Street. Cool refreshments after shopping.

Out of Banjul

Ambassador Bar and Restaurant, Kairaba Avenue (Tel: 91269). Excellent draught beer, fish and chips, grilled half-chicken.

Baalbeck Restaurant, Atlantic Road, Bakau (Tel: 96120). Lebanese-run, delicious soups and grills.

Bakadaji Restaurant, off Kairaba Avenue, Latrikunda (a little difficult to find without a taxi). Delicious African cuisine.

Bamboo Restaurant, off Kairaba Avenue, Fajara (Tel: 95043, 95764). Long established Chinese restaurant. Delicious shrimp balls among other authentic Chinese specialities.

Bobo's, Bakau New Town Road. English-run bar and restaurant, attractive leafy alcoves to sit in.

Dolphin, next to Senegambia Hotel. Small English-run bar and restaurant overlooking sea. Good steak and kidney pie.

Francisco's, corner of Atlantic Road and Kairaba Avenue, Fajara (Tel: 95258). Very attractive Gambian-Danish run restaurant in exotic tropical garden setting.

Golden Dragon, Kairaba Avenue, Fajara (just past Kotu Beach turn-off). Lebanese food served in pitta bread, e.g. *kofta*, chicken, *merguez*, brains, at D12 per generous portion.

Rice Bowl, Cape Point Road (Tel: 95504). Chinese restaurant.

Samou's, Old Cape Road, Bakau (Tel: 95237). Gambian and European food.

Le Saigon, Kairaba Avenue (next to Fajara War Cemetery), Fajara (Tel: 96026). Vietnamese restaurant. Delicious soups and *nems* (Vietnamese spring rolls served with fresh green salad, mint and coriander).

Yellow Gate, off Kairaba Avenue. Malaysian-Chinese restaurant. Excellent satay.

Weinstube, just before the Senegambia Hotel. Sister restaurant to Braustuble Restaurant in Banjul with similar cuisine.

Palma Nova Bar and Restaurant, off Bakau New Town Road (Tel: 95220).

Paradise Beach Bar, on beach between Fajara and Bungalow Beach Hotels. Very popular beach bar for cool drinks and snacks.

Ilmondo Bar, on beach next to Bungalow Beach Hotel. Popular beach bar with shade, sunbeds, drinks and snacks.

Avenues Bar and Restaurant, Kairaba Avenue. Open-air bar, Gambian cuisine.

Sofanyama Bar and Restaurant, opposite Senegambia Hotel. Tables on shaded verandah for drinks, snacks and light meals.

Lamin Lodge, Mandinari (out towards airport, turn left and two miles down track to river). Picturesque floating restaurant on the creek. Freshly fried fish and chips.

Senegal

A greater range of dishes is available in Senegal, the Gambia being, in effect, a small sub-region of its larger neighbour from a gastronomic point of view. In addition, the French influence has been beneficial, providing much superior non-indigenous cuisine as well as a range of French-African compromise dishes, which are excellent.

Fish is a very important feature. The big white sea-bream known as a *thiof* is a superb fish simply grilled, stuffed à la St Louisienne or as part of a stew with rice. Senegal's most famous dish, *thie-bou-dienne*, is known throughout West Africa. (It consists of rice cooked with fish and vegetables.) Other well known dishes are *mafé* (peanut stew with meat and *yassa* (onion and lemon stew with chicken, fish or meat).

Shellfish are also excellent. Oysters, which are farmed as well as gathered in Siné-Saloum and Casamance, are excellent and pose less of a health risk than Gambian ones. Huge prawns are caught off most of the coast, as well as clams, mussels and superb lobsters and crayfish.

Unlike the Gambia, Senegal contains a variety of restaurants from the little *dibiteries* which serve grilled meat, through French-style brasseries (though do not expect a full-scale Alsace-style establishment under this name), up to quite classy and therefore pricey restaurants.

The following is a list of establishments in and around Dakar. Elsewhere in the country, the best restaurants belong to the hotels already listed. Outside the capital, it is rare to find high-quality restaurants existing independently of hotels, although there are always plenty of little *dibiteries* and cafés.

Chez Loutcha, Rue Blanchot (Tel: 21 03 02). Reasonably priced Euro-African menu.

Terrou Bi, Corniche Ouest (Tel: 22 02 47). Luxurious fish specialities including live lobsters from tank.

Le Ramatou, Route de N'Gor, Dakar-Yoff. Medium-priced French and Senegalese dishes.

Le Bilboquet, Avenue Roume (Tel: 22 17 42). Good French traditional cuisine in mock Normand setting.

Le Virage, Route de N'Gor (Tel: 20 06 57). Panoramic view of sea, good fish and seafood specialities.

Le Lagon, Route de la Petite Corniche (Tel: 21 53 22). Excellent fish with view over ocean in smart modern setting.

Brasserie Sarraut, Avenue Sarraut (Tel: 22 55 23). Good Parisian-style family restaurant with terrace.

Le Kermel, Place du Marché Kermel. French café-restaurant.

Le Rustic, Avenue Georges Pompidou (Tel: 22 18 76). Standard and quite well-run French café-restaurant.

Le Ponty, Avenue Georges Pompidou. Busy café/restaurant with terrace on main shopping street.

La Dagorne, Rue de Dagorne (Tel: 22 20 80). Good moderately priced French fish dishes.

Chez Charli, Route de Rufisque, Thiaroye sur Mer (Tel: 34 07 42). Tables under straw roofs, fish specialities.

Le Rond-Point, Place de l'Indépendance (Tel: 22 10 29). Fish and shellfish.

Maitre Boeuf, Centre Nautique Pehoa-N'Gor (Tel: 20 03 64). French-style meats grilled on wood fire, plus fish.

Le Forum, Avenue Lamine Gueye (Tel: 21 93 88). Café/restaurant/tea-room. Popular with journalists from ORTS nearby.

La Voile D'Or, Copacabana Beach, Bel-Air (Tel: 21 86 48). Fish restaurant in beach setting with palm-trees.

Le Coq Gaulois, Boulevard Dial Diop (Tel: 22 19 11). French and Senegalese specialities.

La Marmite, Rue Felix-Faure (Tel: 21 41 98). Senegalese and other West African dishes.

Le Wallame, Avenue Bourguiba (Tel: 22 78 24). Good African specialities.

Café de Paris, Avenue Georges Pompidou (Tel: 21 56 20). Another reliable French establishment.

La Croix du Sud, Avenue Albert Sarraut (Tel: 23 29 47). Elegant old-style hotel restaurant serving excellent and expensive French-Senegalese cuisine.

Le Chevalier de Boufflers, Gorée Island (Tel: 22 53 64). Small restaurant in pretty Gorée hotel serving excellent French seafood.

L'Auberge Rouge, Rue Blanchot (Tel: 21 72 56). Pretty old hotel courtyard with good French food.

Safari 2000, Rue Parent (Tel: 21 27 19). Expensive, classy French cuisine.

Hotel de la Paix, Rue N'Doye (Tel: 22 29 78). Well-run traditional French country restaurant, with pleasant bar adjoining.

Hotel-Restaurant Saint Louis, Rue Félix-Faure (Tel: 22 54 23). Lovely old courtyard with plants, reasonably priced tasty cooking.

Le Cauri, Rue Bourgi (Tel: 22 55 59). Good Senegalese cooking, including *thiebou-dienne*.

M'Baye Barik, off Avenue Bourguiba. Senegalese dishes served in a Sahelian ambience.

Le Djolof, Marché Soumbédiounne. Good Senegalese cooking.

Le Trastevere, Rue Mohamed V (Tel: 21 49 20). Pizzas and home-made pasta.

La Pizzeria, Rue Bourgi (Tel: 21 09 26). Pizzas and Italian and French dishes.

Restaurant Farid, Rue Vincens (Tel: 21 61 27). Lebanese specialities.

La Tonkinoise, Rue Dagorne (Tel: 21 60 80). International menu including Chinese specialities.

Hanoi, Rue Carnet (Tel: 21 32 69). Chinese and Vietnamese dishes.

DRINKING NOTES

Both the Gambia and Senegal are predominantly Muslim, but, though Islam disapproves of alcohol consumption, neither country imposes restrictions on its sale.

The Gambia

Beer is very much the favourite Gambian drink. Gambia has its own brewery, producing a refreshing light lager "Joyful" Julbrew, which can be served bottled or draught. The same brewery also makes soft drinks.

There are no opening hours in the Gambia. A cool beer or other drink can be taken at any time of the day (electricity and fridge permitting). Pubs and bars are open most of the day and evening, many serving snacks as well as drinks.

Many restaurants which have restricted eating hours will, however, serve drinks throughout the day.

WATER

On the whole, tap water is safe to drink unless otherwise stated, but many people, to be on the safe side, buy bottled mineral water which is easily (but expensively) available. Boiling and filtering water makes it doubly safe. Carry plenty of water with you if you are on safari, to prevent dehydration in the heat. Take water-purifying tablets if you are travelling long distances and do not know where the water might come from.

Some of the better known bars are:

Uncle Dembo's, next to Senegambia Hotel
Sambou's, Old Cape Road
Tropic Smile, Bakau
Rising Sun, Bakau
Avenues Bar and Restaurant, Kairaba Avenue
BBC Bar, Kairaba Avenue
Martha's Bar and Restaurant, Kotu Beach Complex.

(See also under Restaurants and Hotels.)

There are innumerable other little bars by the roadside and around the hotel complexes, some more, some less appealing.

Senegal

The Senegalese also drink a good deal of light, continental-style beer to quench thirst. The most popular local brand is Flag; imported beers are readily available but more expensive.

In addition, wine is imported from France, Spain and North Africa, but is reasonably expensive because of the cost of importing and storing it. Moroccan wines are often worth considering as a good compromise between quality and expense.

There are no set drinking hours. Many restaurants double as café/bars in the French manner.

Here is a selection of some bars in Dakar where the prices are reasonable and the atmosphere is pleasant. Conversation is easy if you say "hello" to anyone there. Senegalese people are very responsive to greetings and they will open up if you show them you are ready to enter into a discussion.

Auberge Rouge, rue Moussé Diop

Bar Yang Yang, Avenue Blaise Diagne

Bar le Mama Guedj, Avenue Lamine Gueye

Bar Odeon, Sicap Liberte 6

Le Fouquets, Avenue Lamine Guèye.

In addition, particularly in the suburbs, there exist little unofficial back-room or back-yard bars known as *clandos* (short for clandestine). If you are adventurous and persistent (they are not advertised), a visit to a *clando* will give you real insights into the lives of ordinary working Senegalese.

THINGS TO DO

The pleasures of Senegambia are relatively simple ones. Dakar is not Rome or Paris and Banjul is scarcely a suburb of either. Most of the holiday attractions of the region are described in the sections dealing with beaches, hunting and fishing, sports and so on. Many visitors do little more than lie in the sun.

Another large area of activity concerns excursions, from half a day to a week, to visit other parts of the country. Many people on a two-week holiday in Cap Vert or the Little Coast visit Casamance briefly, for example, to get an idea of the very different type of terrain in the south. Visitors to the Gambia often take a day's return flight to Dakar for big city thrills, while French holidaymakers in Senegal frequently hire a car and check out little Anglophone Gambia. Vacationers in either country might go overnight to Guinea-Bissau in the south, or the Cape Verde Islands out in the Atlantic. The possible variations are numerous. A list of the principal tour operators in both the Gambia and Senegal is printed below; between them, they cover the whole range of excursions available. In addition, the Places section describes the main features of interest across the region.

THE GAMBIA

You wouldn't expect such a little country to be rich in museums, opera houses and so on, and the Gambia isn't. In Banjul, the National Museum, Independence Drive, is a pleasant little museum with clean, well-kept exhibits of local jewellery, clothes, utensils, housing, customs and rituals, supported with photos, maps and other clear explanations. A full-size groundnut sailing boat, formerly used to carry the groundnuts down river to Banjul but now replaced by motorised lighters, is being built in the grounds outside, commissioned by President Jawara.

The African Heritage Gallery, Wellington Street, is the only art gallery in the accepted tourist sense of the word. Local carvings, paintings, clothes and jewellery are tastefully displayed and all for sale as well. Set in lofty, cool rooms with a balcony overlooking the river.

In addition, artists display their paintings and sculptures in their own local galleries. Several will be found in Bakau, at Cape St Mary near Sambou's restaurant, along Atlantic Road, off New Town Road – each with their own signboard pointing the way.

Otherwise, one can simply wander and observe Banjul's architecture. Disregard the pot-holes, the dusty buildings, the open drains and walk, if it is not too hot, round the streets, not forgetting the back streets behind Independence Drive. (Or take a taxi drive.) Notice the style of architecture, the two-storeyed houses with shady courtyards through open gateways, and balconies overlooking the road, pastel-coloured walls of pink, blue or cream (needing a coat of paint maybe, but possibly all the more attractive in their run down mellowness), the corrugated iron pagoda-style roofs.

For concerts, film screenings and other cultural events, you will either be obliged to use the tourist hotels or watch local posters and the media for the occasional public event.

SENEGAL

This bigger, more sophisticated country is better equipped with cultural infrastructure, much of which is described elsewhere in this book.

Senegal has few museums. In Dakar, visit the IFAN museum, Place Soweto, with its collection of rare masks.

Art Galleries: Despite the government's genuine efforts to help the arts, art galleries are something of a miracle in the country.

In Dakar, visit the Galerie 39 (Avenue Georges Pompidou), a French-run gallery which manages to put on several exhibitions every year, and the National Art Gallery (Avenue Albert Sarraut).

Concerts: These are held fairly regularly in the main towns. The two stadiums (Iba Mar Diop and Demba Diop) and the Sorano National Theatre host most concerts in Dakar.

Theatres: The Sorano National Theatre is the main venue for most plays. In the popular areas, actors use houses and government-sponsored youth and sports centres to perform.

Movies: Senegal gets, sooner or later, the latest movies produced in the west. The Senegalese are very fond of cinema, their country being the most important in Africa in film production. Names like Ousmane Sembène are world famous in the cinema industry.

In every major city, there is a cinema. Most films are in French, but there are many films from India in original Hindi with French subtitles.

TOUR OPERATORS

The Gambia

Gamtours (Gambia National Tours Company), Kanifing Industrial Estate (Tel: 92505, 92259, 91497).

Gambia Safari, c/o Gamtours.

Gambia Tours, Senegambia Beach Hotel, Kololi (Tel: 92727, 92718).

West Africa Tours, Bakau New Town, P.O. Box 222, Serekunda (Tel: 95258).

Black and White Enterprises Ltd., Serekunda (opposite Police Station near market), P.O. Box 201, Banjul (Tel: 92815).

Gambia Sportfishing Ltd., see Black and White Enterprises.

Mass Cham, c/o Atlantic Hotel, Banjul (Tel: 28601; Home Tel: 28043).

Damel Travel Services, c/o Atlantic Hotel, Banjul (Tel: 28601, 28602).

Gambia River Excursions (Tel: 95526).

Graham Rainey for *Spirit of Galicia* tours up-river, (Tel: 95915).

Columbus Travel Agency, 112 Kairaba Avenue (Tel: 96135).

Senegal

Afric Tourism, 9 Boulevard Pinet-Laprade, B.P. 2576 (Tel: 23 17 65).

Car Afric, 100 rue de Bayeux, B.P. 1881 (Tel: 23 88 67).

Intertourisme, 3 allée R. Delmas, B.P. 1122 (Tel: 23 45 29, Tlx: 51683).

Express Sun Travel, 2 place de l'Indépendance, B.P. 1578 (Tel: 23 31 81, Tlx: 61371).

Sénégal Tours, 5 place de l'Indépendance,

B.P. 3126 (Tel: 23 31 81, Tlx: 21699).

Sénégal Contact, 8 Boulevard Pinet-La-prade, B.P. 3662 (Tel: 23 60 63 / 23 45 30, Tlx: 21672).

Sénégal Tourisme International, 12-15 rue Docteur Thèze, B.P. 8117 (Tel: 21 05 76).

Sénégal Découvertes, 51-53 Boulevard Pinet-Laprade (Tel: 21 74 98).

Nouvelles Frontières, 18 Rue Sandinieri, B.P. 145 (Tel: 21 34 34, Tlx: 21837).

Socopao Voyages, Boulevard Pinet-La-prade (Tel: 21 68 72).

Teranga Voyages, Avenue Malick Sy (Tel: 22 32 74).

Vacances et Loisirs, Place de l'Indépendance (Tel: 21 45 31).

Tour Operators and Travel Companies in Europe who arrange packages and other forms of travel to Senegal and the Gambia:
UK
Hayes and Jarvis (Travel), 200 Sloane Street, London SW1X 9QV (Tel: 01-245-1051).
Horizon Holidays, Broadway, Edgbaston Fiveways, Birmingham B15 1BB (Tel: 021-643 2727).
Wings, as for Horizon.
Kuoni Travel, Kuoni House, Dorking, Surrey RH5 4AZ (Tel: 0306-740500).
Select Holidays, Centurion House, Bircher-ley Street, Hertford SG14 1BH (Tel: 0992-554144).
Thomson Holidays, Greater London House, Hampstead Road, London NW1 7SD (Tel: 01-387 8484).
Intasun Travel, Intasun House, 2 Cromwell Avenue, Bromley, Kent BR2 9AQ (Tel: 01-290 1900).
Sovereign Wintersun, Groundstar House, London Road, Crawley RH10 2TB (Tel: 0293-517868).
Redwing Holidays, as for Sovereign.
Serenity Holidays, 17 Bell Street, Romsey, Hampshire SO51 8GY (Tel: 0794-514646).

Sweden
Vingressor, Sveavagen 25 S-105 2, Stock-holm, Sweden (Tel: 46 8 22 23 60).

Norway
Vingressor, Akersgt 35, Oslo, Norway (Tel: 02 429170).

Denmark
Spies, Nyropsgade 41, DK 1602 Copen-hagen, Denmark (Tel: 01 11 42 00).

Switzerland
Jelmoli Reisen, Nansenstrasse 5, CH 8050 Zurich, Switzerland (Tel: 01 316 7130).

West Germany
Jet Reisen, Kaiserstrasse 64D, 6000 Frank-furt, Federal Republic of Germany (Tel: 069 26811, Tlx: 413034).

Netherlands
Arke Reisen, Touroperator-Wholsaler, 7500 AJ Enschede, P.O. Box 365, Deurnin-gerstraat 16, Netherlands (Tel: 053 33105).
Sonar Interservice, Zakkendragerssteeg 7, 3511 AA Utrecht (Tel: 030 322497).

France
Africatour, 23 rue Linois, 75015 Paris (Tel: 40 59 41 41).
Resinter, 2 rue de la Mare Meuve, 91021 Evry Cedex, France (Tel: 64 97 70 04) and 5 rue du Ventoux, 91021 Evry Cedex (Tel: 60 77 95 40).
Jumbo, Quai de la Megisserie, 75001 Paris (Tel: 1-42 61 84 22).
Uniclam, 63 rue Monsieur le Prince, 75006 Paris (Tel: 1-43 29 12 36).
Creation Voyages, 31 Avenue Jean Jaures, 75019 Paris (Tel: 1-42 45 53 87).
Republique Tours, 41 Avenue de la Republi-que, 75001 Paris (Tel: 1-43 55 30 00).
Nouvelles Frontières, 87 Boulevard de la Grenelle, 75016 Paris (Tel: 1-45 68 70 00).

Italy
Frankorosso International, 366 Via Roma, 10121 Torino, Italy (Tel: 11 531443/ 11 549357).

Belgium
Alfonso Marroquin (Uniclam representa-tive for Benelux countries), AC1 s.a., Rue de l'Association 4, 1000 Bruxelles.

Canary Islands
Columbus Agencia de Viajes, Edif. Taidia, Avenida Tirajana 11, Playa del Ingles, Las Palmas (Tel: 76 38 38/ 76 20 02).

The Gambia

There is only one National Park open to the public in the Gambia: **Abuko Nature Reserve**, between Serekunda and Yundum Airport. Started by Eddie Brewer, a former forestry officer who was later made the first Director of Wildlife Conservation by President Jawara, and his daughter, Stella, these 22 acres (nine hectares) of original Gambian forest have been preserved in their natural state for visitors to walk through at leisure. Pools hide crocodiles and attract colourful birds to their banks which can be watched from carefully constructed hides. Monkeys, squirrels, the occasional iguana and, if you are lucky, the shy sitatunga antelope, can be seen among the trees.

The BBC2 film *Jewel in the Sun* (May 1989) gives a vivid picture of the bird and other wild life in Abuko.

Abuko's sister project, **Baboon Island**, is not open to the public so as to protect the chimpanzees from intrusive visitors while they learn to survive on their own in their natural habitat. It was started as a conservation island by Stella Brewer for this purpose.

Senegal

Senegal is well equipped with National Parks, which are particularly rich in bird life. For details of all parks, contact **Direction des Parcs Nationaux,** Point E, Dakar B.P. 5135 (Tel: 21 06 28).

The following is a list of the parks. For further details, see the relevant section of "Places".

Parc National du Niokolo Koba: One of the largest big mammalian reserves in West Africa, this park occupies a total area of 180,000 acres (73,000 hectares) in the southeast of Senegal. You will find elephants, lions, gazelles. Accommodation is available in campsites and hotels (see Tambacounda Hotels).

Parc National des Oiseaux du Djoudj: In the north east, not far from the mouth of the River Senegal, 40 miles (60 km) from St Louis by good sand road. This is the gathering place for millions of migrating birds. The best time to visit is between October and April. Camping is possible, with excursions by canoe.

Parc National du Delta du Saloum: 50 miles (80 km) west of Kaolack. The park is dotted with small islands made up of mangroves and sand dunes. You will find pink flamingoes, storks and many other birds. Tourist camps are available.

Parc National de la Langue de Barbarie: A refuge for birds and sea tortoises, this park is a narrow strip of sandy land between the Atlantic Ocean and the River Senegal. Easily reached from St Louis.

Parc de la Madeleine: Just by Dakar, on the Corniche, an archipelago used to protect the numerous colonies of sea birds. The park is accessible every day by canoe.

Parc National de la Basse Casamance: In the extreme south, 12,000 acres (5,000 hectares) of forests and mangroves. By road, seven miles (12 km) from Oussouye and 45 miles (75 km) from Ziguinchor. Camping possible, with excursions by canoe.

NIGHTLIFE

Nightlife is rather limited in the Gambia, to the disappointment of both Gambians and some visitors. The larger tourist hotels have their own nightclubs, open to members of the public as well as to their own guests. Some are open every evening, some only at weekends. Some are free, some charge an entrance fee.

During the tourist season, the larger hotels stage entertainments for their visitors. This is a good chance to see local dancers, drummers, fire-eaters, acrobats or fashion shows. Cabaret shows as in Europe are not common. Occasionally a hotel will put on its own cabaret, drawing talent from its visitors; sometimes an artiste is hired for the six-month season, doing a tour of these hotels. For performances by visiting African popular groups, watch out for posters and listen to the radio. Large concerts occasionally take place in the National Stadium.

These are some of the major nightclubs:

Atlantic Hotel: Dunda Nightclub (Tel: 28601). Disco music. No entrance fee.

Kombo Beach (Novotel): Bellengo Nightclub (Tel: 95605). Disco music. Entrance D20.

Senegambia Beach Hotel Nightclub (Tel: 92717/8/9). Live bands sometimes, e.g. during Monday night barbecue. Otherwise disco music. Entrance D30.

Musu's Disco, Cape Point. No entrance fee.

Tropicana Nightclub and Disco on the way to the Senegambia Hotel. In among the trees. Disco music.

Oasis, Clarkson Street, Banjul. Disco. No entrance fee.

Tropic Garden Hotel Nightclub. Disco music. No entrance fee.

Gambling –

Amis Casino, Cape Point.

Fajara Casino.

Most towns have at least one disco/nightclub. As one would expect, Dakar has many.

SENEGAL

In addition, live popular music is available both at large open-air concerts and in clubs reasonably regularly. Watch the press and listen to the radio for details.

Top Dakar groups such as Youssou N'Dour and the Super Etoile de Dakar and Super Diamono de Dakar often have residencies for periods at a particular club, playing every night or two or three times a week. Both the clubs themselves and the resident groups change regularly, however. Check with your hotel for latest news.

Nightclubs open, and continue, late. At midnight they might still be three quarters empty and 4 a.m. is about the time of maximum activity. Usually you pay at the door (between CFA 1500 and 3500) and this price entitles you to your first drink free.

Some addresses are:

Harry's Club, Boulevard de la République (Tel: 21 90 88)

Miami, Rue de Rheims (Tel: 21 39 69)

Kilimanjaro, Village Artisinale Soumbedioune (Tel: 21 99 89)

Play Club, Rue Jules Ferry (Tel: 21 24 84)

Sahel Night Club, Boulevard Gueule Tapée (Tel: 21 21 18)

Gambling –

Casino du Cap-Vert, Ngor (Tel: 20 09 74)

SHOPPING

There are two sorts of buying transactions in Senegambia, which represent the modern, European, systematised method as against the traditional, African, informal one. The first is in the modern shops and supermarkets where prices are fixed and displayed by the goods and everything is very simple. The second, which still applies in many markets and small shops and stalls, involves bargaining and is therefore not simple.

How best to bargain? It would be seen as madness to pay the first price requested. The proper price is probably between a half and two-thirds. To get to the correct price, however, you must play a leisurely game in which it is perfectly acceptable to feign impatience, walk off, pause, turn back, think, discuss details of the goods, etc. The vendor will not understand at all the idea that you might be in a hurry. The best method is probably to start at around one-third of the asking price, so that you can be seen to increase your offer at least once.

WHAT TO BUY

Shopping hours in the informal sector (markets, etc.) are very flexible, more or less from dawn to dusk. An African vendor will never turn away a visitor just because he has half-finished packing up his wares.

The Gambia

Popular purchases include Gambian tie-dye or batik cloth, sold in lengths or made up into shirts, shorts, skirts, dresses, trousers, children's clothes, tablecloths or napkins. Local cloth called *Lagos*, printed not tie-dyed, is brightly coloured with original designs. Dutch and English wax prints are also popular but slightly more expensive. There is also local indigo-dyed cloth (dark blue/light blue patterns) at certain stalls in the markets.

Tailors, machines whirring all day long, will run up anything from a pair of shorts to a man's suit in a matter of one or two days.

Other souvenirs are wood carvings, silver filigree jewellery, masks, bead necklaces, bangles of silver or copper, wooden bowls, traditionally dressed dolls, batik cloth pictures of Gambian scenes. A set of posters of Gambian flowering trees and shrubs, birds or butterflies can be found in some hotel shops. Musical instruments are also for sale.

Books on Gambian history, myths and legends, flora and fauna, and novels by Gambian writers can be found in the Methodist Bookshop and in some hotel shops.

Senegal

All of the same items as in the Gambia are available in Senegal.

As far as cloth is concerned, it is worth remembering that in the Gambia it is considerably cheaper; indeed every bus from the Gambia into Senegal carries a number of women returning from an expedition to stock up on cheap materials.

As in the Gambia, markets throughout Senegal abound in tailors who will run up a costume – perhaps a magnificent flowing *boubou* gown – in 24 hours.

Gold and silver jewellery are both available, the latter particularly from Mauritanian silversmiths (though the 1989 exodus of Mauritanians has reduced this trade enormously).

SPORTS

SPECTATOR

Wrestling is the national sport, taking place on a Saturday or Sunday evening (except during Ramadan). The atmosphere and audience reaction are to be enjoyed as much as the wrestling itself. The wrestlers are usually draped in amulets to bring luck and often pour over their bodies and drink "magic" potions to protect themselves. Between bouts, followers of each wrestler dance, drum, blow whistles and flutes, playing to the crowd, whipping up excitement and spurring their hero to flaunt himself and show off his strength. The actual wrestling round lasts no time by comparison. First one to touch the ground loses.

Excursions to wrestling matches are organised from the hotels, but anyone can attend by simply turning up.

Canoe Racing takes place irregularly (check with local hotels, tour operators, etc.) but can be quite spectacular, with up to 30 men propelling the large craft. The most active areas are Cap Vert and St Louis in Senegal.

Football is popular as a street game with improvised equipment but both countries have major stadiums where organised matches take place. Again, the events are irregular. Watch local press, talk to local people to get advance warning of a match.

PARTICIPANT

The Gambia

In such a small country, facilities are obviously limited. The major activities obviously relate to the beach and swimming pool, and these are available in abundance. Most beach hotels will have windsurfers, surf boards and perhaps small yachts available, usually with instructors.

Facilities are available at the Senegambia,

Kombo Beach (Novotel), Fajara, Sunwing and Atlantic Hotels for tennis. Some of the above also have squash and badminton courts and facilities for volleyball and basketball. Short-term visitors can also join the Fajara Club, opposite the Fajara Hotel, and enjoy their 18-hole golf course, squash, tennis and badminton courts, snooker table and swimming pool. Tennis courts are also available at the Cedars Club, Serekunda and the Reform Club in Banjul.

Hunting: The Gambia takes very seriously its duty to conserve wildlife and hunting in virtually all forms is heavily discouraged. You will often see printed, as posters, etc., the text of Sir Dawda Jawara's so-called "Banjul Declaration" of 1977: "It is a sobering reflection that in a relatively short period of our history most of our larger wildlife species have disappeared together with much of the original forest cover. The survival of the wildlife still remaining with us and the setting aside of protected natural habitats for them is the concern of all of us. It would be tragic if this priceless natural heritage, the product of millions of years of evolution, should be further endangered or lost for want of proper concern. This concern is a duty we owe to ourselves, to our great African heritage and to the world. Thus I solemnly declare that my Government pledges its untiring efforts to conserve for now and posterity as wide a spectrum as possible of our remaining fauna and flora."

The only form of hunting permitted is a limited participation in the culls of wild pigs occasionally ordered by the police when the animals threaten the rice crops. Application to the police at such a time, which is entirely unpredictable, may result in permission to participate.

Fishing: Sea or river fishing with a line from the beach or bank is popular and needs no particular organisation. Up-river, piroques may be hired everywhere informally for short excursions. Game fishing for the wide variety of species which abound offshore is organised through all of the major hotels and also by Sportfishing Ltd. (See Tour Operators).

Senegal

Since independence, Senegal has an active sports policy. At colleges, sport is a subject taught and included in the two main exams, that of BFEM (the equivalent of the British O-Level) and the Baccalauréate. So popular are the sports activities in Dakar that the authorities have made available a long stretch of running track on the Corniche Ouest, facing the University. Every day, from around 5 p.m., hundreds of people are to be seen along the Corniche doing push-ups, hurdling or simply having fun. Similarly, throughout the country groups of joggers in the morning and evening are a common sight.

As far as beach sports are concerned, all major centres of tourism supply the full range of windsurfers, etc. All of the big hotels in the most popular regions – Cap Vert, the Little Coast – have private beaches. Dakar is also surrounded by fine beaches.

All are clean and well looked after by the authorities. In areas where swimming is forbidden, there is a red sign in French saying *Baignade interdite*.

The best beaches are Yoff, les Almadies and Anse Bernard. For the young, the beaches of Bel Air, Hann Plage are the most popular as waves are almost non-existent.

Tennis: Although tennis courts are common in the tourist hotel complexes, public facilities are few. Tennis clubs in Dakar are: the Tennis Club Dakarois (Tel: 21 16 07) and the Union or Olympique Club Corniche (Tel: 22 21 98).

Golf is similarly not a widespread game, being regarded as exclusive and a rich man's sport (which it is, of course, in Africa). Apart from the Cap Vert and Little Coast hotels, courses exist at: the golf club on the Route de Cambérène (Tel: 22 40 69); the Lagon 1, Dakar (Tel: 21 53 22); Les Marinas, Bel Air (Tel: 22 25 77).

Equitation: Many major beach hotels offer horse riding facilities. Public riding stables are rare, however. Up-country, the Ranch de Doli hunting lodge in the Djourbel Region offers horse treks. In Dakar, the Centre de l'Etrier (Tel: 32 52 63) and the Cercle Hippique Sportif (Tel: 34 02 33) provide facilities.

Flying: There is only one flying club in the country, the Aéroclub Iba Guèye at Dakar Yoff airport (Tel: 20 04 12).

Dance Schools: After the closure of the Mudra Dance School, a ground-breaking institution engaged in the propagation of traditional African dance, several former teachers and students set up their own schools. All of them offer a full range of styles (jazz, classical, etc.), but they are particularly good in African dance. These are the best known:

Lorenzetti, 4 rue Mage (Tel: 22 12 37); Manhattan Dance School, 127 rue Carnot; Marie Eve, Rue Victor Hugo (Tel: 22 00 14); Atelier Sobo-Bade, 50 rue Mohamed V; Xarit Dance, 14 Avenue A. K. Bourgi (Tel: 21 32 63).

Hunting: The hunting season in Senegal is from 15 December until 30 April. Hunting is strictly controlled. The Water and Forests Bureau in Dakar issues hunting permits to those with insurance, firearm certificate, regulation permit papers and dues. Permits come in three categories: the Small Game permit is issued for one day's shoot, taking not more than 15 in total of stone-partridges, guinea-fowl, bustards, francolins or hare; the Medium permit includes the small game but also the shooting of one of each of the following – gazelle, oribi, waterbuck, cob, warthog or two great bustards; a Big Game licence is issued only through authorised hunting guides, and then rarely. It covers all of the large game. Rare species, such as lion, however, require the personal permission of the President to hunt. It is not often given.

In addition, there is a special permit covering water game-birds available.

Permission to bring firearms into the country must be obtained from the Ministry of the Interior. Authorised guides may obtain this permission on behalf of their clients, or, of course, provide guns for their use. It is forbidden to import ammunition, which must be bought in Senegal. Insurance is obligatory for all hunters.

All questions and applications should be addressed to: **Direction Des Eaux, Forêts et Chasses,** Parc Forestier de Hann, B.P. 1831 Dakar (Tel: 23 76 14, 23 06 28).

Fishing: Senegal is rich in fish of all descriptions, and a major centre for fishing of different categories. As in the Gambia, simple "surf casting" with a line or rod and line from the beaches or reefs will bring in a wide range of fish, even including sharks and rays on occasion.

From a boat in the bolongs off the rivers Casamance and Saloum and their substantial estuaries, a whole range of river and sea fish can be caught. Again, not only small speci-

mens – barracuda may be taken in this way.

Underwater fishing, for which insurance is obligatory, takes place, particularly in the Cap Vert region, for large grouper and barracuda among the species.

Finally, Senegal is a major centre for big game fishing, for the much prized sailfish, marlin, wahoo and sharks. Cap Vert and the Little Coast are the main regions for this activity.

The following is a list of centres specialising in the various categories, all of which supply full equipment and arrange all possible details of a trip from an amateur's afternoon dozing in a pirogue to a full big game fishing holiday including stuffing and mounting of the catches. See also the list of Tour Operators, and the big hotels, particularly Club Méditerranée at NGor and at Cap Skirring.

Sports/Big Game Fishing
Centre de Pêche Sportive de Dakar (Air Afrique), Embarcadère Dakar Gorée, B.P. 3132 (Tel: 21 28 58).

Centre de Pêche des Hotels Meridien, B.P. 8092 Dakar (Tel: 23 10 05).

Centre de Pêche du Savana Frantel, B.P. 1015 Dakar (Tel: 22 60 23).

Africa Safari, Dakar (Tel: 21 07 16, 22 26 84).

Centre de Pêche de la Petite Cote, B.P. 64 M'Bour (Tel: 51 10 75).

Les Piroguiers, B.P. 22 à Foundioungne (Tel: 45 11 34).

Line Fishing by Boat/Pirogue
Les Barracudas, B.P. 14 Dakar (Tel: 21 94 38).

Village Hotel Keur Salouma, Toubacouta, B.P. 334 (Tel: 41 10 19).

Hotel Kabrousse-Mossor, Cap Skirring, B.P. 236 Ziguinchor (Tel: 91 14 26).

Hotel Savana, Cap Skirring (Tel: 91 15 52).

Diving
Oceanium Diving Club, B.P. 3870 Dakar (Tel: 22 19 19).

SPECIAL INFORMATION

DOING BUSINESS

The general atmosphere of approaching a transaction in Africa is more leisurely, roundabout and personal than in Europe and America. Personal contacts are important and middlemen are common and may expect a commission even where no formal agreement exists.

THE GAMBIA

People wanting to set up businesses in the Gambia should apply to the Ministry of Economic Planning, 1/2 Buckle Street, Banjul, for work permits, giving their reasons for the request and proof of being financially independent at least for the first year. The Ministry will also provide information and assistance with all forms of potential or actual business transactions.

SENEGAL

Potential investors and business people seeking information or contacts of any kind may contact either the Directeur, Commerce Exterieure, Ministère de Commerce, Rue Réné N'Diaye, Dakar (Tel: 22 36 41), or the Chambre de Commerce, Place de l'Indépendance, Dakar B.P. 6018 (Tel: 21 71 89).

There is a biennial International Fair in Dakar (1990, 92, etc.). Details from: Centre Internationale d'Echanges, Route de l'Aeroport, Dakar-Yoff, B.P. 3329 (Tel: 20 03 75 or 23 10 11, Tlx: 430 SG).

GAYS

Both Islamic doctrine and the social/moral background of the region are strongly against homosexuality. Senegal is relatively relaxed and cosmopolitan by comparison with the Gambia, where homosexual acts are illegal. In both places, overtly homosexual behaviour may arouse hostility and incomprehension. This is not to say that discreet homosexual activity, including prostitution, never takes place – merely that it is absolutely not viewed publicly in the same way as Europe and America.

DISABLED

Virtually no facilities for disabled people exist in either country. On the other hand, one must become accustomed to the sight of crippled beggars propelling themselves along the pavements by their hands on makeshift wheeled boards.

STUDENTS

No facilities for student discounts exist in either country.

The sole university in the region, Dakar's Cheikh Anta Diop University, organises exchange programmes with universities in Africa, Europe and the United States.

PHOTOGRAPHY

Both countries are perfectly open with regard to photography but people do not like having their photographs taken. This applies particularly to older people and those up-country away from the tourist centres and urbanisation, who believe that photos take away part of the soul of the person being photographed. If you do want to photograph people, you must get their permission first and this may well be refused. A small payment may even be demanded. Street scenes are best shot from a passing car with a fast film or with a long-distance lens from across the street.

Everywhere except in Dakar, supplies of film are limited in choice, and prices are higher than Europe everywhere.

LANGUAGE

English is the official language of the Gambia and is almost universally spoken. French occupies a similar position in Senegal. In addition, the region has more than 10 indigenous languages. The most widespread is Wolof, which is useful in both countries.

USEFUL WORDS & PHRASES

Hello *Sala maleikum* (this is, in fact, Arabic)
Good morning *Jamm ga fanan*
Good night *Fanan jamm*
How are you? *Nanga def?*
I am well *Magni fi rek*; *Jamba rek* (used in the Gambia)
How is your family? *Ana waa keur ge?*
They are well *Nyunge fe*
Are you well? *Ba dara metee wula?*
Thank you *Jerejef*
Yes/No *Waow/Deedeet*
Come/Come here *Kai/Kai fi*
I would like/I want *Dama buga*
I want to eat *Dama buga lek*
To eat/to drink *Lek/naan*
Breakfast *Ndeki*
Lunch *Agn*
Dinner *Rer*
To go/to come *Dem/nyo*
I am going (= Goodbye) *Mangi dem*
I shall come back *Dina nyo at*; *dina delussi at*
The day/the night *Betiek/gudi*
Now/today *Leegi/tey*
Yesterday/Tomorrow *Demb/elek or souba*
See you tomorrow morning *Be soube*
Till next time *Be beneen yon*
Bread/water *Mburu/ndoh*
Meat/fish *Yap/jen*
Just a little *Tutti rek*
I am hot/cold *Dama tange/sedde*
I am thirsty *Dama maar*
I am tired *Dama sonne*
It is hot/cold *Dafa tange/sedde*
Where? *Ana?*

Here/there *Fi la/fale la*
Here/there *Fi/fofu*
Where is the market/hotel *Ana marsé/hotel?*
Do you speak English? *Degg nge Anglais (English)?*
I don't speak Wolof *Degguma Wolof*
I don't understand *Degguma*
How much? *Nyata?*
How much is this? *Bi, nyata le?*
It is too expensive *Dafa jafé*
Lower the price, please *Wanyi ko*
Good (it's good) *Baakhne*
It's bad (no good) *Baahul*
Wait! *Haaral!*
Go straight on *Talal*
Where is the restaurant? *Ana restaurant bi?*
I want to get down here *Fi laay wach*
I have had enough to eat, thanks *Suur naa*
She (it) is pretty *Rafet ne*
It is good (of food) *Neehne*
My friend *Suma harit*
Give me/Sell me *Joh me/Jai me*
Put it here *Bai ko fi*
Bring it *Indi ko*
Bring me a beer *Indi me beer* (*bière* in French)
Take this *Amm*
Excuse me *Baal me*
I am going to rest *Damai dem nopelu*
My wife/husband *Suma jigeen/jekeur*
Tea (Senegalese style) *Ataya*
Money *Halis*
I haven't any money *Anuma halis*
I have a headache *Suma bop dey meti*
I have a stomach ache *Sume biir dey meti*
Charity has already been done (A useful phrase to get rid of beggars) *Sarak be ague na*

Numbers
1/2/3/4/5 *Benn/nyar/nyet/nyent/juroom*
6/7 *juroom (ak) benn/juroom (ak) nyar*
8/9 *juroom (ak) nyet/juroom (ak) nyent*
10 *Fouk*
20/30/40 *nyar fouk/fan wer/nyent fouk*
50/100 *juroom fouk/teemeer*

Money
(slightly different from numbers)
5 CFA francs (Senegal) *derem*
10 CFA *nyar derem*
15 CFA *nyet derem*
20 CFA *nyent derem*
25 CFA *juroom i derem*
30 CFA etc. *juroom benn derem* (= 6 times 5 etc.)
50 CFA *fouk*

100 CFA *nyar fouk*
150 CFA *fan wer*
500 CFA *teemeer*
1000 CFA *nyar teemeer*
5000 CFA *jooni*

Further Reading

THE GAMBIA

Very little has been written specifically about the Gambia in English and virtually nothing modern is in print, apart from a number of guide books which include the country in a wider region, e.g. West Africa as a whole. This is a small selection, beginning with a good paperback edition of the 17th-century explorer Mungo Park's excellent account of his perilous journeys.

Park, Mungo: *Travels Into the Interior of Africa* (Eland, London and Hippocrene, N.Y., 1983)

Rice, Berkeley: *Enter Gambia, the Birth of an Improbable Nation* (Angus and Robertson, London, 1968)

Sonko-Godwin, Patience: *Ethnic Groups of the Senegambia* (Book Production Unit, Banjul, 1985)

Edberg, Etienne: *A Naturalist's Guide to the Gambia* (J. G. Sanders, Sweden, 1982)

Haley, Alex: *Roots* (various editions, from 1976)

Commonwealth Fact Sheet: The Gambia (Commonwealth Institute, London, 1977)

Tomkinson, Michael: *Gambia* (Michael Tomkinson, London, 1987)

SENEGAL

A considerable body of literature exists, but exclusively in French.

Adams, A.: *Le Long Voyage des gens du Fleuve* (Maspéro, Paris, 1977)

Amin, S.: *Le monde des affaires Sénégalais* (Grands Documents, Editions de Minuit, Paris, 1969)

Barry: *Le royaume du Walo* (Maspéro, Paris, 1972)

Berhaut: *Flore du Sénégal* (Editions Clairafrique, Dakar, 1968)

Brigaud, F.: *Histoire du Sénégal* (Editions Clairafrique, Dakar, 1964)

Camara, C.: *St Louis du Sénégal* (IFAN, St Louis, 1968)

Chamard, P.-C. et Sall, Mamadou: *Le Sénégal, Géographie* (Nouvelles Editions Africaines, Dakar, 1977)

Delcourt, Père Jean: *L'île de Gorée; histoire religieuse du Sénégal* (Editions Clairafrique, Dakar, 1976)

Deschamps, Hubert: *Le Sénégal et la Gambie* (Presses Universitaires de France, collection "*Que sais-je?*", Paris, 1968)

Diop, Birago: *Les contes d'Amadou Koumba* (Présence Africaine, Dakar)

Diop, Cheikh Anta: *Nations nègres et cultures* (Presence Africaine, Paris, 1954); *L'Unité culturelle de l'Afrique noire* (Presence Africaine, Paris, 1959); *Antériorité des civilisations nègres* (Presence Africaine, Paris, 1967); *Identité culturelle et société postindustrielle* (Presence Africaine, Paris, 1980)

Duchemin, G.-J.: *St Louis du Sénégal, guide historique* (IFAN, St Louis, 1955)

Dupuy, A.-R.: *Le guide du parc national du Niokolo-Koba* (Editions G.I.A., Dakar, 1970)

Fall-Sow, Aminata: *Le Revenant; La Grève des Battû* (NEA, Dakar, 1976 et 1979)

Kane, C.A.: *L'aventure ambiguë* (Julliard, Paris, 1961)

Loti, Pierre: *Le roman d'un Spahi* (Calmann-Lévy, Paris, 1936)

Lunel, A.: *Sénégal* (Atlas des Voyages, Editions Rencontres, Lausanne, 1966)

Monteil, Vincent: *Esquisses sénégalaises* (IFAN, Dakar, 1967)

Saglio, Christian: *Sénégal* (Petite Planète, Editions du Seuil, Paris)

Seck, Assane: *Dakar, mêtropole ouest-africaine* (IFAN, Dakar, 1970)

Sembène, Ousmane: *Le Docker noir* (Audecam, Paris, 1956); *O pays, mon beau peuple* (Press Pocket, Paris, 1957); *Les Bouts de bois de Dieu* (Press Pocket, Paris, 1960); *Voltaïque* (Audecam, Paris, 1962); *L'Harmattan* (Audecam, Paris, 1963); *Véhiciosane* (Audecam, Paris, 1966); *Xala* (Audecam, Paris, 1974)

Senghor, Léopold Sédar: *Liberté I* (Editions du Seuil, Paris, 1964); *Liberté II* (Editions du Seuil, Paris, 1971); *Poèmes* (Editions du Seuil, Paris, 1954); *Chants d'ombre* (Editions du Seuil, Paris, 1956); *Nocturnes* (Editions du Seuil, Paris, 1961); *Ethiopiques* (Editions du Seuil, Paris, 1956).

USEFUL ADDRESSES

TOURIST INFORMATION

In the Gambia

National Tourist Office, Ministry of Information and Tourism, Apollo Hotel Building, Orange Street Wing, Banjul, The Gambia (Tel: 28472, 28497, 26396)

Outside the Gambia

Gambia National Tourist Office, 57 Kensington Court, London W8 5DG, **England** (Tel: 01 937 9689)

Aviation and Tourism Services GmbH, Fichtenstrasse 47, D-6242 Kronberg/Ts. 2, **West Germany** (Tel: 06173-66997)

In other countries, contact nearest Gambian diplomatic representation or tour operator (see separate lists).

In Senegal

Ministère de Tourisme, 5 Avenue André Peytavin, B.P. 4049, **Dakar** (Tel: 22 22 26, 22 53 71, 22 13 80)

Outside Senegal:

Bureau National Senegalais de Tourisme at

15 Rue de Rémusat, 75016 Paris, **France** (Tel: 40 50 07 90)

Sremdewerkchramt, Münchenerstrasse 7, D-6000 Frankfurt-M, **West Germany** (Tel: 23 26 91/92)

Centre de Cooperation Internationale, Largo Africa, 20145 Milan, **Italy** (Tel: 46 44 21)

In other countries, contact nearest Senegalese diplomatic representation or tour operator (see separate lists).

EMBASSIES

The Gambia
Gambian Diplomatic Representation Abroad

The Gambia High Commission, 57 Kensington Court, London W8 5DG, **England** (Tel: 937 6316/8, Cable: GAMEXT London)

The Gambia Embassy, 126 Avenue Franklin Roosevelt, Brussels 1050, **Belgium** (Tel: [02] 640 10 49, Cable: GAMEXT BRUSSELS)

The Gambia High Commission, 162 Awolowo Road, South Ikoyi, Lagos, **Federal Republic of Nigeria** (Tel: 24632, Cable: GAMEXT LAGOS)

The Gambia High Commission, 11 Rue de Thiong, Dakar, **Republic of Senegal** (Tel: 214476, Cable: GAMEXT DAKAR)

The Consul General, Mr. E. Eichner, Frankfurter Strasse 74-78, D-6236 Eschborn, Taunus, **West Germany** (Tel: 06196-46098, 46099)

The Gambia Consulate, Mr. Gerhard Bartels, Kurfürstendamm 102, D-1000 Berlin, **West Germany** (Tel: 030-886051)

The Gambian Embassy, 1030 15th Street NW, Suite 720, Washington DC 20005, **USA** (Tel: 84 21 35 6, 84 21 35 9)

Diplomatic Missions in the Gambia

Embassy of the USA: White House, Kairaba Avenue, Fajara, Kombo St Mary; PO Box 2596, Banjul (Tel: 92858, 92856)

British High Commission: 48 Atlantic Road, Fajara, Kombo St Mary; PO Box 507, Banjul (Tel: 95133/4, 95578)

Embassy of the People's Republic of China: Chancery: PO Box 784, Banjul; 6a Marina Parade, Banjul (Tel: 27351, 28385); Office: 17th Street West, Fajara (Tel: 95380, 95622)

Office of the Ambassador of the USSR: 7 Buckle Street, Banjul (Tel: 28282); 68 Atlantic Road, Fajara (Tel: 95317)

Senegalese High Commission: 10a Cameron Street, Banjul (Tel: 27469, 27680)

Nigerian High Commission: Garba Jahumpa Avenue, Bakau; PO Box 630, Banjul (Tel: 95803/4)

Sierra Leone High Commission: 67 Hagan Street, Banjul (Tel: 28206, 28462)

Consulate of Guinea-Bissau: 16 Wellington Street, Banjul (First floor, next to

CUSO Office)

In Senegal
Senegalese Diplomatic Representation Abroad

Senegalese Embassies at:

2112 Wyoming Avenue, Washington DC 2000, **USA** (Tel: 234 05 50, 234 05 41)

11 Phillimore Gardens, London W8 7QG, **England** (Tel: 937 0925)

14 Avenue Robert Schumann, 75007 Paris, **France** (Tel: 47 05 39 45)

Via Bartolomo Eustachio 12, 00161 Roma Quirinal, **Italy** (Tel: 85 94 99)

Argelanderstrasse 3, Bonn, **West Germany** (Tel: 218 008)

8 Skeppsbron, 1st Floor, Box 2036, Stockholm, **Sweden** (Tel: 14 32 35)

196 Avenue Franklin Roosevelt, 1050 Bruxelles, **Belgium** (Tel: 67 300 97, 67 290 51)

Diplomatic Missions in Senegal
Embassies in Dakar

Algeria: 5 rue Mermoz, PO Box 3233 (Tel: 22 35 09, 22 45 27)

Austria: 26 Boulevard Pinet Laprade, PO Box 3247 (Tel: 22 38 86)

Belgium: Route de la Corniche Est (Tel: 22 47 20)

Canada: 45 Boulevard de la République, 4th Floor, PO Box 3373 (Tel: 21 02 90)

Cape Verde Islands: 1 rue de Denain (Tel: 21 18 73)

Cote d'Ivoire: 2 Avenue Albert Sarraut, 3rd floor, PO Box 359 (Tel: 21 36 73, 21 01 63)

Egypt: 65 Boulevard de la République, Sorano Building, 1st Floor (Tel: 21 24 75, 22 19 64)

France: 1 rue Elhadji Amadou Assane Ndoye (Tel: 21 01 81)

Guinea: KM 4/5 route de Ouakam, PO Box 7123 (Tel: 24 86 06)

Guinea-Bissau: Point E, rue 6 (Tel: 24 59 22)

Italy: Rue Elhadji Seydou Nourou Tall (Tel: 22 05 78)

Japan: 2 Rue Malan, Immeuble Electra 1st and 2nd Floors, PO Box 3160 (Tel: 21 01 61)

Mauritania: 37 Avenue du General De Gualle, PO Box 1209 (Tel: 21 63 43)

Morocco: Route de Ouakam (Tel: 24 69 27)

Netherlands: 37 Rue Kleber (Tel: 23 94 83)

Portugal: 5 Avenue Carde, PO Box 281 (Tel: 21 59 22)

Spain: 45 Boulevard de la République (Tel: 21 30 81)

Switzerland: Rue René Ndiaye (Tel: 22 58 48)

United Kingdom: 20 Rue du Dr. Gillet, PO Box 6025 (Tel: 21 73 92)

USA: Avenue Jean XXIII, PO Box 49 (Tel: 21 42 95)

West Germany: 43 Avenue Albert Sarraut (Tel: 22 48 84)

ART/PHOTO CREDITS

Agence Hoa-Qui/Michel Renaudeau	14/15, 16/17, 18/19, 20/21, 22, 27, 34, 35, 37, 44/45, 46, 47, 49, 50, 51, 52/53, 54, 55, 60/61, 62, 63, 64, 65, 66, 67, 68/69, 70, 71, 72, 73, 74, 75, 78, 79, 80L, 80R, 81L, 81R, 82, 83, 86, 88, 89, 90, 91, 92/93, 94, 96, 97, 98/99, 100, 101, 102, 103, 104/105, 106, 107, 108, 109, 110, 111, 112/113, 114, 115, 117, 118/119, 120/121, 123, 124, 125, 127, 128/129, 130/131, 132/133, 138, 141, 142, 143R, 144/145, 147, 150, 151, 154, 155, 160, 161, 163, 164, 165, 170, 174/175, 176/177, 178/179, 180/181, 182, 184, 185, 188, 189, 190, 191, 192, 194, 195R, 196/197, 198, 200, 201, 202, 203, 204/205, 206, 207, 208, 209, 210, 211, 212, 213, 214/215, 216, 218, 219, 220, 221, 222/223, 224, 225, 226, 227, 228, 229, 230, 231, 232, 233, 234, 235, 236/237, 238/239, 240, 241, 242, 243, 245, 246, 247, 248/249, 250, 254, 255, 256, 257, 258/259, 260, 261, 262, 263, 264, 265, 266, 267, 268/269, 270/271, 272, 273, 274, 275, 278, 279, 280, 281, 282/283, 284, 285, 286, 287, 288, 289, 290, 291L, 291R, 292, 293, 294
Allsport Pictures	116
Associated Press	57, 58/59
Gravette, Andy G.	143L, 159, 251
Louvre Museum	36
Mary Evans Picture Library	24, 26, 28/29, 30, 32, 33, 38/39, 40, 42, 43, 48
Naylor, Kim	87
Pierres, Susan	122, 126, 146, 152, 153, 156/157, 158, 165, 166, 168, 169, 171, 172, 173
Spectrum Colour Library	244
Tony Stone Worldwide	76/77, 195L
Topham Picture Source	9, 56, 84/85, 136, 139, 162

INDEX

N

O-P

U-W

Y-Z

INSIGHT GUIDES

COLORSET NUMBERS

You'll find the colorset number on the spine of each Insight Guide.